THE ENCYCLOPEDIA OF
MOTORCYCLING

George Bishop

G.P. PUTNAM'S SONS · NEW YORK

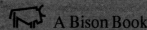
A Bison Book

First published in the USA by
G.P. Putnam's Sons
200 Madison Avenue
New York, NY 10016
USA

Produced by
Bison Books Limited
4 Cromwell Place
London SW7

 Published simultaneously in Canada by Academic Press Canada Limited, Toronto.

Library of Congress Catalog Card Number: 80-80951

ISBN: 0-399-12557-4

Printed in Hong Kong

Phototypeset by Oliver Burridge & Co. Ltd, Crawley

Produced by Colourviews Limited for Bison Books under the direction of Patrick Whitehouse.

Designer: Roy Williams

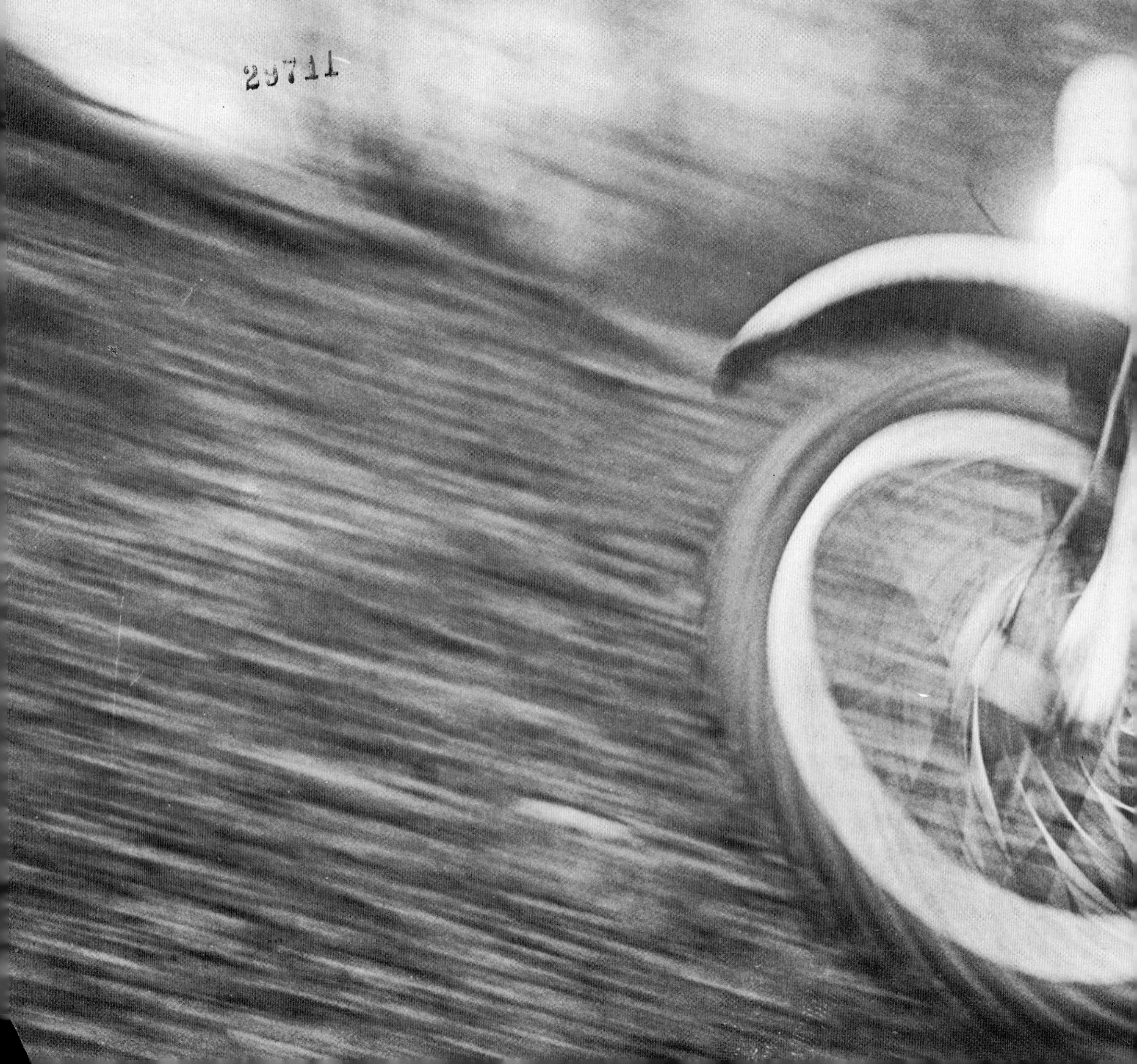

CONTENTS

THE HISTORY OF MOTORCYCLING

Franz Biber winning the Solitude
race on his BMW R32 on 18 May 1924.

The first motorcycle was made in 1885 and more two-wheeled powered machines are being sold now than at any time in the years since they have been with us. There are about 30 million machines in use if we include mopeds with motorcycles, and nearly eight million are made worldwide each year. Statistics are boring but they do bring home the message that the motorcycle is enjoying the biggest boom in its history.

Why? There is no short and simple answer. Initially the two-wheeler offered all the personal freedom of individual transport at a much lower cost than the car, and the motorcycle was used by the man who could not afford a car. Then as living standards rose and the motorcar ceased to be the rich man's toy, the sale of two-wheelers declined. Vehicles like the Austin Seven in England, the Model T Ford in the United States, and similar machines in other countries offered reliable and cheap transport out of the rain and the wind. The motorcycle was used by what used to be called the working man, or the rabid enthusiast who refused to shut himself up in a mobile glasshouse.

Now the picture has changed completely and the motorcyclist is the person who *chooses* to ride on two wheels rather than being forced into it by lack of money. The cutprice transport side is taken care of by the moped with its impressive fuel economy of 150–200 miles to the gallon, while the real enthusiast may pay more for his machine than the family man does for his small car. The superbikes offer the performance of a Ferrari at about one-tenth of the cost, but the rider cannot be categorized as he is drawn from all income brackets and all classes of society.

Although there were early examples of twin- and four-cylinder machines it was the single-cylinder or one-lunger which reigned for about 30 years outside the United States, where, after World War I, only two big-selling makes survived, the Indian and Harley-Davidson, both twins. Then the Indian died, although the name lives on in a small-engined machine, and Harley diversified into bikes of all sizes, although today the company produces nothing under 1000cc.

There have been more than 2500 different makes of motorcycle down the years, but about 20 names dominated the scene for most of the time. For the period between the two world wars the English machine was paramount, and the illustrious name of Norton was on top in racing for something like 30 years. Politics played its part in their decline and virtual disappearance, and innate conservativism dealt the *coup de grâce*. In recent years the Japanese have taken over with multi-cylinder machines and now make more than half the world's production.

Partly because of the special clothing needed to keep out the wind and the cold, the motorcyclist has always had the image of a masculine, sporting figure in the Superman mold. Once upon a time the car driver also needed his leather coat and gauntlets, but the sedan/saloon car with fixed roof and glass windows, heater and other conveniences no longer made it necessary for the driver to be a sportsman pitting his skill against the elements and the tough road conditions of long ago.

The first motorcycle was made by Gottlieb Daimler in 1885 with a wooden frame and a single-cylinder gas engine producing five horsepower from 260cc at 600rpm. It was a test bench for his engine more than anything else, and he moved on to four wheels. It was the Germans who invented the internal combustion engine and the French who made the motorcar work, but in the two-wheel world the movement was worldwide and not so easily pinned down to nations.

There is an English contender for the title of being first—

Edward Butler, who made his machine in 1884, one year ahead of Daimler in Germany, but his machine had three wheels and so cannot qualify as a motor bicycle. There are earlier claimants, but they are not well documented and are open to doubts. A French machine made by M Michel appeared in 1869 as well as an American model from Mr S H Roper, both steam driven, but

neither developed into production models. There were also tricycles from pioneers like Count Albert de Dion and Leon Serpollet, but not two-wheelers.

Daimler's engine followed the principles of Dr D N Otto, in turn borrowed from the Frenchman E Lenoir and Beau de Rochas, and Daimler was assisted by Wilhelm Maybach, another great pioneer. Maybach actually rode the first Daimler machine, but it was the only one. So who was first in production? The Hildebrand brothers of Munich are given the credit. First they made a steam engine, then a gasoline engine which they put into a bicycle, and in the 1890s they were in production with a motorized bicycle with a step-through frame like a modern low-powered motorcycle,

Jake de Rosier on the famous Indian twin racer running on a United States board track in the pioneer days.

A postcard with a French mother with offspring, originally captioned 'Woman on her way to emancipation.'

with the engine where the pedals should be.

In England Colonel H C Holden countered with a four-cylinder motorcycle and in France the pioneer Count de Dion in partnership with a man half his size, Georges Bouton, produced a range of two-wheelers with gasoline engines. Nowadays and for many years past virtually all motorcycle engines have been located in the same place in the frame, but in the early days a dozen different alternatives were tried—in front, behind, under the saddle, over the front wheel, and even in the middle of either wheel.

Motorcycles mostly used belt drive, as they continued to do for many years, and had no variable gears. Yet there were curious glimpses to the future, like a six-speed Douglas in 1912, a twist-grip on the Indian in 1904, a mechanical inlet valve (Indian again) in 1908, electric lights in 1914 (Indian) and on the same machine electric starting in 1914, which virtually disappeared until the Japanese brought it back in recent years.

The British Scott used a rotary valve in 1911, which was abandoned until its reuse in the 1950s, and telescopic forks, another 'modern' device. The 1911 Douglas had a disk brake. The aforementioned Holden also had the first four-cylinder engine in 1896. The sidecar appeared in 1904. Racing began almost as soon as there were two machines to compete against each other, but Grand Prix racing came only in 1920.

Motorcycles in these early days were made in 30 countries, which has now dwindled to a dozen although the overall production is much higher. There are now about 55 makes and 240 models, some of the Japanese companies offering a choice of 20 or so. Most of the great names of today are newcomers, and all the giants of the past have disappeared. Fortunately the boom in classic and vintage machines means that the remaining examples are being restored and run in special races and rallies so that we can see how it was in the heyday of competition between more than 300 marques.

The enthusiasm of the motorcycling fraternity can be measured by the sales of magazines devoted to the sport and pastime. For example, although there are 14,000,000 cars on British roads, few motoring magazines can sell 100,000 copies per issue, yet there are motorcycling publications selling that number to just over one million motorcyclists.

A Royal Enfield 1.5 horsepower with back-pedalling brake at the Stanley Show in November 1901.

Women have always been associated with motorcycles and not only as pillion passengers. In the very early days there were a number of 'ladies models,' which died the death because straddling a two-wheeler was not thought to be ladylike. Today Italian women are still expected to ride sidesaddle on the scooters so popular in that country.

Motorcycling has always attracted its heroic figures, from the back-to-front cap merchants to the leather-clad Barry Sheenes of modern times, and it would take a lot of words to recapture a roll of honor of the all-time greats. A name to conjure with from the pioneering times, although hardly a hero, was the American E J Pennington, who sold the rights of his motorcycle in 1896 in England to the infamous H J Lawson for £100,000. The machine was said to be able to leap over rivers in Evel Knievel style, but only did so in his advertising brochures. Lawson tried to capture the monopoly of the infant motor industry by buying up the patents of just about everything made, but both he and Pennington went broke.

Exactly when the motorcycle became a practical machine rather than an eccentric's toy is hard to determine, but there were signs of future development in 1903 with the use of shaft drive (the Belgian FN). The first recorded race was one year later in France, known as the International Coupe Race. At that time there were more than 21,000 machines in England alone, and the first Tourist Trophy (TT), which has become the Mecca of two-wheelers, was held in 1907 in the Isle of Man off the west coast of England. The world's first purpose-built motor racing course at Brooklands near London was also built that year.

In the United States there were close to 100,000 machines on the roads by 1910, and the following year the Americans astonished Britain by running 1-2-3 in the British TT with Indian machines, in the Senior race for 500cc bikes. Before that there had been single- and twin-cylinder classes, and as there was a curious idea that twins were slower, when the two types ran together the singles had to be under 500cc but the twins were allowed 585cc.

From 1907 to 1910 the TT had been run on the flattish St John's course of 15.8 miles, and Indians won in the first year on the 37.75-mile mountain circuit which is still used today, although the race is no longer the ranking British event in the international calendar, as the Grand Prix has taken its place. Many famous international riders refused to ride on the long course on the grounds that it was too dangerous, and it has claimed more than 100 lives.

The TT Indians were in fact scaled down to 585cc from their normal 5.5 horsepower 800cc and used one of the first counter-shaft gearboxes, with the also unusual chain drive. The only saving grace for Britain was that the riders were British: Oliver Godfrey, Charlie Franklin, and Arthur Moorhouse. One of the Indian riders the previous year had been W O Bentley, later famous as maker of the Bentley car.

This year, 1911, was obviously something of a watershed as it saw the division of the TT into the two classes, Senior for 500s and Junior for 350s, and the Indian victory with chain drive and shifting gearboxes. But it was the forthcoming world war of 1914–18 which proved to be a forcing house for the motorcycle, as it was for weapons, surgery, and many other aspects of technology. Motorcycles were used by dispatch riders, and sidecars carried machine guns and stretchers in their wartime service.

During the war Britain utilized many makes: Clyno, Douglas, P & M, Sunbeam, and Triumph, and the Americans used up 70,000 Harley-Davidsons. The Germans had Wanderer and NSU, the Austrians the Puch, the French the Gillet, and the Italians the Bianchi. Machine-gun sidecar outfits were heavily loaded with ammunition, gasoline, spare tires, and parts, and the guns could be forward or rear facing.

After the war the discharged soldier wanted his own personal transport for the first time, and motorcycling enjoyed a boom. Scooters also came and went, to return again after World War II. There was a flood of machines onto the market—good, bad, and indifferent—and the buyers soon learned which were the best.

An unofficial stop on the English Motor Cycling Club's London–Land's End run for Jack Haswell on his Triumph.

Landmarks were the Ace in the United States, which was designed by Bill Henderson who first worked for the Chicago Excelsior. Later, after his death in a crash, the same four-cylinder engine appeared in the Indian, a four-cylinder 1200cc unit which was continued up to 1941, with changes over the years.

In Germany the DKW (officially Dampf Kraft Wagen but more commonly Das Kleine Wunder, or The Little Wonder) came on the market with a two-stroke engine, and in England two famous names, the ABC designed by Granville Bradshaw, and the Dunelt appeared. There were many others, some to join the list of famous marques, others to fade away. In Britain there were 14 times as many machines on the road by 1920 as in 1904, coming from almost 200 different factories.

By the following year the registrations increased another 100,000 to 373,000, double the number in the United States. Strong on the scene was Alfred Angas Scott, whose water-cooled two-stroke twins began in 1909 but made their mark in the 1920s. Scott died in 1923, but left his memorial in telescopic forks and the use of a rotary inlet valve by 1911. His machines with their distinctive appearance and noise were beloved of enthusiasts many years after his death.

By another of those illogical decisions, like the one which pronounced that twins had less power than singles, the racing powers that be penalized Scott's two-stroke when he was winning everything. They decreed that his 333ccs must be multiplied by 1.32 to give the others a fair chance since he had more power strokes. In spite of this handicap his machine was the first two-stroke to finish a TT in 1910 on the short circuit, and one year later set the fastest lap in the Senior over the mountain course at 50.11mph. In 1912 Frank Applebee won the Senior at 48.69mph.

Scott originally used two chains each with its own sprockets to provide two ratios, but after World War I the machine had a conventional two-speed gearbox as well, giving four ratios. Later still an orthodox three- or four-speed box was used. The Super Squirrel and Flying Squirrel have a special place in the affections of motorcyclists, and a replica is still made today under the marque name of Silk.

The year 1923 was another milestone. It saw the introduction of the first Sidecar TT, won by Freddie Dixon with his banking sidecar, the first Amateur TT which became the Manx Grand Prix, and the first German BMW opposed-twin, which is still in production today in the same basic design. Instead of trying to hide the age of the design the makers advertise the virtues of the more than 50-year-old layout which still comes from their factory —now in Berlin, although their headquarters is in Munich.

This classic design came into being almost by accident when Max Friz, who designed aero engines for BMW which powered German machines in World War I, was unable to continue this occupation after Germany had lost the war. He was asked to turn to motorcycles but was not keen until he was offered an office with a wood-burning stove, a luxury in the Germany of those days. So it was that the flat-twin shaft-driven R32 emerged, forerunner of many similar machines since, right up to the R7 series.

Friz had been a founder with Karl Rapp of the Bayerische Flugzeugwerke AG to build aero engines in Munich, and the company has on file a letter from Baron von Richthofen thanking it for the superiority of the engines with which his famous squadron was equipped. Production ended in 1919 after Franz Diemer had set a world-record height of 9760 meters in his biplane with a BMW engine.

The company then made agricultural machines and castings for

The German BMW company, forbidden to build aircraft after World War I, turned to motorcycles and founded a famous line.

A flat-twin BMW shaft-drive machine.

other companies until it moved on from marine engines and truck engines to a lightweight motorcycle, the Flink, the first moped of all. Then came the Helios, with a horizontally opposed engine but mounted lengthwise with belt drive to the rear wheel. Finally in 1923 came the R32 with horizontally opposed twin engine mounted across the frame as we know it today, with shaft drive and fully floating axle, the first of its kind. It was the sensation of the Paris Salon that year.

By 1925 there were nine motorcycle models; by 1927 BMW had sold more than 25,000 machines, and introduced the 750cc version of the twin, the R62. Then Ernst Henne began his record runs at the Avus track in Berlin and on the Munich-Ingolstadt autobahn, clocking 135mph in 1929 with a supercharged 750. He went on to put this up to 174mph and to take 76 world records, and it was 14 years before his 174mph was beaten by Wilhelm Herz on a blown NSU twin after World War II.

BMW was also the first company to use supercharging in road racing, with a Zoller eccentric-vane blower on a 500cc machine, beating the then invincible Nortons and the Swedish Husqvarna twins and the Italian Moto Guzzis. Then in 1935 came the R12, the first motorcycle with telescopic forks, interchangeable wheels, and a hinged rear mudguard. It was true that Scott had been using telescopics in 1911, but not with hydraulic damping as on the BMW.

By 1939 BMW had even beaten the Norton to win the Senior TT with a blown 500, and picked up 491 gold medals that year. Schorsch Meier was its TT winner and Britain's Jock West second, also on BMW. When supercharging was banned after the War it put an end to BMW victories in solo races, but they dominated the sidecar field instead; Wilhelm Noll did 174mph on the familiar

autobahn stretch in November 1955 in a completely enclosed two-wheeler with a third outrigger wheel attached, becoming the world's fastest.

World War II put an end to BMW production for civilians, but BMW carried on with a 750 R75 for the Wehrmacht with 26bhp and four road gears plus two reverses and four cross-country gears. The sidecar wheel had a differential and brakes were hydraulic. This model was used also in Africa, Russia, Lapland— and on the French Riviera. Aero engines became the staple output again until 1945 when the Munich plant, which had been largely destroyed, was confiscated by the Allies and the Eisenach plant went into public ownership in the East.

Schorsch Meier had hidden his prewar racing machine in a barn, and brought it out again for the first postwar 'Round Bavaria' race, becoming the German Road Champion. The company was banned from making motorcycles and old cylinder heads were turned into saucepans until 1948 when it was allowed to produce the single-cylinder R24 with 12bhp from 250cc, made on the most primitive jigs and tools in a makeshift workshop.

The twin came back in 1949 as the R51/2, and 100,000 machines had been sold by 1953, when a slump in two-wheelers hit the company. By 1959 closure faced the company, but it was saved by Dr Herbert Quandt. In 1968 the single-cylinder was dropped and the days of the motorcycle seemed to be numbered, but a revival in public demand put production up from 4700 to more than 20,000 a year by 1971.

The history of BMW is a microcosm of the industry, going from near disaster to great success according to the whims of the customers. It is worth telling because of that company's extraordinary success for more than half a century with virtually a one-model policy, admittedly made in varying engine capacities, but with an unchanged design basis. Yet the classic English companies who also tried to stick to what they knew failed one by one as the Japanese came in with more and more novel and exciting designs.

The previously mentioned makes which made their mark include BMW, Indian, Scott, Douglas, and the other great American —the last to survive—the Harley-Davidson. That epic British make, the Norton, made a brief appearance, but all motorcyclists with a sense of history would include many others in the honor roll of classics, among them the Brough Superior, the Ariel Square Four, the Velocette, the 'cammy' and Big Port AJS, the Sunbeam, Matchless Silver Hawk, various BSAs, the Vincent HRD, the great Italians MV Agusta, Guzzi, Ducati, Benelli, and Gilera, and the modern Japanese Honda, Suzuki, Kawasaki, and Yamaha.

This leaves out Triumph, whose Speed Twin introduced a new breed which endured a long time, and the Zenith Gradua and Rudge Multi which introduced the idea of variable-ratio transmission. Most of the famous marques of machine had equally well-known riders associated with them, although we know more about those on the scene from about 1920 than we do about the real pioneers who endured the hardships of untarred roads, temperamental tires, and knew all about uncertain journeying. The very early days are perhaps less exciting to read about, as speeds were low, unreliability the norm, and every rider was his own mechanic. But once carburetion, spark, and front suspension had been made to work to a reasonable standard, more rapid development took place, notably when the chain replaced the belt drive, which did not work too well in the dry and hardly at all in the wet.

Zenith with its Gradua provides an early milestone, as it was the first attempt to offer variable gear ratios. In the beginning most makers ran a V-belt between two pulleys, one on the crankshaft and the other, much larger, on the rear wheel. Then someone hit on the idea of moving the driving pulley in and out to vary the ratio. At first the machine had to be stopped to 'change gear,' and a shorter or longer belt put on to replace the one in use. Zenith improved on this with its Gradua gear, which appeared in 1908 but was used right up to 1923 when it was distinctly old fashioned. The company used various engines (JAP, Fafnir, Green, Bradshaw, Villiers) but Freddie Barnes' Gradua suited any of them. This enabled the rider to change ratio without stopping the machine, which was a big step forward.

The Gradua operated by expanding or contracting the pulley flanges, at the same time moving the rear wheel backward or forward in slots to keep the tension right. It was all done with one handle sticking up almost vertically, alongside the tank. At first it was on the righthand side, then moved to the left. It may sound odd, but it worked for 15 years, and Barnes won numerous competition events with its aid.

The Rudge Multi, which came out in 1911, three years later than the Gradua, cut out the need to move the rear wheel by expanding one pulley as it contracted the other, keeping the belt tension the same. This was a logical improvement over the Zenith, but the next step was to discard the belt in favor of the chain and still offer more than one gear ratio.

This was first done by Jonah Phelon and Richard Moore, who first called their machines P & M and later Panther. They used chains from their start in 1900, and by 1904 had a two-speeder with countershaft. But their original device was to use two chains and two sets of sprockets, engaged by a dog clutch onto a countershaft which carried the secondary chain to the rear wheel.

Alfred Scott used the same idea and was sued by P & M, but he claimed that it was not new and quoted Werner and de Dion

Thomas Greene on the Rudge which won the Grand Prix de France, and Cyril Pullin after winning the 1914 Senior TT on his Rudge Multi (below).

A 1913 Australian 980cc Wesson-JAP twin.

Bouton as precedents for its use. Scott took it a step further by providing the first kick start with a chain from one of the pedals used to start (as on a moped today) except that it had to be hinged round first. P & M had another novel idea and dispensed with the frame downtube and used the engine as part of the frame, just as Vincent did later on his high-performance machines.

By 1906 there was a three-speed gearbox from the English company of Chater-Lea, still in business but no longer making motorcycles. Once chain drive and variable gears had taken over, progress really began. Some people tried out epicyclic hubs, like those still used on push-bikes, but they did not stand up to the transmission of power as they did the pedal push.

Frame design was also subject to change, although initially the diamond frame was universally employed except by Scott who used a cradle like many bikes have today. Most engines had settled down over the bottom bracket after the early experiments, and tanks hung from the top tube.

The scientifically minded are always complaining that the motorcycle has developed little over the years, is still crude, and in much the same form as it was in the beginning. There is some truth in this. Whereas the motorcar has some models with front engines driving the front wheels, some rear engines driving the rear wheels, and even some with mid-engines and all sorts of other variations, the motorcycle keeps its classic shape. The comfort, power produced, road holding, handling, and reliability are another matter. Racing did a great deal to improve the breed. The Tourist Trophy was the toughest race, but the Brooklands Track which came into use about the same time (1907) offered several different circuits, and the possibility of continuous high speed to test the stamina of engines and other parts, notably frames on the rough surface. It may come as a surprise that in the first race, for touring motorcycles, twins had to average 75 miles to the gallon and singles 90.

Charles Collier, one of the three brothers behind the Matchless, irreverently known to bikers as the Matchbox, won the singles race with a JAP-engined machine. Matchless and Collier are not names to be passed over. Charlie Collier and his brother Harry either won the TT or finished second from 1907 to 1910 and went on to many other victories. The third brother, Bert, raced in the 1920s on what was really a modified production model.

Matchless used JAP and MAG engines, singles and twins, and when AJS got into trouble in 1932 it bought the company and did

some badge engineering. It also bought Sunbeam in 1937, but passed it on to BSA. Later the great Matchless name disappeared in the conglomerate which eventually owned all the surviving British makes. In its day Matchless mounted many army dispatch riders, racers, and clubmen. Apart from its fairly orthodox machines the firm produced two which are remembered with affection. They are the Silver Arrow, a 394cc side-valve V-twin, quiet and comfortable if not quick, produced in 1929, and the four-cylinder Silver Hawk of 1930, which had an overhead camshaft. Both bristled with novelties. The Arrow had both front and rear brakes coupled to the pedal, but a separate hand lever for the front. The Arrow, designed by Charlie Collier, also had dry-sump lubrication.

These machines also had a sprung rear end on Silentbloc bushes, working on coil springs under the saddle with an adjustable damper. The Arrow did not sell too well at £55, and ran for only four years. The Hawk, in which brother Bert took a hand, had coil ignition, an instrument panel on top of the handlebars, and

an oil-bath primary chain case. This one sold about 500 models over only five years, yet it must be considered a milestone in the development of the motorcycle.

If the Arrow was a bit slow because it was overweight, the Hawk could top 80mph (half a century ago) and also dawdle in top gear. It cost £75, and that was the problem. An American writer called it: 'A sterling example of ingenuity by British designers. . . . It is very probable that it was discontinued because of its complexity and high cost of manufacturing in the limited numbers that such an expensive machine would require.'

Matchless was not alone in attempting the four-cylinder theme in the days before knowledge of metallurgy and production machinery made it all easier. There were at least a dozen makes, some not well known, some which did not reach the production stage, but were worthy attempts at something different and better. Best known perhaps is the Ariel Square Four, which *did* get into production and lasted 25 years. The Squariel, as the fans knew it, came in three forms from 1930 onward: 500, 600, and 1000cc, but

In the 1920 Scottish Six Days Trial Ariel entered its new 4.5-horsepower single-cylinder machines as a team.

Rex Judd on his flat-twin horizontally opposed
Williamson 1000 in the 1913 Scottish Six Days.

all with the four cylinders in a square. It was really two twins contra-rotating, with linked crankshafts, designed by Edward Turner who later produced another milestone, the Triumph Speed Twin.

He used a chain-driven overhead camshaft in the 500 and 600 models, but went to pushrods for the Thousand, which was the one to have. The 500 was 51 by 61mm, and in the 600 the bore size went up to 56mm. The Thousand was 65 by 75mm. The Four was a sensation in 1930, and the 600 pleased the sidecar men when it came out in 1932. It had more power than most machines of the time, and it came smoothly and quietly, which was even more unusual. The Thousand also ran to dry-sump lubrication, pioneered by Ariel in the 1920s.

Once the early overheating problems had been solved the Squariel could cruise at hitherto unheard of speeds. The Thousand came back after the war with telescopic front forks and a sprung rear end on option, and to cut the weight the engine went from iron to aluminum, saving more than 50lb.

In the United States, home of the big car engine, big motorcycles with four-cylinder units were more common. We have mentioned Ace, Henderson, and Indian, but they were all predated to the market by the Pierce Four in 1909 from the Pierce Arrow car company of Buffalo, New York.

Some people looked a little sideways at the Pierce Four as it had more than a passing resemblance to the advanced Belgian FN, which was sold from Boston, Massachusetts. While both were in-line Fours, the FN used an automatic inlet valve, suction operated as in many early engines, while the Pierce had a T-head with a camshaft on either side for positive operation of both sets of valves. This followed the design of the successful Pierce Arrow car engine.

Percy Pierce, only son of George Pierce, was given the company by his father, and brought an FN home with him from Europe. The Pierce Arrow car was in the Cadillac class, and the motorcycle followed, using shaft drive and costing $325. There was no starting clutch; the engine was pedalled into motion with the machine on the rear stand, then bike and rider (hopefully) shot off together. Later models had a multi-plate clutch. Another novelty was that the gasoline and oil tanks were part of the tubular frame. The price went up from the 1909 figure of $325 to $400 in 1912 and the machine was available in black, carmine, or royal red. But it was costing more to make than the selling price, and disappeared in 1914.

From 1903 the Belgian FN on which the Pierce Four was based was a pioneer in four-cylinder engines and shaft drive. In fact the firm made the first practical four-cylinder machine at the Liège factory of the Fabrique Nationale d'Armes de Guerre in 1904. The designer was Paul Kelecom, and the machine was ridden through six countries to the 1905 Paris Salon without trouble. He crossed France, Italy, Switzerland, Germany, Holland, and Belgium before appearing at Paris, and this was in bad winter weather in November and December.

The motorcycle was said to be smooth and vibrationless, and produced 3bhp at 1800rpm from 362cc. The shaft drive ran inside a frame tube, and the ignition cut out to stop the engine was worked by a twist grip. A curious feature was that the starting chain and pedal bracket, held on by one big bolt, was made under license from the American Colombia Works of Hartford, Connecticut. Later a special American model was made with various modifications.

An Englishman, Sidney Horstmann, designed a two-speed gear which could be installed on the FN. The very advanced twist-grip stop was not successful because it sometimes caused explosions which destroyed the silencers. It was dropped in 1906 in favor of a valve lifter on the now-bigger 410cc engine. In 1914 the size went up again to 750cc.

The Germans occupied the FN works in 1914 and made the 750 Four for army use, and kept it on afterward. It was not easy to ride solo as the engine torque resisted left-hand bends, but it was continued up to 1923. The Four died in 1926.

Another little-known Four which had a similar life span but less success was the Militaire Four, later the Militor; probably fewer than 100 machines were made by eight companies from 1910 to 1922. The first model looked rather like the Ner-a-Car, also American designed, with hub-center steering, an armchair seat, and even a steering wheel. It also had outrigger wheels as on a child's bicycle to keep it up when stationary, both front and rear suspension and shaft drive. The makers persisted in calling it a car, which did not improve sales. This model was begun in Canada and moved to Cleveland, Ohio, but it had not appeared by 1913 when a new model offered handlebars instead of a steering wheel. Then the Champion Motor Car Company of St Louis, Missouri, took over and called it The Champion. Car dealers still said it was a motorcycle and would not sell it.

Next N R Sinclair took over and moved operations to Buffalo, New York, but he went broke in 1917, and was followed by the Militor Corporation of Jersey City, New Jersey. That company sold some models to the US Army with sidecars attached, but they were heavier than Indians or Harleys and certainly no better. Knox Motors finally took over, in Springfield, Massachusetts, opposite the Indian factory. This was in 1920, and the Militor died in 1922 after a sea of teething troubles. It was a good try.

William G Henderson had more success with his Four, which ran from 1912 to 1932. Carl Stevens Clancy rode one around the world in the launch year, covering 18,000 miles. Henderson offered a hand crank for starting when all the other machines had to be put on a stand and pedalled to start. It was a straight air-cooled Four, selling for $325. One of the many publicity stunts was a ride round a roller-coaster track by Blick Wolter in 1917.

Henderson began in 1912 with a single-speed model but by 1914 had a two-speed gearbox in the rear hub. He also shortened the wheelbase, as a very long machine was a handicap on rough and rutted roads. The new models ran on a 58-inch wheelbase. This was partly achieved by removing the two-foot footboard which ran right across the machine in front of the engine and putting individual ones on either side. A three-speed gearbox in unit with the engine with car-type clutch came in 1917.

Another of the Henderson stunts was to take the coast-to-coast record from Los Angeles to New York City, 3296 miles in seven days 16.25 hours, beating that set up by the famous and colorful Canonball Baker on an Indian Twin in 1914. The Henderson rider was Allan Badell, 21, who died of influenza in the 1917 epidemic. Roy Artley then did the Three-Flag Route from Blaine, Canada, to Tijuana, Mexico, covering 1667 miles in three days and 25 minutes on a Henderson—again taking the record from Canonball Baker.

Roads were of course rudimentary in those days, and riders had to ford streams, dodge rocks, and plow through mud. Henderson also won speed, hill-climb, and endurance records until he sold out to Ignaz Schwinn of the Excelsior Motor and Manufacturing Company, makers of the Excelsior Twin, and the machine became the Excelsior-Henderson. William and his brother Tom soon left, William to start making the Ace Four.

The old Henderson had used a splash-lubrication system, but the designer of the new Model K put out by Excelsior, Arthur O Lemon, who moved on from the old firm, put in a full force-feed system and Roy Artley rode for 300 miles at 77mph on a California track. The K sold well and was followed by the De Luxe which could do 100mph and was bought by many police forces in the United States.

The stunts went on, with Wells Bennett covering 1562.54 miles in 24 hours on a board track at Tacoma in 1922, a record which stood for 15 years. Again he took it from Canonball Baker. Then in 1928 Excelsior hired A R Constantine from Harley-Davidson to design the KJ Model, sometimes known as 'the Streamlined Henderson.' This was a 110mph machine much used by police since it could catch any car. In 1931 Schwinn became alarmed by the Depression and suddenly stopped production, going back to bicycle making, which his company is still doing.

William Henderson also designed the Ace after he left Excelsior in 1919, and this was another great American Four which lasted until 1926. American machines of the period went in for house colors: Henderson blue, Harley-Davidson khaki, Indian red, Reading brown. Ace favored blue with white wheels and gold lettering on the tank, and offered $10,000 to any machine which could run faster.

Henderson and Arthur Lemon produced the design for the air-cooled straight four, which sold for $395 in 1924 and dropped to $335. Lemon took over completely when Henderson was killed in 1922. Ace followed Henderson in putting on stunts and record attempts, and Red Wolverton covered the mile at 129mph in 1923 on a road near Philadelphia, riding a specially-prepared and lightened machine, and 106mph with sidecar.

But, like other famous mounts, the Ace was selling for less than it cost to make, and production eventually stopped in 1924. A few more were made by new owners (Michigan Motors Corporation) in 1926, and then Indian Motorcycle Company bought what was left, producing the Indian Four which lasted until 1941.

Acquisition of the Ace gave Indian a single, twin, and now a Four in their range, which they proclaimed as the most complete in the world. Indians featured a quarter-elliptic leaf-spring in their front suspension, and when it featured the Ace engine it produced vibration which it had never done in its 'own' frame. Indians switched to a cradle frame, after using a steadying brace as an interim measure. The new model was called the 402, and it also featured a five-bearing crank in place of the Ace's three bearings.

There followed an unfortunate model in 1936 known as 'the Upside-down-Model' because the usual Indian setup of inlet over exhaust valves was turned round with the exhaust valves on top and inlets down below. This spoiled the appearance of the 437 series and the public did not buy it. Later models went back to the old arrangement.

The last models, from 1939 to 1941, featured telescopic rear springing and mudguards with enormous valances almost enclosing the wheels. Two prototype Indians with shaft drive designed after the war were never produced.

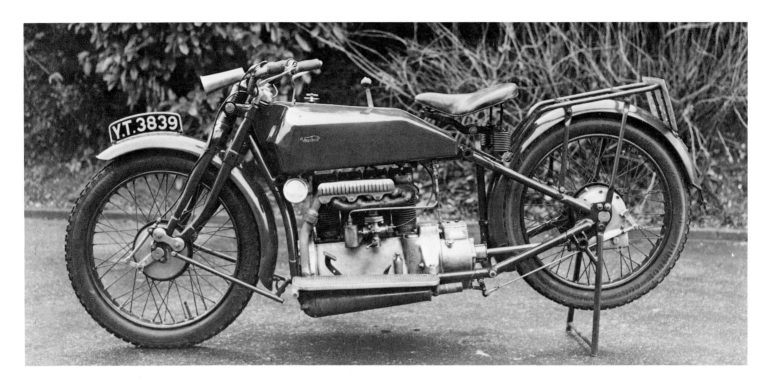

The last American Four which we have not discussed was the Cleveland, made in Cleveland, Ohio, from 1925. This excludes unrealized projects like the Gerhart and Cannonball Baker's own machine. Cleveland, makers of lightweight machines from 1915, produced its first Four in 1925 with a 37-cubic-inch T-head engine, but it did not handle or perform as well as expected. The company then hired E H DeLong, who came from Ace and Henderson, and drew up a new model called the '4-45' with a monobloc casting, ioe valves, unit gearbox, and cradle frame. But the rival Ace and Henderson had engines nearly twice the size, so Cleveland moved up to 61 cubic inches, or 1000cc. The last model, the Century, was sold with a 100mph guarantee and a foot clutch in the American way, but was killed by the Depression.

The Gerhart was suspiciously like the Belgian FN but had differences. It used a four-cylinder pushrod engine and leafspring front suspension and was made in Philadelphia in 1913, but very few machines emerged from the factory.

The other unrealized dream came from the record-breaker Cannonball (E G) Baker, who died before the machine was built. It was a joint project with E H DeLong of Ace/Henderson/Cleveland, with a four-cylinder V engine of 73 cubic inches. An engine was built and tried in an Indian frame, but was unsuccessful. This was in 1920.

England and mainland Europe were also the source of some unfulfilled dreams in the four-cylinder world, including one which even had the name of the Golden Dream. This came from George Brough, who made the famous SS 80 and 100 models ridden by Lawrence of Arabia, among others. George Brough showed his first Four at the 1927 Olympia Motor-Cycle Show in London, with a V engine of 998cc. He went on to show four prototype Fours in subsequent years, culminating with the Golden Dream with a transverse Four, like two twins on top of each other. Before that he tried an Austin Seven car engine, but none of the models was ever sold.

The Wilkinson Four, which looked rather like the American Ner-a-Car with a car-type seat, was similar in some ways. This was designed by P G Tacchi but not produced, although one—presumably a prototype—still exists. The designer moved on to the Touring Auto Cycle (TAC) in 1911, which also had a car-type bucket seat, but was water cooled. The second version was called the Touring Motor Cycle (TMC), and only a few were made.

Another stillborn English venture was the Vauxhall motor-cycle, made by the car firm which is now part of America's General Motors but was independent in 1921 when it designed the four-cylinder 930cc ohv machine with three-speed gearbox. It had flutes on the fuel tank like the ones that used to be on the hood of their cars. An aircraft-engine designer, Major Halford of the Ricardo Engineering Company, drew the engine and the rest of the machine, which had shaft drive, interchangeable wheels, and an American-style foot clutch. Apparently only two were made.

Even sadder was the story of the Wooler Four, another British effort. John Wooler produced designs from 1912 to 1954, but few ever reached the market. Curiously the Wilkinson Sword Company, who was behind the Wilkinson Four also agreed to make John's single-cylinder machine in 1912, but it did not happen. He went on to make some twins himself, announced a Four in 1943 which was built as a prototype but never went into production, and another of different design in 1954. The 1943 Four appeared at the 1948 London's Earls Court show, with 500cc flat-four light-alloy engine, shaft drive, and the novel feature that the whole machine could be dismantled with one open-ended wrench as only two nut sizes were used. Unhappily, although production plans were made, they never came to anything.

The longest production-run record must go to Nimbus of Denmark, who made a four-cylinder machine from 1920 to 1957, with 746cc ioe engine and a frame made from pressed steel welded and bolted up. There was, however, a gap between 1928 and 1934 when Nimbus was too busy with vacuum cleaners. Many of the machines were sold to the army.

The Ner-a-Car, designed by the American Carl Neracher and made from 1921 onward in Syracuse, New York, was not in the four-cylinder class but valuable as a curiosity. It had a 211cc single-cylinder two-stroke engine, mounted in a frame which later sprouted a bucket seat, a car-type dashboard and a windshield. Some had different engines, and the steering was from the front hub centers. The Ner-a-Car was a cross between a car and a motorcycle, which was its downfall, because users of both types of vehicle were too conservative to buy something different. In America it cost $225 in 1921 but was sold for 66 guineas in England.

A British version was then made by Sheffield-Simplex at Kingston-on-Thames with a 285cc engine. Transmission was by friction drive with a fiber-clad ring pressing on a bronze disk, and by chain to the rear wheel. Later models had bigger Blackburne

Far left: The only Vauxhall motorcycle, the
survivor of six made by the British car firm in 1924
with a four-cylinder engine, integral clutch and
gearbox, and shaft drive to the rear wheel. It is in a
private collection in the Isle of Man. Vauxhall is
now part of the American General Motors concern.

Left: Arthur Hind's 350cc single-cylinder
Connaught with Burman gearbox with hand
change. This is a 1925 machine photographed
taking part in a run for old machines. The one
behind is a Royal Enfield.

350cc engines and normal three-speed gearboxes. Most of the
works were hidden, and the hope was to attract women riders.
Many stunts were tried, and the Ner-a-Car did well in trials and
other competitions, but it was gone by 1926.

The scooter had a brief spell of glory, with makes like ABC,
Kingsbury, Reynolds, and Quadrant in the 1920s. Some had to
be ridden standing up, which was not popular, although one of
these types—the Kingsbury—had a two-stroke engine and chain
drive. However they could not compete with the motorcycle and
faded away.

There are so many great names which have departed among the
makers that we can pick out only the household ones for a brief
history. The greatest English name is perhaps Norton, which
started up in 1901. Ironically enough James Lansdowne Norton
used foreign engines, Swiss and French, in his first machines.
Although his bike won the 1907 TT in the twin-cylinder class, the
great Norton era was from the 1920s on, after the founder's death
in 1925.

Model names which stick in the enthusiast's mind are the International, at one time the favorite of newspaper dispatch riders for

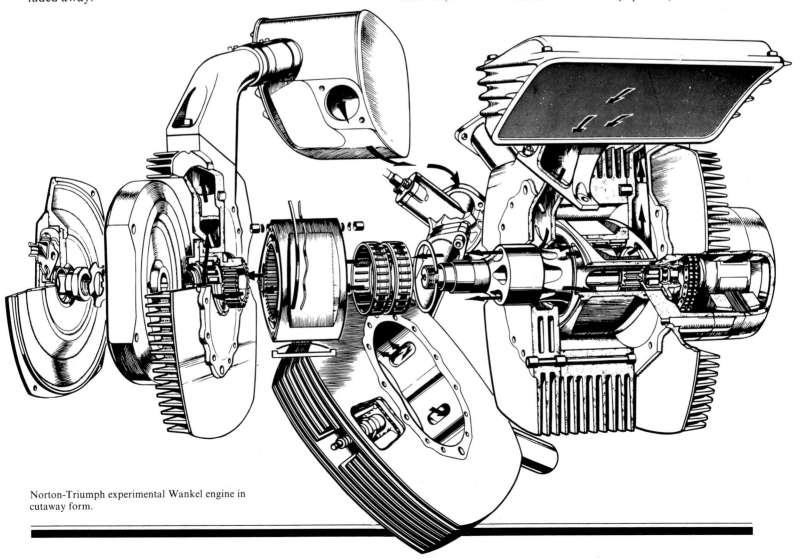

Norton-Triumph experimental Wankel engine in
cutaway form.

rushing photographic plates to their offices, the Manx, the 16H (a side-valve model much used by the British Army), and the Featherbed. James Norton himself rode a 490cc side-valve machine in the TT races of 1909, 1910, and 1911 but failed to finish each time.

He became ill after his last run and the business almost closed in his absence, but another firm by the name of R T Shelley and Company, who had done work for Norton, formed Norton Motors Limited which kept the great name going. A famous tuner, D R O'Donovan, also helped by rebuilding engines before they were installed in new machines with a guaranteed speed of 70mph for his Brooklands Racing Special or 75mph for the Brooklands Special.

Norton did not contribute much to World War I until a late stage when it supplied some machines to Russia, and after the war rebuilt old military models for sale to the public. The next step was an overhead valve in 1922 which James Norton had designed long before but not marketed, but this retired in the Senior TT that year.

It went on to be sold as the Model 18, and in 1923 this model—or the racing version—ran second and fourth in the TT, and with

Right: Brian Stonebridge on his 347cc Matchless in the 1950 International Six Days Trial in mid-Wales.

Below: James was a name famous in the British industry for small machines, but this 1914 model was a lusty 600cc suitable for hauling a box sidecar, and equipped with acetylene lighting.

a fifth place as well took the Manufacturers Team Prize. Norton began winning the TT in 1924, one year before .the founder's death. Two other famous names then came on the scene, Walter Moore, who had left Douglas to join Norton and produced the overhead camshaft engine, and Joe Craig, a racer who became the mastermind behind Norton racing victories for many years to come.

The 'Cammy' Norton won the Senior in 1927 ridden by Alec Bennett and went on winning for some 30 years, with development by another designer, Arthur Carroll. The names of the riders read like a *Who's Who* of the best in motorcycling: Stanley Woods, Tim Hunt, Jimmie Simpson, Jimmy Guthrie, Freddie Frith, Harold Daniell, Geoff Duke, Artie Bell, Reg Armstrong, the Rhodesian Ray Amm and, on three wheels, the sidecar ace, Eric Oliver.

Norton domination continued up to World War II and on into the 1950s, when the Featherbed frame gave them a second lease of life. The heart of the machine, the 500cc engine, was a straight-forward single developed from the iron-block 1927 version with single camshaft. The later Craig model used light alloy and two camshafts to produce 50 horsepower.

Compression ratio eventually went up to 10.8:1 on the 350 and 10.4:1 on the 500 by the time the end came in 1954, and the Nortons were also using telescopic forks and a sprung rear end. After 1953, when they were bought by Associated Motor Cycles who also made Matchless and AJS, the downhill slide began. In 1966 AMC too went under, and a new company known as Norton-Villiers Limited took over. There was a minor revival with the 750 and 850 Commandos, but the great days of the 'Garden Gate' frame (so called because that was what it looked like), the International and Manx models were long gone.

The older generation still cannot understand what happened, the young perhaps do not care, but the naked brute glory of the big-banger single slogging under that massive tank is still impressive.

One of the architects of Norton success outside the factory orbit was Francis Beart, tuner extraordinary, who made the machines do undreamed of things from the 1930s into the 1970s. He learned his trade from the late Eric Fernihough, a top Brooklands rider and record-breaker on Brough Superior, and first turned his

Left: Back in 1935, long before the 'kneelers' for sidecar riders were invented, W Graham shows how it is done on his 495cc AJS with his passenger hanging out in traditional style. The race was at Alexandra Park, north of London.

talents to the JAP engine, but soon became a Norton man, coaxing out the hidden horses as no one else could.

Beart came from Suffolk in eastern England, born in 1905, but his family moved to London where he was educated, in matters motorcycling more than anything else. He began as a racing rider himself in his spare time, but eventually became the high priest of the Norton engine, entering his own riders in the big events. His specialty was meticulous preparation, saving of weight with his own alloy parts, and the inevitable infinite capacity for taking pains.

Norton's competitors in the great one-lung era were principally AJS, BSA, Matchless, and Velocette, plus machines from other countries like the DKW supercharged two-stroke, Benelli (although both these were lightweights), Gilera, BMW, and of course Rudge and Excelsior. There were others among the dozens of makes on the market at that time who will emerge in their rightful place.

The AJS company, which took its name from the five Stevens brothers, or more accurately from Albert John Stevens, originally sold engines to other people to put in their machines. These were made at the Wolverhampton works from about 1902, but in 1911 they produced their own machine after experience in competition themselves. Their machine was a single, with the option of direct belt drive or chain drive, and a two-speed gearbox.

AJS stuck to this 292cc (70 by 76mm), or 2.5 horsepower under the British rating, until it became involved in the TT. The company ran a 350cc to win the 1914 event from the twins of Royal Enfield and Douglas, which expired. The rider was Eric Williams with Cyril Williams, also AJS mounted but not related, in second place. This began something of a tradition, interrupted by World War I. No civilian machines were made until after 1918, but Jack Stevens was back with a new 350 in the Junior of 1920.

He had now progressed to push-rod actuated overhead valves and a six-speed transmission, achieved by using two primary chains and a three-speed gearbox. Unfortunately his team members fought a private battle with each other which put them all out except Cyril Williams who won at 40.74mph, but AJS went on to win the Junior for four years in a row.

AJS was among the first British makes to use overhead valves, and was also early with chain-driven overhead-camshaft models in 1927—the immortal Cammy Ajay, which had as big a following as the 'Big Port' which had come in earlier. As well as the successful racing singles there were production V twins, first side-

valves up to 990cc and then ohv and even an in-line Four. Then the company diversified into cars, trucks, and radios and did not survive the 1931 slump. It went through the hands of another company on the way to becoming part of the Collier brothers empire, makers of the rival Matchless machine.

AJS became a Matchless painted another color, part of Associated Motor Cycles which eventually was the British motorcycle industry, owning Francis-Barnett, James, and Norton, and at one time Sunbeam as well before selling it to BSA. There were famous models still to come after the war—the Porcupine and the so-called Boy Racer. The Porcupine fell down because it was designed during the war to be supercharged, but the use of blowers was

banned by the time it was produced. The name came from the spiky fins on the cylinder heads.

The Porcupine was a twin ohc of 500cc inspired by the racing successes of BMW and Gilera. When blowers were banned AJS tried to recoup some power with higher compression but the induction tracts were all wrong. It should have produced 60bhp but initially only produced 40, later painfully pushed up to 55. Similarly peak power should have come at 9000 but was actually at 7600rpm. In spite of this and the handling, which could have been better, the Porcupine won races, notably the Dunholme Grand Prix, but it did no better than places behind the Nortons in the TT.

Les Graham came close to a Senior win, and in addition to the two Williams already mentioned 30 great riders did well on AJS. The Boy Racer, officially the 7R, came on the scene in 1948 as a copy of the successful Mk VIII Velocette KTT ohc 350cc single. It even had the same (74 by 81mm) dimensions. It never won a TT except in experimental three-valve form in the hands of Rod Coleman in 1954. The front forks were different and the AJS was lighter than the Velo. The Boy Racer did well in the amateur Manx Grand Prix of 1952 when, with Bob McIntyre, it won both the Junior and the Senior for 500cc machines. Eventually the production two-valve machine put out more power than the factory's experimental three-valve racer.

The AJS name is not dead, and 248 and 358cc two-stroke motocross machines are now being made under the banner of the old marque. Its great rival of the 1920s was BSA. It was a company with a different kind of image, initially for reliable touring machines like the 1924 Roundtank and later 1928 Sloper, although in later years the Empire Star and Gold Star moved them into the sporting class.

BSA stood for Birmingham Small Arms Company, which produced various kinds of guns from the Crimean War onward. When it ran into financial trouble it was discovered that machines which made shells could also make bicycle spindles and hubs, and an industry was born. BSA progressed from bicycle parts to complete machines by 1910, and the BSA motorcycle was born. The first was a 499cc single with belt drive and no gears, finished in the green and cream which was to become its livery.

World War I took the company back to gun making, but the bikes came back with peace, with a big V twin added to the singles. BSA made a big assault on the TT with a £10,000 program and six machines; unfortunately not one finished and that marked the end of racing for a long time. The little 250 Round Tank and the Sloper were very successful, even if the parent company was not. A total of 35,000 Model Bs (official designation of the Round Tank) were built, and the Sloper, with 350 and 500 versions, both side and overhead valve, was a steady number for a decade.

The big V twins were the standard sidecar machine in Britain, and in the sporting field the Gold Star was invented (a 350 single) when Walter Handley won a Brooklands Gold Star for lapping at over 100mph. The fact that he rode a 500 is irrelevant as there was also a 500 production model. With World War II the company returned to gun manufacture again, except to produce the 500cc side-valve M20, used by the services to the tune of more than 120,000 machines. The M20 survived the war and was joined by more exciting models. The vertical twin A7 500 was not a success,

The 1922 BSA trials team with their sidecar outfits and Harry Perrey on his 493cc solo (center). The other riders are Bertie Bird (left) and J H Walker, who was killed the following year.

but led to the 650cc Golden Flash A10 twin and the Star Twin, which won three gold medals in the 1952 International Six Days.

Now there were singles, twins, two-strokes and scramblers and ultimately the three-cylinder 740cc Rocket capable of 120mph. A half-million Bantams, copied from DKW, were made with 125cc two-stroke engine up to the 1973 demise of the company, when it was swallowed by Norton-Villiers-Triumph. Although BSA never came back to racing a factory team after its TT debacle, the Gold Star dominated club racing in private hands in the 1950s and won great affection among riders and watchers alike.

The Ariel Company, also located in Birmingham, was big in singles until it was bought by BSA and the two firms began to share common parts in the 1960s. Ariel has left behind famous model names like the Red Hunter as well as the famous Fours. The company began in 1898 and made its first motorcycle in 1902,

Right: Bill Nicholson again, this time with a pudding-basin helmet (No 20), leading Basil Hall on an early BSA Gold Star in the Experts Grand National in 1952.

Below: W Nicholson on his 500cc BSA in the first section of the famous Burn Bottom during a trial in 1952 before helmets were compulsory wear.

after producing tricycles and quadricycles. Ariel never undertook much racing as a factory, although owners did well with tuned machines.

One of its publicity stunts was to mount a 500 single on floats which successfully crossed the English Channel and back again, carrying rider and pillion passengers, both trials riders. Ariel went bankrupt in the Depression of 1932, but Jack Sangster, who later owned BSA, kept the company running with a smaller range of models. The Red Hunters appear in this era in 250, 350, and 500 guise with the fashionable twin upswept exhaust pipes and a dashing appearance.

The war stopped production except for an Army model, the 350 W/NG, which was actually a modified Red Hunter. After the war this model was joined by the revamped Four and some vertical twins in 500 and 650 sizes. Then came the curious Ariel Leader, a device with a pressed-steel frame open ended at the front, with a 250cc two-stroke twin engine suspended from above. The engine was enclosed, the machine had leg shields, and the 'tank' was really a luggage trunk. The real tank was under the hinged dual seat.

This machine was quite different but it did not sell well. Ariel simplified the machine by removing some of the panelling and the leg shields and called it the Arrow, which was more successful. There was even a sporting version which had some success in private hands, as the factory did not race.

BSA sold the old Ariel works at Selly Oak near Birmingham and moved the remnants of the company into its own Small Heath factory. They tried to make a 200cc Arrow and finally a three-wheeler with a 50cc unit called the Ariel 3, but the public did not like that either. The end came in 1966. They tried to make a new Four to sell as a portable generator for service use, with the idea of putting some of the 600cc units into a Leader frame.

A 1914 Royal Enfield with sidecar in a modern run for veteran machines.

Service spending was cut, and that marked the sad end.

Excelsior was another great name among the singles competing with Norton; they were most effective in the 250cc class whereas Norton were always in the 350 and 500 class. The 250 Manxman was the machine on which Excelsior fame rested, but it was selling production machines in the same market, as opposed to the racing specials.

There has been confusion because there were four unconnected Excelsior makes, two German, one American and one English, and it is the latter which made the grade in the Isle of Man and elsewhere. The English machine was made by Bayliss Thomas from 1896 in Coventry and faded away in 1964. All sorts of engines were used in the early days: Blackburne, JAP, Villiers, MMC, Minerva, and Excelsiors' 'own' engine in the curious Mechanical Marvel was made by Blackburne.

This 250 which won the 1933 Lightweight TT on its first outing, ridden by Sid Gleave, had a complicated valve gear, with two camshafts working four radial valves through pushrods, pistons, rollers, bushes, and bearings. It was all too much to make for production, and gave way to a straightforward overhead-cam 250 single Manxman, followed by a four-valve version and then a twin 250. The various racing Manxmen in 250 form (they also made a 350 and 500 road-going machine) were most successful in the 1930s, but after the war Excelsior turned to Villiers-engined, two-stroke bread-and-butter machines which were practical but dull, although the company also still made its own 250cc twin two-stroke.

Rudge Whitworth, also big in singles and racing in the golden age of motorcycling, built one machine of nearly as much complexity as the Excelsior Mechanical Marvel. It was the four-valve or Radial Rudge which ran 1-2-3 in the 1930 Junior TT on

its first outing, and went on to other great victories. There were various versions of the complex valve gear, which was the last pushrod engine to win a Junior TT.

Rudge began making motorcycles with the familiar red hand badge in 1911 with a 499cc inlet overexhaust single. The Rudge Multi of 1912 was famous for its introduction of variable gears, and the Rudge Ulster was yet another motorcycling milestone and a model beloved of two-wheel enthusiasts the world over.

The forerunner of the Ulster was the Rudge Four, a single-cylinder 350 and later 500cc machine with four valves and four-speed gearbox offered in 1924. The Ulster model came four years later when Graham Walker, the sales manager, won the Ulster Grand Prix at a shade over 80mph, the first 80-plus win. The machine came first and the name later, and went on to be used on works-replica machines sold to the public. In spite of the success of the Ulster the Rudge was not selling well enough, and the company went bankrupt in 1933. It limped on in other hands up to the war, but the factory was needed for more important things and another great name bit the dust.

The history of the British motorcycle industry reads like a long obituary, and yet another once competitive name on the list is that of Royal Enfield—'Made like a gun.' In spite of this sober slogan the factory raced and was successful in trials until it faded away in 1967 like so many others. It had begun in 1899, gone out of business in 1907, and come back in 1910; altogether it spanned a long life.

Royal Enfield's most famous models are probably the big side-valve V twin of 972cc, the K model, which pulled many a British family sidecar in the 1920s and 1930s, and the later Bullet range of more sporting machines, which had first four valves, then three, then four again. They also used internal push-rod tubes cast within the barrel walls.

The 692cc Meteor twin and the 736 Interceptor were fore-runners of the modern Superbike but did not sell well enough. The Continental GT of 1965 was advertised as Britain's fastest 250, but it was not enough to save the company. One can still buy an Enfield Bullet, but it is made in India and is not the most modern machine available.

New Imperial is another name from the past with a ring to it, but that model did not have the success or the aura of Norton and others, and died out in 1939 after being on the market since 1903. One of its claims to fame is that it was the last British machine to win the Lightweight TT in 1936. The great racer Bert le Vack rode a New Imperial in the 1922 Junior TT, with a special machine dohc JAP-powered which had already taken the world one-hour 350cc record and the flying kilometer, the latter at 83.56mph. He led the race until he fell out, which is typical of the New Imperial story.

A one-lunger favorite perhaps even less distinguished but remembered with affection is the New Hudson. It ran from 1909 until 1952 without making much impact, although the racer Bert le Vack was involved with this one, as was Jimmy Guthrie. New Hudson departed from one-lung practice with a big 770cc V twin

in 1913, which is hardly remembered now among its subsequent models.

Under le Vack, New Hudson did come second in the TT once, but production ran out in 1933. In the 1940s there was a New Hudson autocycle or moped made by BSA, but that was the last. The Bronze Wing appeared in 1930, and the New Hudson 500 in 1932 with the speedometer inset in the fuel tank.

Historians may record the facts but do not always weigh the sentiment accurately in terms of how the public remembers various machines. A case in point is the Levis, which was also lost with the war (1939) but has a big place in the affections of old-time motorcyclists. Levis was first known for two-strokes from 1912 when it brought out the 211cc Baby Levis which went on for about 15 years. It used racing as a publicity tool, but did not always win. After the first war Levis produced a 250 for the 1920 TT with the same stroke (70mm) as their two-strokes, but with a 67mm bore to compete for the trophy for 250 machines. They ran 1-2-3 in the new class. In later years these machines were outclassed.

The two-strokes endured and there were nice-looking 250 and 350 machines with chain-driven ohc, but the best one was the 1930 model 350 A2 ohv machine. The 500 developed from it was not as good, but the last fling, the 600 single was a success, if orthodox.

Italian Pietro Ghersi taking Governor's Bridge on the Isle of Man TT course on his way to second place in the Lightweight.

It would have had a sprung rear end but for the war.

A curious story is that of Raleigh, now one of the biggest English bicycle makers, but lost to the motorcycle world. Its three-wheel cars with one front wheel are not easily forgotten. Raleigh also made some motorcycles before 1906, and returned after World War II when it produced big flat twins and singles up to 500, and a V twin.

During its second spell Raleigh also supplied engines to a number of other makers, notably Coventry Eagle, Dunelt, and Cotton, although they were actually sold under the label of Sturmey-Archer, part of Raleigh and better known for making

The BAC Lilliput of 125cc, made in 1951 by the Bond Aircraft Corporation of Blackpool, England, and powered by the ubiquitous JAP two-stroke engine in a simple tubular frame.

gearboxes and hub gears for bicycles. Raleigh used a twist grip in 1903, an advanced device, but the company was not otherwise innovative. It dabbled in racing, but was more involved in reliability trials until it stopped making motorbikes in 1933.

Although Raleigh had not had much success with its TT entries, it was bold enough to market a 'TT Replica' in 1930 with a foot

gear change, which was also *avant-garde*. It made a brief return to the powered two-wheel scene in 1958 with the 50cc Runabout still with what was called a Sturmey-Archer engine but made by BSA. Raleigh also made the French Mobylette and the Italian Bianchi under other names without great success.

Single-cylinder great names from the past also include the British Sunbeam, which came from a company making both cars and bicycles from the very early days. It was the bicycle company which produced the motorcycles, and it was already famous for its 'Patent Little Oil Bath' in which the bicycle rear chain lived away from road dirt. The first motorized machine appeared in 1912, a 347cc single finished all in black, including the handlebars.

The 'Little Oil Bath' came with the motorcycles too, plus a split rear spindle so that the wheel could be removed without disturbing the bathing arrangements. As the company had made 'The Gentleman's Bicycle' the motorized device had to be 'The Gentle-

man's Motorbicycle' as well. Soon the single was joined by a 770cc V twin, but with a bought-out JAP engine. The next step was a 500cc single which did quite well in the 1914 Senior TT, with a second and two lower places. During World War I Sunbeam made some machines for the French army, and the twins served as sidecar ambulances and machine-gun outfits. Afterward both the founder, John Marston, and his son died and the company changed hands.

Sunbeams had always sold under a quality label, and the new owners kept this up, as they did the TT entries. Sunbeam's best-known rider was George Dance, a market gardener when out of the saddle, but others included Graham Walker.

Walker became competitions manager in 1924 and played with an overhead camshaft design, but it did not win races and the company went back to a pushrod operation. This brought victory in the Ulster Grand Prix, the Grand Prix d'Europe on the German Nurburgring and elsewhere, while Sunbeam was also notching up wins in reliability trials.

The 500cc racer was now called the Model 90 and its 1928 win in the Senior TT in the hands of Charlie Dodson, defeating former chief Graham Walker who had now gone to Rudge. Dodson won at 62.98mph and Walker did not figure among the leaders. Sunbeam also picked up the manufacturers' team award, as it did the following year when Dodson won again, although this was the last win by a pushrod two-valve-per-cylinder machine.

After this the sporting side remained in the background until

Sunbeam joined AJS and Matchless under the Associated Motor Cycles umbrella. They faded away with World War II, apart from producing an army design which was not made, until Sunbeam came back as part of BSA, with a 487cc vertical twin with ohc engine and shaft drive, plus large fat tires. The S7, as the model was called, was not a success due to weakness in the shaft drive and vibration. A later S8 was made with modifications, but apart from some BSA/Sunbeam scooters in the late 1950s the famous name declined.

Triumph, another British maker, had long been a Sunbeam rival, although strangely this very English company was started by two Germans in Coventry in 1903. Like many other companies Triumph first used imported engines—Minerva, Fafnir, and JAP —until it made their own 499cc single which won the TT in 1908. Originally it appeared in a small size and was developed for racing.

There was also a Triumph factory in Germany, at Nuremberg, and both businesses co-operated until 1929 when they went their own ways. During World War I Triumph sold more than 30,000 of the Model H 550cc side-valve to various armies, and in World War II did the same with their 350cc single. There was to have been a vertical twin, but German bombs destroyed the factory.

Most Triumph models were worthy but unexciting, except the 'Riccy,' an ohv four-valve single designed by the famous cylinder-head man Harry Ricardo and Major Frank Halford in 1921. It finished second in the 1922 TT, but in 1924 the rider, Walter Brandish, fell and no more was heard of the four-valver.

Triumph had one more big model in store: the Speed Twin which made motorcycling history in developed form as the Tiger, Bonneville, and Thunderbird. It began when Triumph, who were now making cars, decided to close the motorcycle side of the business, and Ariel boss Jack Sangster bought it up. He had the Ariel Square Four designer Edward Turner with him, and Turner designed the 500cc vertical twin marketed in 1937 as the Speed Twin. There had been an earlier Val Page-designed 650cc vertical twin which did not last long in the catalogue. In 1939 a sportier version was named the Tiger 100, following up the Tiger 70, 80, and 90 already being sold. The twin which never was would have been a 350cc version. After World War II Triumph was in a new factory at Meriden built in 1942. The 350cc Twin arrived, and also the TR5 Trophy, which had unusual parentage. It was Tiger 100 with the cylinder heads from a portable generator produced to charge the batteries of RAF bombers while in flight, made of light alloy to save weight.

Mac Hobson and passenger, G Atkinson, cornering fast on the Scarborough circuit, England, in 1970 on their 654cc BSA.

The twin grew to 650cc as the Thunderbird, mainly for the United States, and the more sporting Bonneville. Then came the last model, the three-cylinder Trident with 741cc. Triumph and Ariel belonged to BSA since 1951 and the BSA Rocket Three was similar to the Trident except that it used a different engine. The BSA group was now in financial trouble, and it decided to close Meriden.

Just before this happened the British government had persuaded Norton-Villiers to take on the BSA remains. The Triumph men refused to be shut down with the loss of 1500 jobs, and 'sat in' for 18 months until they won. The government put up £750,000 plus a loan of £4.2 million to keep a workers' cooperative going, producing the Bonneville, the rights to which they had bought, together with the Trident from Norton-Villiers with another £500,000 of government money.

By 1979 the Cooperative was making and selling bikes steadily after sorting out problems which began in 1973, but its machine was originally designed in 1937 and due for replacement. There was a revised engine on the stocks.

A famous name which arises in connection with twins is that of Douglas, pioneer and old faithful of many British riders until it disappeared as a make in 1956. Douglas was always known for the flat-twin mounted along the wheelbase of the bike, and this was its classic design. Later it turned the engine round BMW-style to make a transverse twin, which did not please the die-hards. Their dirt-track bike, born in 1928 when speedway came to England, was also a winner, with the gearbox over the rear cylinder.

The company began in 1907, and the 'Duggie' was soon a firm favorite with British riders with the 348cc flat twin, although the under-engine gearbox first used made the center of gravity unnecessarily high. Many of these machines were ridden by World War I dispatch riders. Freddie Dixon won the first sidecar TT in 1923 on a Douglas, but it was a 600 with his inimitable banking sidecar in which the passenger sat still and the machinery did the leaning over. Douglas also won the Spanish TT and was fourth in the French Grand Prix 10 years earlier.

In 1923 Douglas raised the gearbox and shortened the wheelbase; it had been using overhead valves for racing since 1920 and now went for light-alloy cylinder heads and a four-speed gearbox. Dixon won the TT again, and another Douglas rider, Len Parker, won the sidecar event. From 1928 onward the dirt-track machines sold highly successfully, but in 1932 the Douglas family pulled out of the business and quality gave place to low price. The manufacturers tried shaft drive and cross-mounted engines, but the old Duggie was gone, and the customers did not want a substitute.

Another twin of which relatively few were made, yet which held a special place in the affection of all motorcycle enthusiasts, is the Vincent. Philip Vincent, father of the machine, and George Brown, who raced it with such success, both died in 1979, bringing an era to an end. The grandfather of the Vincent HRD as it was first called, was Howard Raymond Davies, born in 1895, who became an AJS apprentice with the five Stevens brothers. Davies did well in racing on Sunbeam and AJS until he decided he could build a better bike himself, which he did under the HRD banner in 1924. His JAP-engined machines did well in the TT and elsewhere, and about 500 were made before 1927 when the money began to run out following the British General Strike of the year before and anti-motorcycle propaganda in the newspapers. Howard Davies sold the HRD name to Philip Vincent, and went to work first for Alvis and Star and finally for Bill Lyons, who was running the company, Swallow Coachbuilding, which eventually became Jaguar cars. He and Vincent did not meet until shortly before Davies' death in 1973.

Philip Vincent was the son of a cattle rancher in Argentina, who owned his first motorcycle when still at Harrow public school and built the first of his own machines when he was a Cambridge University engineering student. He had designed the frame as a schoolboy, and bought the HRD name, stocks, and tools for about £400 in 1927 when he was 19. Thus the first of a famous line began, leading to the 1000cc twins which might have been dubbed the Rolls-Royce of motorcycles if George Brough had not already pre-empted that title for his Brough Superior. Perhaps 'the Bentley of motorcycles' might be more appropriate in view of the sporting aspect of the Vincent. The HRD part of the name was dropped in 1949.

The famous names began with the Rapide and variations called Black Knight, Black Shadow, and Black Lightning under the general slogan of 'the world's fastest,' as they held the speed record at one time. Attempts on short-distance records were less successful than the long time and distance ones.

Although the Vincent twins and even the single-cylinder Comet were considered the best among riders of the day, the company was never successful financially and eventually was sold after years in the hands of receivers. One of the reasons was that Phil Vincent hated to buy in parts and wanted to make everything himself, which was expensive. He told Roy Harper, who has written three books about the man and his machines, that he dropped the HRD label because Americans thought it had something to do with Harley-Davidson. Curiously enough there was an attempt at a marriage between Vincent and the American Indian in 1949 when a Rapide engine was put in an Indian Super Chief frame, to be called the Vindian. There was also a Vincent-Indian, which was a modified Black Shadow with American lighting and controls, but neither model was ever sold as the Americans preferred the straight Black Shadow or Rapide. Vincents suffered from lubrication problems and brake troubles, although the brakes were marvellous at low speed. However they stand alone as an attempt to make the best motorcycle ever, regardless of cost.

Although Vincent was always a small-production firm there were parallels between its situation and that of Velocette, also a high-quality manufacturer who had a very checkered beginning and end but a successful period in the middle. After starting in 1896 the company went broke in 1905, did not make much impact until 1923, and went out of business in the face of Japanese competition in 1971.

But Velocette, like Vincent, had a special place in the hearts of enthusiasts and could do no wrong. The immortal models are the KSS and KTT, and Velocette was the first to use the positive stop foot gear change in the 1929 Junior TT. The company's attempts to make an 'everyman' machine as opposed to one for the sporting rider never quite succeeded. The nearest to success was the quiet-running, water-cooled, shaft-driven LE model of 1948 onward, with enclosed mechanical parts and full weather protection. Although it sold well to the police, the public did not make it a best seller—perhaps because it was too expensive.

The company was originally called Veloce Ltd, and the forerunner of its successful line of overhead camshaft models came in 1925 with 348cc, designed by Percy Goodmann. There were also some good two-strokes, but the ohc is the Velocette hallmark, allied to dry-sump lubrication. The first was the K model, which fathered the KSS, and later the KTT which was a racer sold over the counter after its TT victories. Another curiosity was that it placed the secondary chain outside the primary chain, making ratio changes easy and the crankcase narrower.

The popular M series also sold well from 1933 onward, but it lacked the magic of the Ks, except for the pushrod MAC 350, and was a cheaper substitute for the 'cammy' models. The 350 was always Velocette's winning class, but 500s were made from 1935 onward. Velocette made a famous bike-that-never-was under the title of the Roarer, a supercharged 500 twin with shaft drive. It was not ready before the war and afterward the racing authorities banned the supercharger. The designer, Harold Willis, died in 1939. Velocette's last fling from 1956 was the V models, Venom and Viper, sporting machines which did well. There was also the Thruxton push-rod single of 1964, which had a good specific output, but the great models and great days were gone.

Britain was dominant in the motorcycle world up to 1939 and a few years after the war, but some intruders did make their mark. One was the Swedish Husqvarna, which is also the name of a town and of a famous armament maker, which was active from 1903 onward. Like many others the company began by using other people's engines, but soon developed its own. There were all sorts and sizes, but the classic is the 498cc V-twin racer which demonstrated what was to come in the 1934 Senior TT when Stanley Woods made the fastest lap and was about to win the race when he ran out of petrol. The 500 Husky twins were the fastest machines in the Isle of Man with 118mph top speed in their day, and the 350cc machines were challengers too. Husqvarna ran for six years in the major races before giving up, eventually producing 44bph at 6700rpm—and this in the 1930s. It is still in business but now with small motocross machines with two-stroke engines of its own make.

The Italian firms of Moto Guzzi, Benelli, and Gilera were also challenging by 1937, and the German DKW had joined the BMW twin with its buzzing two-stroke, all in the racing field, which was the mirror of motorcycling progress at the time. The Italians were dominant for 10 years, roughly from 1950 to 1960, and then the Japanese moved in and have stayed at the top. We will come back to the Japanese machines in a later chapter and consider meanwhile the scene of combat.

The most important venue in world image value was the Isle of Man, where four different circuits have been used over the years, although only the 37.75-mile Mountain Circuit counts in most people's eyes. The first was the 52-mile network of roads used by

Harold Daniell winning the 1938 Senior TT in the Isle of Man on his 500 Norton.

the Royal Automobile Club in 1904 to select the British team for the international Gordon Bennett Cup car races. (Racing was not permitted on the public roads of mainland Britain, which could only be closed for that purpose by a special Act of Parliament that stood no chance of being passed.)

The car circuit took in a climb of Snaefell Mountain, which was obviously too steep for the early two-wheelers; when the Auto-Cycle Club decided to run its selection trials for the British team for the International Cup races it mapped out the 15.8-mile St John's Circuit. This started and finished at the village of St John's, near Douglas. This short circuit followed some of the roads used in the Mountain Circuit, but not always in the same direction. This was used from 1907 to 1911 when the races were moved to the Mountain Circuit. The fourth circuit in the island, last used in 1959, is the Clypse Circuit of 10.79 miles, on which the 1954 Lightweight and sidecar TT events were held, and subsequent similar races up to 1959. Whereas in 1954 it was over 10 laps or 107.9 miles, in 1955 the length was cut to 97.14 miles or nine laps, and extended to 10 laps again in 1957.

The Lightweight TT was for 125cc machines and for 250s, the Junior for 350s, and the Senior for 500s. In 1947 when the races were resumed after the war, as a sort of celebration the Isle of Man also ran three races in the same gradings for Clubman's machines. Clubmen were road bikes which had to be kick started rather than pushed off, and they were allowed up to 1000cc in the Senior. But the difference with the race was that all the riders ran together, the smallest and slowest starting first, with the assumption that all the winners would arrive at the same time. This meant that the fastest riders had to overtake the whole field. The Club-

man races lasted until 1956—in 1955 on the Clypse Circuit—and were then moved to the mainland. They have been succeeded by the Production Machine TT. The Manx Grand Prix for amateur riders, at the time of writing, is still a regular event taking place in September.

The name Tourist Trophy has become something of a misnomer for events for pure racing machines, and the Isle of Man TT is no longer the qualifying British round in the international calendar after some star riders had complained about the safety aspects of such a long course which is hard to learn and cannot be protected all the way round.

An Open Formula 750cc Classic International TT was added in 1974. The number of laps run has varied over the years, but generally the bigger-engined machines have to cover a longer distance than the 'tiddlers.'

Other British circuits include Aintree, where the Grand National over-the-sticks horse race is held. This three-mile circuit opened in 1954 and was used by cars and motorcycles for 10 years. Similarly Brooklands, which opened in 1907, came to an end with World War II. It offered a 2.75-mile circuit plus a road course combined with the concrete saucer. Brands Hatch near London started as a motorcycle grass track and now has 2.65-mile lap used for many car and motorcycle races.

Castle Combe in the West of England has a 1.8-mile circuit used mostly for club events for cars as well as bikes, although not for major events. London's Crystal Palace circuit opened in 1937 with a two-mile lap, later cut down to 1.39 miles, but has not been used for some years. Donington Park Circuit opened in 1933 for motorcycles, was closed by the war, and recently (1977) reopened on a slightly different lap of less than the original 3.1 miles after considerable argument with various authorities. Two other park circuits are Mallory and Oulton, both north of London. Mallory began as a grass track but progressed to a 1.35-mile road circuit, used for the Anglo-American motorcycle races among others. It is about 100 miles from London. Oulton Park is 70 miles further

north, also used for the Anglo-American, and is 2.76 miles long with lakes and trees.

Snetterton in Norfolk, 2.7 miles around and near Norwich, opened in 1951 and is in the same ownership as Mallory, Oulton, and Brands. Thruxton in Hampshire is an old airfield first used for motorcycles and has a 2.35-mile lap.

Of the Continental circuits, France has several which are used for the Grand Prix. They are the Clermont-Ferrand, a five-mile track in mountainous central France; Paul Ricard, a brand new artificial circuit in the south; and a selection of others utilized over the years at Le Mans (Sarthe), Rouen, Reims, Nogaro.

One of the most famous and popular motorcycle circuits in Europe is the home of the Dutch Grand Prix at Assen, the Van Drenthe circuit of 4.796 miles on normal public roads, permitting very high speeds. It rivals the Spa-Francorchamps 8.77-mile lap used for the Belgian Grand Prix for many years, one of Europe's fastest.

Germany offers the incomparable Nurburgring in the Eiffel Mountains which is 14.17 miles round the normally-used northern loop, and the Hockenheim ring which is smaller and less interesting with a 4.2-mile lap. The old Avus track in Berlin has not been used since 1967.

Italy has the high-speed Monza Circuit in a park near Milan and Imola, where a 200-mile race like the United States Daytona event is staged around the 3.1-mile Autodrome Dino Ferrari of artificial roads.

The Imola 200 is one of the fastest and riches races, although not up to the Spa course, where Barry Sheene won with a race average of 134.98mph in the 1977 race for the 500cc Belgian Grand Prix. The other Belgian tracks, such as the 5.9-mile Chimay and 4.8-mile Mettet, do not compare, although even at Chimay in the Grand Prix des Frontières Sheene won at 127.296mph.

The Spanish Grand Prix has two homes between which it alternates. One is in the Montjuich Park in Barcelona where the motor show is held, offering a 2.35-mile lap, and the other the newer Jarama circuit of 2.2 miles near Madrid.

Switzerland no longer allows road racing since the Le Mans disaster in the French 24-hour car race. In Northern Ireland the Ulster Grand Prix for motorcycles was run on a true road circuit

Barry Sheene, former World Champion, on his 750 racing Suzuki before he left the works team.

Brian Smith about to win the final in the first Santa Pod, England, drag meeting of 1973.

of 16.5 miles near Dundrod until the security situation and lack of money brought it to an end in 1973.

Back in England the flat and featureless Silverstone track on an old airfield is one of the fastest and best-equipped tracks with a 2.9-mile lap which permits fast average speeds, run by the British Racing Drivers Club. The lap is 2.932 miles and the record held (1978) by James Hunt (Marlboro McLaren M23 Ford) at 1 minute 18.81 seconds or 215.539kph.

North America has many circuits in both the United States and Canada, but the most famous for motorcycling is Daytona International Speedway where the Daytona 200 is run, the most prestigious race on that side of the Atlantic. The track opened in 1959 with a 2.5-mile lap, and a 3.81-mile (now 3.87) road circuit was later created by adding 1.31 miles of infield road to the banked tri-oval. Speeds are very high for both cars and motorcycles.

The machines and the tracks make the setting, but it is the men of skill and courage who make racing possible and, since the first TT in 1907, have been doing what to the ordinary man does not seem possible. In this chapter we have space to pay tribute to only some of the many heroes who put the sport on the map, but many others will be found in the alphabetical A-Z section, from all countries of the world.

The most famous Italian is Giacomo Agostini who has won 15 world titles and more than 123 Grand Prix races. With his film-star good looks 'Mino,' born on 16 June 1942 at Lovere, Brescia, northern Italy, home of the great Mille Miglia car race, is a natural crowd puller. Most of his wins were on MV Agusta machines until he switched to Yamaha in 1974. He led the top riders' opposition to the danger of the British TT races in 1972 when his fellow countryman, Gilberto Parlotti, was killed. He had also tried his hand at car racing.

American Steve Baker, born September 1952 at Bellingham, Washington State, is short, slight and wears glasses and looks a most unlikely world champion. He won the FIM 750 World Championship in 1977 for Yamaha, and was second in the 500 Championship. He lives near the Canadian border and began his racing in that country, winning the Canadian Championship in 1974 and 1975. He also came second in the Daytona 200 that year, and came to Britain with the American team for the Anglo-American races. He won Daytona in 1977, and the previous year three of the Transatlantic match races.

George Brown, who died in 1979, held world and British national records on his Vincent machines until forced to retire at 55 years of age in 1967, and was still the fastest—car or bike—up the Shelsley Walsh hillclimb in England. His favorite machines were Nero of 998cc and Super Nero of 1147cc, both from the Stevenage, Hertfordshire, works of Vincent where he was a road tester. Nero was built from a wreck after he had left the company, and his other pet was Gunga Din, a 1000cc racing machine which was the prototype of the Black Lightning.

Johnny Cecotto from Venezuela was a prodigy who won the 350cc World Championship in 1975 when he was only 19 years old. He was the son of a racing father who won local championships in South America before competing in Italy and the United States. After a Daytona third place he came to Europe and beat Giacomo Agostini in the 350 Championship for Yamaha. Success so young made people call him a playboy, but nevertheless in 1976 he won Daytona and was second in the 350 Championship. In 1977 he was all set to challenge Barry Sheene in the 500 class when an accident put him out in a 250 race, but he came back to win races again in 1978.

Charlie Collier is famous as the winner of the first-ever TT race in 1907, but there were two races, one for singles and one for twins, and it was the singles class in which he conquered. He and his brother Harry founded the British Matchless company and both brothers raced; their father Harry A was also involved in the business from 1899. Charlie went on competing up to 1914 when war stopped play and earned many places and one more win. He died in 1954, active up to the last at 69 years of age.

Harold Daniell, great Norton rider, could always raise a laugh by recalling that he was turned down as an Army dispatch-rider in 1939 owing to his poor eyesight. Yet he rode in competition for 16 years and had many places in both Junior and Senior TT, including two Senior wins, always on the inimitable single-cylinder Nortons, except for his first three apprentice years on AJS. He rode in the TT for 10 years from 1934 onward and several times set the fastest lap.

Howard Davies gave his name to a marque, the HRD, and this in turn was incorporated in the Vincent-HRD. He rode for Sunbeam at the age of 18 in 1914, his first TT, to finish second. He was most amused when he read his own obituary during his service in the Royal Flying Corps when he became a German prisoner. He came back to ride AJS of which company he was designer and competitions manager until he produced his own machine under his own initials, then sold out to Phil Vincent. He was born in 1895 and died in 1973.

Freddie Dixon became a legend in his own lifetime as Fearless Fred who was up to all sorts of antics and would never behave himself in a way that the authorities thought he should. He first raced in the Isle of Man in 1912 and died in 1956, leaving a chain of worried hotel proprietors and track records behind him. He was an inveterate practical joker, but a winning rider, sidecar pilot, and car driver as well. He rode many makes and introduced the Banking Sidecar which lent over with the machine, and was the only man to win both solo and sidecar races in the Island.

Geoff Duke was a more serious man who won six world titles from the time he came on the scene in 1948 in the Manx Grand Prix. He retired in 1959 after many successes on the Island and elsewhere. He first rode as an army dispatch rider in World War II and went in for trials riding before turning to racing. He joined the then all-conquering Norton works team in 1950, won the Senior, and did the first 90-plus average. Next year he won both 350 and 500 World Championships and the Segrave Trophy.

Helmut Fath from Germany won the world sidecar title twice and produced an engine of his own design. His first win was on the Munich-based BMW in 1958 when he was third in the world-title rounds, and he won the title in 1960. The following year he crashed at Nurburgring, when he was badly injured and his passenger killed. He came back in 1963 and later made his own URS engine, a four-cyclinder dohc 500cc with fuel injection. The machine's name came from his home town of Ursenback, and on this he won the 1968 title to break a 14-year BMW sidecar run of wins. He retired in 1971 but the URS went on to win again in 1971 in the hands of Horst Owesle.

Freddie Frith from Grimsby, England, was one of the great Norton riders who dominated the scene in the 1930s. He first won the Junior for the company in 1936, did the first 90mph lap in 1937, and went on to win the Senior for the first time. He came back after the war on a Velocette, won the 350cc World Road Racing Championship, and was the first motorcyclist to be awarded the OBE (Order of the British Empire). Freddie, always the gentleman, was also always in the first three in any TT in which he finished over the years.

Rem Fowler, like Charlie Collier, won the first TT in 1907, but he won the Twin class, riding a Norton, at 36.22mph. Harry Rembrandt Fowler, to give him his full name, was still taking an interest in the Isle of Man races more than 50 years later when he was in his late eighties. The Norton he used for that first victory had a French Peugeot engine. He rode again on Norton and Rex, then New Hudson and Ariel, but failed to capture the glory again. Nevertheless his name is a milestone in motorcycling history.

Mick Grant is a man of the present rather than the past, a Yorkshireman in racing since 1969 who came to notice in 1971 and has been battling with Barry Sheene round the circuits. He won the Swedish and Dutch 250 Grand Prix on a Kawasaki in 1976, and the following year set the outright lap record for the 37.75-mile Isle of Man Mountain Circuit at 112.776mph. He also won the British MCN/Brut 33 series in 1975 and is after a world title on a Kawasaki in the 250 or 350cc World Championships.

Jimmy Guthrie is a great name from the past, another Norton man who was killed in the German Grand Prix of 1937. There is a memorial to him on the TT course at the point where he retired in his last race there in 1937. Guthrie won six TTs—one Lightweight, three Juniors, two Seniors—and rode in 24, winning other places also. He was a Scot from Hawick.

Mike Hailwood from Oxfordshire, England, won 12 TTs and set more records in the Isle of Man than anyone thought possible. He was a whirlwind until he moved out of motorcycles to car racing, and then made a comeback after 11 years to win the TT again. He won the first race he entered in 1957 and went on win-

Skip Aksland at Brands Hatch near London in 1977.

ning for 10 years when Honda paid him not to race again. In between he won both Junior and Senior TTs and the Lightweight, was the first man to win a Senior at an average of 100mph on a single-cylinder, plus the 350 and 500 World Championships, and one year almost won all three TTs except for an engine failure in the Junior.

Walter Handley, usually known as Wal, was an English rider who after 13 years of successful motorcycle racing was killed in a wartime air crash. He had won all four TT races—Ultra-Lightweight, Lightweight, Junior, and Senior—and set lap records in

Two world champions in battle at Brands Hatch, near London. Britain's Barry Sheene is being led by Kenny Roberts of the United States.

all three major races. His first TT was in 1922 and his last in 1934. In between he rode OK, Rex-Acme, AJS, and Rudge and was regarded as one of the finest riders of his generation by those who followed the sport.

John Hartle was a later performer who first appeared in 1954 and was killed in 1968 racing at the same place, Oliver's Mount in England. He did well in the Isle of Man and rode in the Norton team in its last racing year, 1956. He rode an MV Agusta, then reverted to his own Norton when the factory had given up, and a spell on Gilera before going back to Norton. Injuries kept him out from 1961 to 1963, and again in 1965 and 1966, but he kept coming back. He was a great and popular rider with a polished style.

Pat Hennen from Phoenix, Arizona, born 1953, won the New Zealand Marlboro Series in 1975, 1976, and 1977 and became a Suzuki works rider with Barry Sheene in 1977, when he ran third in the World Championship and won the British Grand Prix. He also won the most points in the John Player Transatlantic Series in both 1977 and 1978. He began racing at 20 as a professional, after dabbling on scramblers from 16 onward and competing in minor events, winning the American Junior title in 1974. In 1976 he won the 500cc Championship race at Imatra, the first American to win such an event.

Gary Hocking from Rhodesia was Welsh born, started racing in 1958, and was killed in South Africa in 1962 practicing for a local car race. He made a big impression in the Continental circus, winning places at Assen in Holland, the Nurburgring, and in France. He started on his own 350 Norton but won a works ride with the East German MZs and won races. In 1961 he won the 350 Championship and also the 500. He won the Senior TT that year and retired from motorcycle racing.

Bill Ivy, known as Little Bill because of his 5-foot 3-inch stature, began racing in 1959 on his local Kent circuit of Brands Hatch and was killed in East Germany in 1969. He fought a bitter duel with his teammate Phil Read on Yamahas in 1968 for the 250cc Championship and lost by two minutes on time when they both had the same number of points. Bill liked fast cars and the glamour life of the racing star, but also won races, including the 125cc World Championship with eight Grand Prix victories.

The Japanese Takazumi Katayama, inevitably known to the bike world as Zooming Taxi, was the first man from his country to win the 350cc World Championship in 1977. Although he has spent most of his life in Tokyo he came originally from Korea, and is a successful rider as well as a pop singer. He was a test rider for Yamaha before becoming a competitor and is said to have an aggressive style, but won second place in the 1976 250cc World Championship.

Teuvo Lansivuori comes from Finland and also answers to Tepi as a nickname. He moved on to road racing from ice racing, speedway, and motocross and won the 1971 Spanish Grand Prix as an unknown. He then rode Yamaha, running fifth in the 250 World Championship, then joined the Yamaha works team in 1973, finishing second in both 250 and 350 Championships. He switched to the Suzuki team, was third in the 500 Championship in 1974, and third in 1975. Since then he has run his own racing team.

Italian Marco Lucchinelli has had more crashes than wins so far, but he is quick and is still in his twenties (he was 26 in 1979). He comes from the marble town of La Spezia, and rode in hill climbs before moving to road racing on a Yamaha in 1975. Next year he was on a 500 Suzuki, and was third in the French Grand Prix, his first championship race, and second in Austria, making him runner-up in the championship. He crashed twice in England, once in Italy and in Holland but won the Dutch race in 1977.

English rider Steven Parrish is an up-and-coming young man, 24 in 1979, who started as a Hertfordshire farmer and was taken up by Barry Sheene. He began racing in 1973 and by 1976 had won the British Championship and a 1977 ride in the Suzuki works team, after also winning the Grovewood Award for the most promising rider in 1975. Suzuki dropped him in 1978, but he was still placed in international races and is on the way up.

Phil Read has a marvellous riding record but became something of an *enfant terrible* among the fans when he criticized the Isle of Man course and refused to ride there. He began racing in 1955 and was winning two years later at the age of 18. He rode in the Yamaha works team, then for MV Agusta and beat his teammate Agostini for the 500 title, then Honda. He has won many championships and major races but proved a hard man to deal with; he was nicknamed 'The Mouth' for his outspoken comments.

Kenny Roberts is an American from Los Angeles who was on top in his own country when he decided to try the European scene. He began at 14, and was American Champion in 1973 after winning the Junior Title in 1972. Riding Yamaha he was third in 1976 and fourth in 1977, the year in which he also won four of the six Transatlantic Match races. In 1978 he won the Daytona 200 and attacked the 250 and 500 classes in the World Championship and is a leading contender among the stars of today.

Kel Carruthers, another American (by adoption) looks after the machines of Kenny Roberts and keeps them in shape. He was born in Australia and has won races there, in Europe, and in the United States. He won the 250 Championship for Benelli in 1969, then the 1970 Daytona 200 on Yamaha, and was second in the 250 and 350 world classes. In 1974 he retired to run the Yamaha team and take care of Kenny's machines in particular.

Bob McIntyre from Glasgow, Scotland, born in 1928, was a great Scottish rider who set the first Mountain Circuit 100mph lap in the Isle of Man on a Gilera Four in 1957. He started racing in the 1950s and was killed at Oulton Park in 1962 after a meteoric career. He rode Nortons and AJS originally before turning to works Gileras and Hondas, and was always within sight of a title but did not quite make it. He took the world hour record on a 350 Gilera Four at Monza in 1957 at 141mph.

Derek Minter, the British rider known as the King of Brands Hatch, began racing in 1948 and went on to take records like winning five races in one day. Then in the Isle of Man he beat the works Hondas on an old machine in the 1962 TT in the 250cc class. He rode Norton, Gilera, EMC, AJS, REG, MV Agusta, Benelli, Honda, and Matchless among others. He was impeccably professional but lacking a works ride decided to give it all up in 1967.

Barry Sheene has become the idol of the crowds in a way that no other rider has done, perhaps because he has happened in an age of easy communication when more people are aware of such stars, allied to an immense talent. He is also still the boy-next-door despite his very successful career, formerly as a Suzuki rider. Barry Stephen Frank Sheene was born on 11 September 1950 in London, son of a former rider. He has won all the big events and championships, survived a 170mph crash, and can make himself understood in six languages.

Jimmie Simpson is another of the great band of Norton riders, but although much respected and talented he only won one TT in his life, the 1934 Lightweight, and that on a Rudge. He began riding in 1922 and competed in 26 races on the Island and finished in half of them. He moved to Norton in 1929 after riding Scott and AJS, but still failed to figure in the winning slot, although he did come in second in the 1933 Senior. He did do the first 80mph

Continental sidecar battle with Britain's Eric Oliver (No 55) on Norton being led in the Grand Prix de Mettet by a European team.

lap, and also the first 60 and 70, and rode sidecars as well as solos.

John Surtees is the only man to win the World Championship on both cars and motorcycles. He was also alone in winning both Junior and Senior TT races in two consecutive years. John, a Londoner, son of a motorcycle dealer, began racing at 17 on a single-cylinder Vincent, then on Norton. Later he was a works rider for MV Agusta, and won both the 350 and 500 World Championships in the same year, 1958, when he also won both the major TT races. He did it again in 1959 and almost in 1960.

Eric Oliver was the first sidecar racer to use a streamlined 'kneeler' in or on which the rider is kneeling down rather than sitting, and all the others had to follow suit. Eric, born 1911 in Sussex, England, was a solo racer on grass and road before he took to three wheels on grass. He began in 1931 and when he retired in 1955 had been champion of the world four times, in 1949, 1950, 1951, and 1953. But in 1958 he appeared again in the Sidecar TT, riding a Norton Dominator touring machine with a Watsonian Monaco 'chair' in which his lady passenger sat in an upright touring position. He finished tenth at almost 60mph average.

Stanley Woods from Dublin rode in his first TT at 17 and went on competing for 17 years, on two occasions winning both Junior and Senior in the same year, 1932 and 1933. He was a favorite with the fans and after riding Cotton, New Imperial, Scott, and Royal Enfield settled down with the unbeatable Norton until tempted away by Guzzi, Husqvarna, and finally Velocette with whom he stayed until his 1939 retirement.

A-Z

Barry Sheene in action, knee-out style.

A

AAMRR

The American Association of Motorcycle Road Racers is one of the bodies concerned in the management of racing in the United States. It is now on friendly terms with the AMA, but has not always been.

ABC

The All-British Engine Company began in 1913 and the machines were made, finally only in France, until 1925. The designer was Granville Bradshaw and his layout was similar to the modern German BMW machine, with a transverse flat-twin air-cooled engine, but unlike the shaft-driven German machine it used chain drive. The model by which the company is remembered is the 398cc ohv flat twin of 1919 onward made by the Sopwith Aviation and Engineering Company Limited, at Kingston near London. It had a four-speed car-type gate change, and used quarter-elliptic leaf springs at both front and rear gears before many other machines had sprung frames. The price rose from £70 to £150 due to inflation and there were production problems leading to faults, particularly in the valve gear and with lubrication. By

1921 the British company had closed down, but machines were made in France by Gnome and Rhone for several years longer. ABC also made a scooter called the Skootomota with a 123cc engine from 1919 to 1922 which sold well but failed to survive.

Aberg, Bengt

Born in June 1944 in Sweden he won his first World Championship in motocross in 1969; he won again the following year and is one of the leaders in this sport. Aberg began riding in competition at 16 and has ridden Matchless, Metisse, Husqvarna, and Bultaco and was victorious in four of the 12 ranking races in 1970.

Continental favorite Giacomo Agostini on his 500 Yamaha in the course of winning one of his many championships. He has now turned to car racing

Abingdon

This British machine lasted more than 20 years from 1903 to 1925. It was made by a famous toolmaker, Abingdon King Dick, at Birmingham, originally with various imported engines, but later with its own side-valve. After 1925 the bikes were called AKD and made with side-valve single-cylinder engines in various sizes up to 350cc.

ACC End-to-End Trial

This was a trial from the south of England

to the north of Scotland (Land's End to John o'Groats) run by the Auto Cycle Club around the turn of the century in which many famous riders like George Brough took part.

Ace
A classic American motorcycle made from 1920 onward until absorbed by the Indian company who used the Ace engine, it was designed by William Henderson who was first involved with the Excelsior. The Ace used a four-cylinder 1229cc air-cooled engine and comprised many special features.

Acme
The Acme was an English machine made from 1902 until the company amalgamated with Rex of Coventry to produce the famous Rex-Acme motorcycle which did well in competition. The original Acme machines were made with bought-out engines, originally singles and later 997cc V twins. See also Rex-Acme.

Adler
Adler was a German manufacturer also known for cars and office machinery including typewriters. It made motorcycles intermittently for more than half a century from 1900 to 1957, mainly before 1907 and after 1949. They were two-strokes, the later ones inclined parallel twins which did well in the smaller classes in racing, motocross, and trials.

Aermacchi
Another Italian aircraft maker, Aeronautica Macchi Spa, turned to two-wheel machines at the Varese factory. It later became the Italian branch of the American Harley-Davidson and is now Cagiva. It started with scooter-like machines and later moved to high performance and racing bicycles, winning many races.

Aero-Caproni
This Italian aircraft factory at Trento manufactured motorcycles from 1948 onward for 15 years. The designs were the company's own creation, in small engine sizes, from 50cc to 150cc using both ohv and ohc and also a variety of frames, both pressed and tubular.

AFM
The American Federation of Motorcyclists was a rival body to the AAMRR before the AMA took control of the motorcycle sport in the United States.

Giacomo Agostini of Italy, one of the most successful riders ever.

Agostini, Giacomo
One of the great names of modern motorcycling, this Italian star, who has recently taken to car racing, has won more than 120 motorcycle Grand Prix races and many world titles. He made his name with MV Agusta and did equally well on the entirely different 750 two-stroke Yamaha. He was born in June 1942, has won races on every size of machine, and is one of the great riders of all time.

Agusta, Count Corrada
The man behind the Agusta machine which carried Agostini to the top, he took over when Count Domenico Agusta died. The family business originally made aircraft and entered helicopter and motorcycle manufacture in the late 1940s.

AJS
AJS was one of the leading British makes for many years, from 1909 onward until it was absorbed into a bigger combine. It was taken over by a competitor, Matchless, in 1931 which was in turn swallowed up. The Stevens brothers who started the company also supplied the engines to AJW, another British maker. Famous and remembered models are the Big Port and the Porcupine.

AJW
The AJW was a small production British machine made from 1926 on by A J Wheaton with engines of various makes, including JAP, Anzani, Villiers, Rudge,

and Stevens. In the post-World War II period machines with 500cc JAP vertical twin engines were planned but never marketed because JAP was unable to build engines. Later mopeds were produced with 50cc Italian power units. AJW imported slightly larger Italian machines up to 125cc which were sold under the AJW marque label.

Alba

Alba was a German make which began after World War I and operated for about five years, although it went on making spares after the production of motorcycles had stopped. They were four-stroke side-valves of 200 and 250cc except for one ohv at the end of the production. The factory at Stettin is now in Poland, and at one time also made engines for other makes and built light three-wheel vans.

Alcyon

A French make that went on for more than half a century from 1902, Alcyon ran in the Isle of Man TT in 1912 with single-cylinder 350cc machines with four valves and at various times absorbed other French makes. The range included a wide variety of specifications, two-strokes side and overhead valve units ranging from 100 to 500cc and used shaft drive on some of the heavier models. After World War II Alcyon moved down to smaller bicycles for the economy market with bought out engines, and eventually went out of business.

Aldana, Dave

Dave Aldana was an American professional racer, born in 1949, from Santa Ana, California, who was known for wearing a white skeleton embossed on his black leathers. He did well on dirt tracks, then turned to road racing and was in the American team for the Anglo-American series in 1970. Aldana rode for BSA/Triumph in the United States, then in the Norton team, and later for Suzuki. After that he bought a Yamaha and Harley-Davidson, but was out of action in 1976 with a broken wrist. His skeleton leathers caused him to be suspended at one stage in the United States, but the authorities relented and he was allowed to ride again.

Allegro

A Swiss machine made from 1925 for more than 30 years, the Allegro was successful in racing in the 175cc class. It used Villiers two-stroke engines and there was also a 350 version, with two engines coupled, ridden by the maker, Arnold Grandjean, in 1929. Production bikes also came with other makes of engine. Toward the end Allegro produced utility machines rather than sporting ones.

Allright

The Allright was an early German machine made from 1901 and sold under different names in different countries, for example, Tiger, Roland, and in England the Vindec-Special or the VS. Various engines were used until Allright joined forces with another German company, Cito, and went on to make the KG (Krieger-Gnadig) machine. The products included a shaft-drive motorcycle, and the machines were successful in competition with German riders. Eventually Allright stopped making machines about 1930 and continued to manufacture component parts for a time.

AMA

There are two organizations with this set of initials: the British Amateur Motorcycle Association and the American Motorcyclist Association. The British one is a body controlling amateur sport, while professional racing is run by the Auto Cycle Union which is the British representative body in international racing. The American Motorcyclist Association with headquarters in Westerville, Ohio, has been the American representative body on the international scene since 1970, and is affiliated to the FIM which runs the sport worldwide.

Ambassador

A British company which sold motorcycles with Villiers two-stroke engines from 1947 to 1964, Ambassador also imported the German Zundapp. The former racing driver Kaye Don was behind the company, which was sold to another British maker, DMW, when Ambassador ceased production.

AMC

This set of initials represents three organizations: (1) the British Associated Motor Cycles Limited, former makers of Matchless, AJS, James, Francis-Barnett, and Norton, (2) the American Allied Motor Corporation of Chicago, which made a big V-twin machine from 1912–15, and (3) the French AMC company which manufactured engines for sale to other companies.

AMF

The AMF is the American Machine and Foundry Group which owns Harley-Davidson and has owned the Italian Aermacchi motorcycle makers since 1969. Both brands of machine were known as AMF Harley-Davidsons, until AMF closed down.

Amm, Ray

A great rider who came from Southern Rhodesia (as it was known then), Ray Amm raced in Europe and was killed riding an MV Agusta for the first time in the Imola 350 event on Easter Monday, 1955. He was 29 and had ridden in the Norton team from 1952, winning many races including both Junior and Senior TT in the same year, 1953.

Ancilotti

These Italian machines were used mostly for trials and motocross in the 50 and 125cc sizes, and were also sold as the Scarab. Ancilotti has been in business very successfully since 1967.

Ancora

An Italian machine made from 1923 up to World War II using the British Villiers two-stroke engine, the Ancora won lightweight races and other events in its heyday. Eventually the production facilities were taken over by the Italian Umberto Dei who continued with the small bicycles until after the war, when he began using Italian Garelli engines.

Anderson, Fergus

Fergus Anderson was a road racer born in Britain in 1909 who was killed racing a BMW in 1956 when he was 47 years old. He rode Rudge, Velocette, NSU, and DKW before World War II and became works rider for Moto Guzzi in 1950, finishing second in the 250cc class of the World Championship. He won the 350 in 1943 and again in 1954, and he also won the Lightweight TT on a 250 in 1952 and 1953. Anderson worked as a journalist before the war and served in the Navy, coming back to racing in 1947. When he gave up racing he ran the Guzzi racing department, but left in 1955, and then rode for BMW until he was killed in Belgium.

Anderson, Hugh

Hugh Anderson was a road racer who was four times World Champion. He was born in New Zealand in 1936 and retired to Holland in 1966. He first rode AJS and Norton and then joined Suzuki in 1962 to ride its small-capacity racers, and won the

Top American, Dave Aldana (inset), leaping his Norton in typical style.

Mick Andrews on his 250 Ossa climbing the rough in the 1972 Scottish Six Days Trial.

Championship in both 50 and 125cc classes. When he retired from road racing Anderson took up motocross on a less serious basis before devoting all his time to his motorcycle business in Assen where the Dutch Grand Prix is held.

Andersson, Hakan

The Swedish Motocross Champion, Hakan Andersson was born in June 1945 at Uddevalla. He began riding at 16 on Husqvarna, and then moved to Yamaha. He has been out of action several times due to serious crashes but has always come back. Andersson was World Champion in the 250 class in 1973 when he won 11 of 22 races. His last mount was the Spanish Montesa.

Andersson, Kent

A Swedish road racer born in 1942 now living in Gothenburg, Kent Andersson rode Bultaco, Adler, Husqvarna, Yamaha, and MZ. He won the 125cc World Championship in 1973 for Yamaha and retired from racing in 1966 after many wins in international Grands Prix in the 125 and 250 classes. After retirement he worked for Yamaha developing racing machines.

Anderstorp Circuit

This Swedish track was used for the annual car Grand Prix between 1973 and 1979 when the race was cancelled, and also for the motorcycle Grand Prix. It has a 2.497-mile lap on an artificial circuit in the south of Sweden, accessible to the main towns.

Andrees

The Andrees, a German motorcycle, was made from 1923 onward for six years, using British Bradshaw engines in 350 single and 500 twin sizes at first, and later Blackburne and MAG units. These machines were successful in competition with German riders, but were killed off by the Depression of 1929.

Andrews, Mick

Mick Andrews is a successful trials rider who has been European Champion twice. He was born in 1944 at Elton in Derbyshire, England, and when very young started riding on a James. After he became a Yamaha works rider he went to live in Holland. Before that he rode Bultaco and won the Scottish Six Days five times in six years, sometimes on the Spanish Ossa. With Yamaha he was said to be the world's highest-paid trials rider.

Anglo-American Transatlantic Series

The Anglo-American Transatlantic is a series of road races between British and

Monterey Park Police Department in the United States used 1000cc Ariel Square Fours in 1949 for a time.

The famous Ariel Square Four in 1951 form.

United States teams, which began in 1971, using 750cc Superbikes.

Anker

Anker was a German bicycle maker who also produced mopeds with 50cc engines and motorcycles up to 250cc for 10 years from 1949. The company gave up two-wheelers in favor of business machinery, but went out of business altogether in 1976.

Anscheidt, Hans-Georg

This German rider has been supreme on the miniscule 50cc Kreidler machines since 1962, when he was second in the World Championship. Anscheidt also won the Spanish Grand Prix three times in this class, and was runner-up in the World Championship in 1962 and 1963. He then switched to Suzuki and won the title for that firm as well.

Antique Motorcycle Club

The Antique Motorcycle Club, an American organization for the owners of old machines, was founded in 1954 and caters for bikes made before 1930. The first president was Henry Wing, Senior, and the secretary was Emmett Moore, with collector Ted Hodgdon a vice-president. The club holds regular meetings with *concours* competitions in various parts of the United States.

Aprilia

Aprilia is an Italian two-stroke used mostly in trials, manufactured since 1968. The company uses 123 Hiro and Sachs engines for its sporting, trials, and motocross bikes, but has also used Minarelli and Franco-Morini power plants, some with six-speed gearboxes. Aprilia also makes road-going 50cc bikes, some of which are sold under the Scarabeo marque name.

Ardie

Ardie, a German make, came on the market after World War I in 1919 and lasted for 40 years. From about 1925 it used British JAP engines in various sizes from 250 up to 1000cc, some single and some twins. Later three or four other engine makes were used as well, and after 1945 there were two-strokes. In the 1920s and 1930s Ardie was active in racing.

Ariel

This British machine was made from 1902 until it was absorbed by BSA in the 1950s. Memorable models were the Square Four and the Red Hunter.

Giacomo Agostini on his 500 MV Agusta at Mallory Park, England, in 1971.

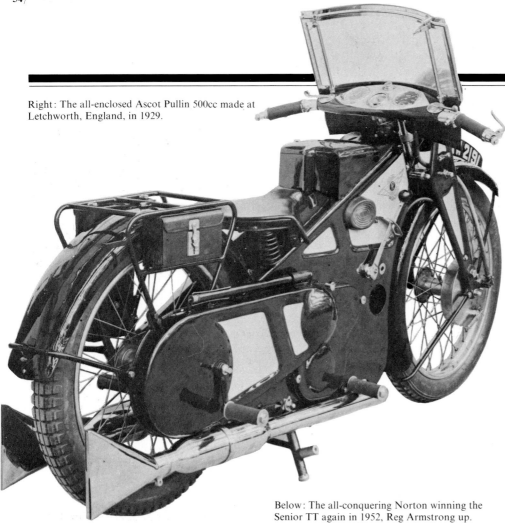

Right: The all-enclosed Ascot Pullin 500cc made at Letchworth, England, in 1929.

Armstrong, Reg

Reg Armstrong was an Irish road racer from Dublin who started at 17 and retired after a successful career when he was only 28. He rode as a professional for AJS, Norton, Gilera, and NSU. He rode the famous AJS Porcupine and was then second string to Geoff Duke on Norton and Gilera. His most famous win was in the 1952 Senior TT when the primary chain of his works Norton snapped and fell off as he crossed the line to take the winner's checkered flag.

Ascot-Pullin

This was an advanced British machine for its year, but failed to make much impact. It came on the market in 1928, offering hydraulic brakes, enclosed chains, and dry-sump lubrication on a single-cylinder machine partly enclosed and with windshield and leg shields, all for £75. It was made at Letchworth, Hertfordshire, north of London. Front and rear wheels were interchangeable, but in spite of its elaborate specification it lasted only a couple of years. The engine was a flat 500 ohv.

Below: The all-conquering Norton winning the Senior TT again in 1952, Reg Armstrong up.

American Steve Baker (inset), leading (32) at Oulton Park, England.

Aspes
Aspes is an Italian maker of motocross and cross-country machines which are also run in trials, using various small engines of 50 and 123cc Minarelli or Franco-Morini. Although they have usually five- or six-speed gearboxes, these little machines are very light and can weigh 200lb fully equipped.

Association of Pioneer Motor Cyclists
This English club was formed in 1928 for those cyclists who had held a license in 1904 or before. Later, as the members died off, the rules were changed to bring in Companion members who have been riding for 40 years and Pioneers who have ridden for 50 years. The Association normally holds several meetings a year.

Austrian Grand Prix
Held since 1971 on the new Salzburgring near the town of Salzburg, the Austrian Grand Prix has been much criticized by riders on safety grounds. The circuit is also used for car races and is surrounded by metal Armco barriers, which do not please the two-wheelers. Before Salzburgring the Austrian race was held on a number of different circuits but did not rank in the World Championship series.

Auto Cycle Union (ACU)
The Auto Cycle Union is the controlling body of motorcycle sport in England, having begun in 1903 as the Auto Cycle Club, an offshoot of the Royal Automobile Club. It now issues about 10,000 licenses a year to racers, and runs events like the British Grand Prix and the Isle of Man TT. The organization consists of more than 50,000 members belonging to more than 700 motorcycle clubs, based in 20 centers.

Automoto
Automoto was the French machine made from 1901 onward until absorbed by Peugeot, who also hold the old Terrot machine and others. The Automoto used various makes of engines (Chaise, JAP, Villiers, Zurcher) all usually under 500cc and tended to be solid and reliable rather than fast and sporting.

Autry, Scott
Scott Autry is an American speedway rider from Maywood, California, born in 1953, who was a scrambles specialist before he took to the dirt track. He is one of the few American riders to move over to Europe and achieve success in this branch of the sport. He has also ridden all over the world and reached the final of the World Championship in 1976.

Avus Circuit
This Berlin circuit composed of two straights linked by U-turns was opened in 1920 and last used in 1967. In 1927 the banked curve linking the two parallel straights was added, but after World War II the circuit was split up by the division of Berlin. The original 12.43 miles came down to 5.151 miles with a new south curve, used from 1951.

AWO
The AWO was a German machine built at Suhl, Thuringia, East Germany, in a former car factory from 1949 onward and incorporating a 246cc single-cylinder ohv engine with shaft drive. There were also racing models with ohc, both single- and twin-cylinders. The name was later changed to Simson after Simson-Supra, a sporting car made in the 1920s in the factory now producing bikes.

B

Baker, Cannonball
Cannonball Baker is the famed American record breaker who started the cross-America run from Los Angeles to New York, 3332 miles, in 1922 riding an Ace motorcycle. He went on to make many long-distance rides over the years.

Baker, Steve
American road-racing star from Bellingham, Washington State, Steve Baker was born in 1952. He started on dirt tracks, but won the FIM 750 World Championship in

his first year in Europe in 1977 and was second in the 500. Short and bespectacled, Baker is very fast. He won the Canadian Championship in 1974 and 1975, and was first seen in Britain with the 1975 Transatlantic Team. He won three of the six Transatlantic races in 1976, joined Yamaha for 1977, and Suzuki for 1978.

Baldet, Andre
Andre Baldet is a motorcycle dealer from Northampton, England, who specialized in records on the Italian Vespa scooter which was also assembled in England by Douglas. He rode up Snowdon, the Welsh mountain, on a 125cc machine with sidecar, and did 100 laps of the Isle of Man TT

circuit (3775 miles) in 100 hours on a 150cc Vespa, with Dennis Christian as co-rider. He also rode through nine countries in 10 days with a 150cc and sidecar, covering 3620 miles.

Ballington, Kork
This South African road racer had his first

South African Kork Ballington (left inset) seen in action (below) at Silverstone, England.

Right: John Banks leaping in the Belgian 500 motocross Grand Prix in 1973.

season of European Grand Prix racing in 1975 and has made a big impression. In his first outing at Barcelona he won the 350 event that year. He won both the 250 and the 350cc world titles on a Kawasaki in 1978. Ballington set a class lap record in the Swedish Grand Prix at Anderstorp on a Yamaha in 1977 at 87.875mph to finish second. He won both the 250 and 350cc world titles in 1979.

BAM
The BAM was a German motorcycle in the 1930s which was really an imported Belgian FN. Germany did not permit imports at this time, so FN manufactured machines under the label of Berlin Aachener Motorradwerke (BAM) from the works at Aachen near the border. The range included a 200, 350, and 500cc model.

Banks, John
British Motocross Champion John Banks is from Bury St Edmunds, Suffolk, where

he was born in 1944. Has been four times British 500cc Champion and runner-up twice in the World Championship. He started in 1960 at 16 on a Dot, and finished third in the Swiss Grand Prix in 1961; in 1968 he rode in the BSA works team.

Baragwanath, E C E

Generally known as Ted or Barry, this famed British Brooklands rider retired in 1933 when he was 50 years of age. He liked to race in a winged collar under his leathers, and rode supercharged Brough Superior twin-cylinder machines which he prepared himself. Baragwanath used a Power Plus blower on the 1000cc JAP twin, pulling a streamlined sidecar, and set many lap records. His sidecar design was copied

The famous record-breaker ECE Baragwanath on his 996 Brough Superior twin JAP at Brooklands, England, in 1928.

from one of the floats of the Supermarine seaplane which won the Schneider Trophy for Britain, and the outfit is now in the Stanford Hall collection.

Barcelona Circuit

The modern Barcelona Circuit used since 1966 is in the Montjuich Park in the city center at the back of the building where the motor show is held each year and has a lap of 2.35 miles. It is a pleasant wooded setting and is a natural road circuit rather than an airfield-type one.

BAT

This British machine whose initials stood for 'Best After Tests,' was made from 1902 to 1926. The company was the Bat Motor Manufacturing Company of Penge in London, named from a Mr S R Batson who ran it, and the slogan followed. It

started with De Dion engines and originally made many sporting bicycles and offered a sprung rear wheel. A Bat finished second in the twin-cylinder class in the 1908 TT ridden by W H Bashall at 37.18mph using a JAP engine. From 1904 the company was owned by the Tessier family, and S J Tessier finished in the 1913 TT in eleventh place. In 1923 Bat took over Martinsyde and called the machine the Bat-Martinsyde, but it did not survive.

Batavus

Batavus was the big Dutch bicycle manufacturer which began in 1904 and produced its first motorcycle in the 1930s. It took over the Dutch company of Magneet in 1969, and some German companies a year later. In 1970 it became part of the Laura Group and used Laura engines in most of

its mopeds, with Sachs in the sporting machine. Batavus is essentially a maker of mopeds rather than motorcycles, with a reputation for high quality.

Bauer

Bauer was a German bicycle manufacturer from 1936 which went into mopeds with Sachs engines. After the war it continued on with small motorcycles up to 250cc but ran into financial trouble; Bauer gave up motorcycles in 1954, but kept going in the cycle market.

Bauer, Willi

Willi Bauer is a German motocross expert born near Stuttgart in 1947. He has ridden Maico, Montesa, CZ, in the works Suzuki, and in the Austrian KTM teams. He won the 500cc Championship in 1973, and was sixth in the 250 class in 1974.

Beardmore-Precision

Beardmore-Precision was a British company with factories in England and Scotland from 1921 to 1924. They made 250, 350, 500, and 600cc motorcycles with their own Precision engines and also special racing models with a different specification. The range even included a sleeve-valve model.

Beart, Francis

A British tuning expert best known for his work on Nortons, Francis Beart was born in 1905 near Beccles, Suffolk, England, and began racing himself before turning his attention to engine tuning. He prepared machines for many successful riders for many years.

Beaulieu

Beaulieu, in Hampshire, England, is the home of the National Motor Museum which houses many famous and historical motorcycles as well as cars and other transport exhibits. It was founded by Lord Montagu, whose father was a pioneer motorist.

Beeston

Beeston was a pioneer English model made in Coventry and owned by the infamous H J Lawson who tried to control all motor manufacture in England. The motorcycles had cycle frames with the engine in an unusual position behind the bottom bracket and in front of the rear wheel. The 1.75-horsepower De Dion engine, made from about 1897 to 1910, was incorporated into the motor bikes.

Bekamo

The Bekamo was a German machine originally made in Berlin, and later produced at Rumburk in Czechoslovakia from 1923 to 1930. It had some unorthodox features including a big diameter top tube to the frame which functioned as a fuel tank, an idea used by other makes later on. The first models were 124cc but later they were 174 and 250cc.

Belgian Grand Prix

Between 1921 and 1937 the Belgian Grand Prix was held on various circuits, but since 1937 it has taken place on the Spa-Francorchamps track, which is mainly public roads that have been abandoned by car drivers as too dangerous. The circuit is 8.76 miles to the lap and is sometimes dry on one side and wet on the other. Race average speeds are of the order of 110mph.

Bell, Artie

A road racer born in Ulster, Northern Ireland, in 1915, Artie Bell rode in the works Norton Team until he crashed in the 1950 Belgian Grand Prix and had to give up racing because of a paralyzed arm. He joined Norton in 1947 and was placed in four Isle of Man TTs. He was also a trials and grass-track rider before taking to road racing, and was associated in business with the McCandless brothers who developed the Norton racers.

Benelli

The Benelli is an Italian machine produced by the Benelli brothers from 1911 onward. In addition to production machines in various sizes they have been successful in racing since the 1939 Lightweight TT with Ted Mellors on a 250cc mount. The factory was taken over by Alessandro de Tomaso, who also owns Moto Guzzi, in the 1970s.

Bennett, Alec

Alec Bennett was an Irish rider born near Belfast in 1898 who rode in only 29 top events but won 11 of them. He first rode dirt track in Canada, but returned to Britain and worked for Sunbeam as a road tester. He also rode in its racing team with the famous George Dance and Tommy de la Hay. Bennett later rode Douglas, and won the French and Belgian Grands Prix and the Senior TT on a Norton, and the Junior TT on Velocette.

Beta

The Beta was manufactured in Italy and sold in the United States under the name

of Premier from about 1950 onward. It ran up in size from 50cc to 350 and included motocross and trial versions, and some with five- or six-speed gearboxes.

Betts, Terry

Terry Betts is an English speedway rider born in 1943 who has reached the top. He started at 17 and rode for Norwich in eastern England, then the London West Ham Club, Long Eaton, and Kings Lynn. He won the World Pairs title with Ray Wilson in 1972, and has been a consistently high scorer for more than a dozen years.

Bianchi

A great Italian company, Bianchi produced many varieties of machine from 1897 until it closed down in 1967. Edoardo Bianchi made his first machine by fitting an engine to a bicycle but went on to much greater things. He made many models over the years and first appeared in the Isle of Man TT in 1926, when Luigi Archangeli finished fourteenth on his 350. Bianchi stayed away until 1960 when it returned with six machines, but failed to make any impression on the results. Meanwhile there were successful road machines, ranging from 50 up to 500cc, from singles to fours.

Bickers, Dave

A British trials and scrambles rider, Dave Bickers was born in January 1938 near Ipswich in eastern England. He started at 15 on a Dot and went on to ride BSA and Jawa, then Greeves, on which he won two European titles. In 1966 he was taken on by the CZ company, whose machines he imported into Britain, to ride in the 500 World Championship, and won the British title. He retired from world class events in 1968.

Blackburne

The British Blackburne motorcycle was made from 1908 until 1921, when the two Burneys, Alick and Cecil, proceeded to make engines for other people after designing both engines and complete machines. Another British maker, OEC (Osborn Engineering Company), continued to make the Blackburne. Many makes, including Cotton, had success with the Blackburne engine.

BM

BM is an Italian manufacturer which began operating from 1950 onward, using various engines: Ilo, Franco-Morini, and some of its own design with ohv or ohc,

in sizes ranging from 50 up to 175cc. The initials stand for the producer, Mario Bonincini.

BMW

One of the great success stories of the motorcycle industry, this German company based in Munich now has its motorcycle factory in Berlin. The original flat-twin horizontally-opposed design by Max Friz was produced in 1923 with shaft drive and is still selling well today, although this basic format has been much refined over the years.

Bohmerland

Some extraordinary machines were produced by this Czech factory between 1925 and 1939. Some were also sold under the name Cechie, and they were very long, sometimes with seats for three people. Bohmerland used a 600cc single-cylinder ohv engine designed by Albin Liebisch. The last model was a 350 two-stroke single on more normal lines. Bohmerland was using cast aluminum wheels before World War II.

Bonniksen Speedometer

The Bonniksen chronometric speedometer with two needles gave an accurate reading, and was used on early high-performance machines. One needle held the reading achieved while the other went back to start again.

Boocock Brothers

These two British speedway riders, Nigel born in 1937 and Eric 6 years later, were both at the top and as a pair won third

place in the 1970 World Pairs competition. They came from Yorkshire; Nigel rode for Coventry for 17 years before retiring in 1976, and Eric rode for Halifax, retiring in 1974 after winning the British Final.

Left: BMW 750cc world-record machine ridden by Ernst Henne in 1935 at 256kph.

Right: BMW R100 RS with 980 flat-twin engine.

Below left: Heart of the R100RS.

Below: The big Bee Em cruising.

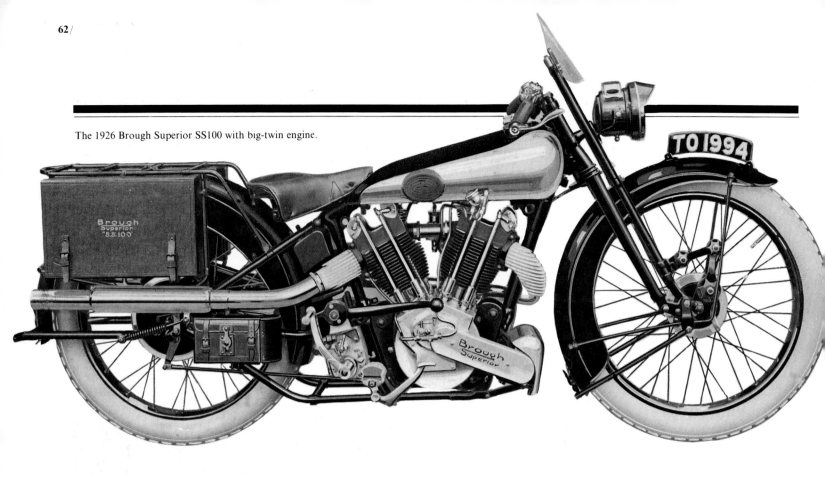

The 1926 Brough Superior SS100 with big-twin engine.

Borgo

This Italian make ran from 1906 to 1926 and was successful in competition. The two Borgo brothers founded the company and a third designed engines which they used. They ignored the economy market and made machines from 500cc upward, both single and twins, some with four valves per cylinder, and one as early as 1921 which peaked at 6000rpm.

Boulger, John

An Australian speedway rider from Adelaide, John Boulger became an overnight sensation in British speedway when he scored 11 from a possible 12 points at Long Eaton, Derbyshire, England, on his first appearance in 1967. He has since become a top rider in Australia and twice National Champion, led the Australian team to win the 1976 World Cup, and was second in the World Pairs final with Phil Crump in 1974. Boulger moved from Long Eaton to Cradley United, still in the British Midlands, in 1974.

Bradbury

An important British model in its day, the Bradbury was produced from 1901 to 1925 in a factory in the north of England at Oldham, Lancashire. The company made models in various engine sizes, mostly the larger 500 and 750cc singles and twins, but the last was a 350 single.

Bradshaw, Granville

Granville Bradshaw was a British designer who produced the ABC in 1919, having worked out details during the war when he was working on aircraft engines which used air cooling. He was associated with many other machines later, but the ABC which was ahead of its time is one of his monuments. It was similar in layout to the BMW, which came on the scene later, with a chain final drive through bevel gears.

Brands Hatch

Brands Hatch is the British racing circuit 20 miles south of London which started as a grass track in 1926, originally for bicycles, and has been used for motorcycles from 1932. It was extended from time to time and now has a 2.65-mile lap on the main course, plus a shorter club circuit achieved by cutting out a loop which had been added in the course of the development. This circuit has always been a special favorite with motorcyclists.

Braun, Dieter

This German road racing star was born in 1943 at Ulm, began his career in motocross, and switched later. He started road racing on a Yamaha, won the German Championship on an Aermacchi, and then rode MZ and Suzuki, on which he won the 125cc title. Subsequently Braun moved to Maico, and won the 1973 350cc Championship. He was riding a Morbidelli 350cc in the 500cc race at Nurburgring in 1976 in the West German Grand Prix when he crashed heavily and suffered serious injuries.

Bridgestone

Bridgestone is a Japanese firm better known as a tire manufacturer, but which also made motorcycles for about 20 years from 1952 onward. The machines were mostly small fry, but later there were models up to 350cc with twin-cylinder engines but still using the rotary valve two-stroke like the mopeds. Bridgestone exported special versions to the United States before deciding to give up motorcycles and concentrate on tires, which it supplies to most Japanese makers of bike and car.

Briggs, Barry

This New Zealand speedway rider, born in December 1934, has taken world speedway by storm. He came to ride for the Wimbledon, London, team in 1950 at 17, won the world title in 1954 and qualified to run and was placed in every final up to 1971, winning three times more. He rode for New Cross, Southampton, and Swindon Robins, and has 'retired' three times, the last in 1976.

British Cycle & Motorcycle Industries Association (BCMIA)

This body succeeded the British Cycle and Motorcycle Manufacturers and Traders Union and in turn became the Motor Cycle Association. It promotes motorcycling and lobbies on behalf of the industry and allied interests.

British Cycle & Motorcycle Manufacturers & Traders Union (BCMMTU)

See above entry.

British Drag Racing & Hot Rod Association

This is the body which organizes sprinting and drag racing for both cars and motorcycles. It also runs meetings at the Santa Pod Raceway on a disused airfield in Northamptonshire, north of London, which has been in use since 1966.

British Grand Prix
The British Grand Prix is the British round in the road-racing World Championship run by the Auto Cycle Union, the British delegate to the FIM. The Isle of Man was the British round until 1973 when riders said the 37.75-mile circuit was too dangerous. Since then the annual race has alternated between Brands Hatch and Silverstone.

British Motor Cyclists Federation
This organization formed in 1963, originally as the Federation of National and One Make Motorcycle Clubs (Fenomsee) but now open to all motorcycle clubs. It looks after all interests of riders outside the sporting sphere, which is the province of the Auto Cycle Union.

Brooklands
Brooklands is a British banked circuit for car and motorcycle racing, the first of its kind in the world, which opened in 1907 and closed with the War in 1939. There were three tracks, the 2.75-mile bowl, which with the finishing straight was 3.25 miles, known as the Outer Circuit, the Mountain Circuit around the Members Hill, and the Campbell Circuit which added internal roads to the track.

Brough, George
George Brough is a British maker of luxury motorcycles. His father made a machine under his name with ABC engines, but George left and started his own production under the title Brough Superior, which was also dubbed 'the Rolls-Royce of Motorcycles.' His models were mostly JAP twins, but there were also fours, all very expensively made from 1921 until World War II. George was also a racer, and later other famous riders raced his machines.

Brown, George
In some ways George Brown was a rival of George Brough, although they were not of exactly the same period. Brown was born in 1912 and always rode Vincent machines, made by the firm which employed him. These were also big twins in the luxury class, but most production was after World War II, when George Brown broke many records with his special machines. He died in 1979.

Bryans, Ralph
Ralph Bryans is a road racer from Northern Ireland born in 1948 who was dominant until 1967. He competed in various forms of motorcycle sport before devoting himself to road racing from 1962 onward, when he was signed first by Bultaco and then Honda. In 1964 he was second in the 50cc World Championship, which he won the following year. He won the Isle of Man 50cc TT and set a lap record never broken at 86.49mph.

BSA
BSA was one of the biggest motorcycle producers in England from the early years of the century until taken over in the 1970s. In 1979 the name was brought back on mopeds made by Norton-Villiers-Triumph. Famous models were the Roundtank (1924), Sloper (1928), Gold Star (1960), and big twins for sidecar work in the early days.

Bultaco
This famous Spanish sporting machine was made from 1958 onward by Francesco Xavier Bulto in Barcelona. The Bultaco range includes two-strokes with very high output which dominate four-wheel Kart racing, and trials and motocross models with engines from 74 to 350cc.

The practical BSA Boxer (top) of 1979 and a bigger banger (below), the 500cc Gold Star ridden by J W Davie in the 1954 Clubman's TT.

The young wizard, Johnny Cecotto, from Venezuela (inset) on Yamaha and before the start (below left).

C

Calthorpe

This British motorcycle, made from 1911 up to World War II, made many friends although it was never in the top racing bracket. Calthorpe used different engine makers (JAP, Precision, Villiers, Blackburne) until manufacturing its own 350 and 500cc units. When the firm went broke a member of the Douglas family bought the remains and built a few machines before selling it again to DMW.

Camathias, Florian

Florian Camathias was a popular Swiss sidecar driver, born in 1924, who was killed at Brands Hatch in 1965. He used a BMW most of the time with the sidecar on the right in British fashion, and his privately entered outfit rivalled the official BMW entries to their embarrassment. He had several different passengers, one of whom, Hilmar Cecco, was killed. Camathias tried a new machine called a Florian Camathias Special (FCS) still with a BMW engine, and finally a four-cylinder Gilera. He came close to the world title in 1959 but was just beaten, and was second again in 1963.

Campbell, Keith

Keith Campbell, Australian road racer, came to Europe in 1951 after local success and was killed in a 500cc race in 1958. He rode a works Guzzi in 1956 and the following year won the 350cc class in three Grands Prix; he was second in the TT, and fifth in the Senior on a 500cc single. That year he took the World 350cc Championship.

When all the works teams pulled out (except MV Agusta) in 1957 he went on with his private Nortons until he was killed.

Campion

The Campion is a British machine made from 1901 to 1926 by a Nottingham bicycle maker who used seven different makes of engine in bicycles from 150 to 1000cc. They were Blackburne, Fafnir, JAP, Minerva, MMC, Precision, and Villiers, the larger models with JAP V twins and a very imposing appearance. The New Gerrard was also built at the Campion works for the last two years before they closed down.

Can-Am

This off-road two-stroke machine was made in Canada and Austria by the Bombardier Group whose main output is snowplows and snowmobiles. The company has been going since 1937 but embarked on motorcycles in 1970. It makes a number of other products also. Jeff Smith, who was with the English BSA company for 20 years and a motocross champion, joined Can-Am to help with the design. The factory makes 125, 175, and 250 machines with rotary-valve two-stroke engines and a six-speed gearbox. It has had much success in off-road competition.

Capriolo

Capriolo is another Italian aircraft factory which built motorcycles for 15 years from 1948 onward. It produces various types with both pressed-steel and tubular frames, mostly with small engines either two-stroke or ohc, but there was also an ohv flat twin of only 150cc. Capriolo also makes three-wheel vans with the same small engine.

Carabela

A Mexican maker of both off-road and street machines for the American market, Carabela has been in business from 1971, making two-strokes from 100cc up to 250 for motocross and Enduro. The company started off with imported engines until its own were ready.

Carlton

A British maker of bicycles dating back to 1913, Carlton is now part of the giant Tube Investments Raleigh Group. Before World War II it also produced Villiers engined two-strokes in the 125cc class.

Carruthers, Kel

Kel Carruthers is an Australian road racer born in 1938 who came to Europe in the

1960s and was third in the 1968 World Championship on a 350cc Aermacchi. The next year he won the 250 TT on a Benelli and also the world title, and then went to the United States to race a 250 Yamaha and won six of seven national races.

Casal

This Portuguese machine was made from 1966 onward with two-stroke engines from 50 up to 250cc. Before Casal began making its own engines Zundapp motors were used. Oddities include a water-cooled 50cc and there are also off-road models.

CCM

The CCM is a successful English motocross machine which came on the market in 1971. It was designed by rider Alan Clews, at first using BSA parts but later was manufactured to their own design. Top riders have had success on CCM 500 and 600cc ohv singles.

Cecotto, Johnny

Johnny Cecotto is a Venezuelan rider who won the World 350cc Championship at 19 years of age in 1975. The year before he had won both the Venezuelan and Latin American Championships, and had ridden at Imola and Daytona. In 1976 he won Daytona and was second in the 350 Championship on a Yamaha. In 1978 Cecotto was second at Daytona and has had many other successes.

Australian rider-tuner Kel Carruthers now in the United States.

The British Clyno company was better known for cars than this 1911 model of a 750cc.

CF

An Italian racer, CF began in 1928 and ran until 1937 when it was bought by another company. At that time it was making 175 and 250cc bikes, but later re-entered the market until 1971 with 50cc two-stroke mopeds.

Chater-Lea

Chater-Lea is a British make from Letchworth in Hertfordshire which began in 1900 and is still in business but no longer making motorcycles. The manufacturer used 14 different makes of engine before producing its own. One of the classic models was a big 900cc V-twin popular for sidecar outfits. Chater-Lea held the world flying kilometer record in 1926 at 102.99 mph in the 350 and 500cc classes and also won Continental races.

Cimatti

This Italian firm makes small machines with engines up to 175cc using other proprietary engines. It has been going since 1949, making both street and off-road motorcycles and mopeds.

Cito

Cito was a well-known German maker, originally of bicycles, from 1905. It had a complex history, originally making both singles and twins at Suhl (now in East Germany), where the Kriegner-Gnadig was also built. Cito took over the production of these KG machines, which were larger, in the 500cc class. Allright then took over Cito and continued making the KG in the Cito works until 1927.

Clement-Gladiator

Clement-Gladiator was a pioneer French company in business with both cars and motorcycles from 1899, although the motorcycles came later than the cars. There was also a Clement model, sold in England as a Clement-Garrard. The Clement-Gladiators ranged from 100 to 500cc and there was a 250cc ohv JAP-engined model which did well in competition in the 1920s. Clement-Gladiator lasted until 1935, although Adolphe Clement retired in 1914.

Cleveland

The Cleveland is an American motorcycle with a 222cc single-cylinder two-stroke engine and a two-speed gearbox made from 1915 to 1927 by a car factory in Ohio. Later it went up in size to 269cc with a more robust frame, followed by a 350cc side-valve on similar lines. Finally Cleveland moved into competition with Ace and Henderson with a four-cylinder 600, which

The American Cleveland Four of 1929 used a 996cc inlet over exhaust layout but it failed to sell.

failed to sell. This was followed by a 750 and eventually a 1000cc model with a guaranteed 100mph top speed, but the great depression came before many were made.

Clubmans TT

The Clubmans TT is a race on the Isle of Man course for amateur riders on production machines which began in 1949.

Clyno

This British motorcycle was made by the Clyno Engineering Company Limited from 1909 to 1923, when it abandoned two-wheelers to concentrate on car production. The first machines were of 386 and 744cc with the Clyno Patent Pulley to give variable gears on the belt drive. The next year the pulley was dropped in favor of a normal epicyclic gear, and then came the famous 5-6 horsepower twin for sidecar use. This proved its worth as a machine-gun carrier in World War I. The last model was the 8 horsepower twin with a spring frame, which never really got into production as the car boom occupied the works.

CM

The CM, an Italian make, was produced from 1930 to 1957 by Mario Cavedagna, whose reversed initials supplied the name, and Oreste Drusiani. There were ohv and ohc machines from 173 to 500cc as well as a racing 350, and in later days twin two-strokes in sizes up to 250. A motorcycle with the same name but no connection with the CM (Italian) was made in Germany from 1921 to 1923, with a 110cc two-stroke engine.

Cockerell

This German motorcycle was made by a famous designer, Fritz Cockerell, from 1919 to 1924, with a single-cylinder two-stroke engine. This designer produced many novelties, including water-cooled engines, and his machines won the 150cc German Championship in 1924. He even had a diesel motorcycle engine.

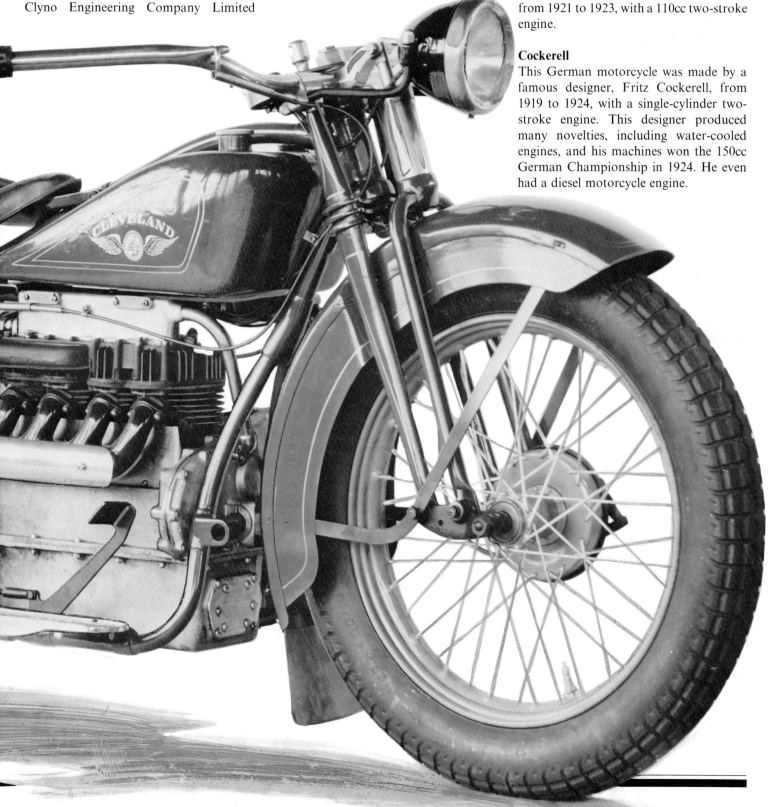

Coleman, Rod

This New Zealand road racer won the Junior TT in 1954 on AJS, giving this make its first win for 24 years, at a speed of 91.51mph. Another AJS ridden by D Farrant was second. Coleman later became the Suzuki importer for New Zealand and sponsored Pat Hennen from California.

Collier, Charles

Charles Collier was a British pioneer rider who with his brother Harry started the Matchless concern; both of them also rode in races. Charles won the first TT in 1907, was second in 1908, and won again in 1910. Eventually the company was swallowed up by a larger group after the death of the brothers.

Collier, Harry

One of the Collier brothers who started the Matchless company, Harry won the TT in 1909 at 49.01mph, and was second in the Junior in 1911 at 40.89 on his own machines.

Above: English champion speedway rider Peter Collins shifting the shale.

Below: The British works Cotton with a 250cc engine arriving in the Isle of Man in 1927, the year after it finished 1-2-3 in the Lightweight.

The 996 Coventry-Eagle Flying Eight.

Collins, Peter

A top British speedway rider born in March 1954 in Cheshire, Peter Collins was World Champion in 1976. He was British Grass-Track 350cc Champion at 17 and turned to dirt track in 1971, riding for Rochdale, Lancashire, and later the Belle Vue Team, Manchester. He won the British Junior Championship in 1973 and did well in World Team Cup events for his country.

Condor

There have been four machines with this name over the years, all unconnected and of different nationalities. The oldest is the Swiss model which used various bought-out engines and was made from 1901 onward. After World War II the Swiss produced 678cc flat twins with their own transverse engines (like BMW) and also a 250 two-stroke twin. They were active in racing in the 1920s and 1930s using the Swiss Motosacoche engines. There was also an English Condor from 1907 to 1914 with an 800cc engine, among other models from this company. Later still the German Condor was a moped-style machine with a 50cc engine made around 1954. The most modern is the AGV Condor 125cc racer on which Henk van Kessel was third in the 1975 Austrian Grand Prix.

Cooper, John

A British road racer, born in Derby in 1938, John Cooper was 350 and 500cc British Champion in 1966, and 250cc winner in 1968. He normally rode British machines (Norton, BSA, Triumph), but won the Race of the Year in 1970 on a Yamsel, a specially developed Yamaha 350 twin. He won this race three times, and also the 250cc Classic at Ontario Speedway, California, and the MCN Superbike Championship in 1972. The following year he retired, after a crash, after nearly 20 years racing.

Cossack

The Soviet Union is number two in the world motorcycle production tables and the BMW-like Cossack Ural and Dnieper models are the best known, usually seen with sidecars. The Cossack name came in 1974, but the machines—not the same models of course—have been made since the 1920s. There has been a wide range from a 125cc single up to the big 650 twins and there are also off-road sporting machines like the 350cc IZH 60. The 175 Voshkod is a good seller, a two-stroke with leg shields, windshield and carrier, which are very useful to the commuter.

Cotton

This British machine started production in 1920 specializing in a rigid triangulated frame which gave good road-holding capabilities. Cotton used six different bought-out engines, but the frame principle held right up to the 1970s. It did well in racing with Blackburne engines and finished 1-2-3 in the 250cc Lightweight TT in 1926 after an earlier win, with Stanley Woods up, in 1923. After 1945 Cotton turned to a different type of machine, with a 250cc Villiers twin two-stroke engine, and was close to closing down. When Villiers ceased making engines, Cotton turned to the Italian Minarelli and did well in off-road events. It returned to road racing in 1976 with a water-cooled two-stroke with an engine from Rotax of Austria with rotary valve. The company also sells a different version to police forces.

Coventry-Eagle

This British manufacturer began making pedal cycles around 1900 and took up motorcycles in the early years of the century, using bought-out engines. Coventry-Eagle was then not much heard of until after World War I when it came back with a 500cc single and a 680cc JAP twin for sidecar use. Later Bert le Vack set Brooklands records with a 996cc JAP-engined twin. It made a high-quality machine until turning to what became its hallmark, the pressed-steel frame with a small two-stroke engine. Motorcycle production ended in 1939.

Coventry-Victor

Coventry-Victor, another British maker, produced engines and motorcycles from 1919 to 1936. The company also made a three-wheel car as well as a speedway bike, and sold engines to more than six other makers. Its own engines were opposed flat twins in the 500, 700 and 750cc classes which had a good reputation in their day.

Craven, Peter

Peter Craven was a British speedway rider who was World Champion in 1955 and

1963, and died after a crash in 1963 at 29 years of age. He was born in Liverpool and began riding at 16 in 1949. He won the Golden Helmet match race title a number of times against formidable opposition, and was captain of the Manchester Belle Vue team at the time of his fatal crash.

Crescent

A large Swedish maker of off-road machines with two-stroke engines, Crescent is part of the Volvo group. The Motocross Champion Ove Lunden has had a hand in its competition models. The company also makes marine outboard engines, although the motorcycles are fitted with 50 or 123cc units from either Sachs or Franco-Morini.

Croxford, Dave

Dave Croxford is a British road racer who was British 500cc Champion in 1968 and 1969. He rode for Matchless, then in the Norton team, and had an enormous number of crashes which he survived. He finished eleventh in the 1965 TT (his first) and won the Production TT in 1975.

Crump, Phil

Phil Crump is an Australian speedway rider from Mildura, Victoria, ('The Mildura Marvel') who came third in the 1976 World Championship in Poland. He rides

Dave Croxford on an unfamiliar-looking enclosed Norton 750 John Player special.

for the Newport team in Wales as well as in Continental events, and amassed a record 434 points in one season. His father-in-law, Neil Street, developed a four-valve head for the Czech Jawa machine which they both ride and also sell to others. He was also a member of the Australian team which won the World Team Cup in 1976.

Crystal Palace

Crystal Palace is the London suburban home of a road-racing circuit and one of England's first dirt-track ovals, used from about 1928. The road circuit began in 1937 in the grounds of the Crystal Palace, which had been destroyed by fire. It was originally two miles around, but was reduced to 1.39 miles from 1953.

CZ

CZ, a Czechoslovak machine, was made from 1932 onward by a firm originally part of the Skoda arms combine. It first made lightweight two-strokes but later tied up with Jawa; CZ has been successful both with off-road and motocross bikes and sophisticated dohc racers in classes up to 350cc. Many of its two-stroke models are twins.

Czech Grand Prix

The Czech Grand Prix is run on a road circuit near Brno, and was given World Championship standing in 1965. The circuit has been cut over the years from 11 miles to just under nine and finally to 6.78 miles. It is the only World Championship race in a Communist country, and has all the usual capacity classes plus sidecars. Race average speeds are well over 100mph.

D

Daimler, Gottlieb

Gottlieb Daimler was the German designer of the first motorcycle, which was produced in 1885. It was constructed of a wooden frame and used a gasoline engine with hot-tube ignition which could turn at the enormous rate of 800rpm. Daimler's

Howard Davies, who won the 1925 Senior TT on his HRD-HAP before he sold out to Vincent.

assistant, William Maybach, rode the machine in 1886, but Daimler then turned to four wheels and abandoned the motorcycle.

Dale, Dickie
This British road racer who had much success in the Italian works teams in the 1950s was killed racing at Nurburgring in 1961. He rode for Moto Guzzi for four years, joined Gilera in 1953, then MV Agusta, and was fifth in the World Championship. Dale rejoined Moto Guzzi in 1955 and was second in the 350 Championship in 1955 and 1956. When Guzzi retired from racing he joined BMW, was tenth in the TT and third in the 500cc World Championship. He also won the East German Grand Prix. Finally Dale joined Benelli and later raced BMW, AJS, Norton, and MZ.

Dance, George
George Dance was a pioneer rider of Sunbeam machines in the 1920s. He was a market gardener by occupation, who put up the fastest lap in the 1920 Senior TT and nearly won the Junior in 1923. His specialty was sprints and hill climbs, in addition to record breaking. He put a 500cc unit into a light frame with a sprint tank to make one of the first 'specials' for short-distance events at which he was unbeatable with a 90mph top speed in the 1920s.

Daniell, Harold
Harold Daniell is a British road racer who has always been associated with Norton. The best-known story about him is that he was turned down by the Military Police as a dispatch rider because of poor eyesight in the year he won the 1938 Senior TT. His 91mph lap record stood until 1950. He began in 1927 and went on until 1950, war years apart. Daniell rode AJS without success and then stayed with Nortons, tuned by his brother-in-law, the famous Steve Lancefield.

Davies, Howard
Howard Davies was the British pioneer rider and designer-producer of the HRD in 1924, on which he won the 1925 Senior TT. He sold his company and the name to Phil Vincent who then produced the Vincent-HRD, sold as 'the world's fastest' after setting motorcycle land-speed records with the big-twin machines.

Daytona 200
The Daytona 200 is a major American race run since 1937, originally on a 3.2-mile oval, then on the new Speedway from 1948. The Daytona International Speedway cost three million dollars and is a tri-oval (with three turns) now 3.87 miles around the lap. When the British Cammy Nortons won in 1950, the organizers of the race banned overhead camshafts to protect Harley-Davidson and its side-valve machines. Eventually they conformed to international rules, and the event is now a Japanese benefit with a race average over 100mph.

De Coster, Roger
A Belgian rider born in 1945, Roger de Coster has been five times World 500cc Motocross Champion. He rode CZ at first, then 250, Suzuki, and began winning cham-

pionships in 1971 on his 400. Before getting into the winning streak he finished fifth in the championship for three years running, 1967, 1968, and 1969, but became unchallenged king of off-road racing.

De Dion

Albert Comte de Dion, born in 1856, is best known for car engines and his special rear-suspension system, but he was also a motorcycle pioneer. With his partner M Georges Bouton, the count made tricycles as early as 1894 when he won a race, but when the tricycle faded from popular favor by 1901 the De Dion engines were sold for use in bicycle frames and later in proper motorcycles. The company also made its own machines. There were also some De Dion Bouton motorcycles made in France from 1926 to 1930, but these were mostly two-strokes and had no connection with the old firm which played such a big part in motoring history.

Degens, Dave

Dave Degens built the Triton, a Triumph-engined Norton, which led to the Dresda, a handbuilt motorcycle which can be based on any make. A road racer himself, he developed frames and engines based on his own experience, and modified machines for other people.

Degner, Ernst

Ernst Degner is a German road-race rider, first on the East German MZ rotary-valve two-stroke. He came over to the West in 1961 after being well placed in the World Championships, but his changeover cost him victory. From 1962 he rode Suzuki in the 50cc category, won the TT and the World Championship. He had many more victories before retiring in 1965, and returned in 1966 to finish fourth in the last 50cc TT to be run.

De la Hay, Tommy

Tommy de la Hay was a pioneer British rider of Sunbeams in the 1920s who finished thirteenth in the 1914 Senior to help the company win the Manufacturers Team Prize, although it was later taken away from them. He rode under the great team manager Graham Walker and was one of the heroes of the golden age of motorcycle racing.

Della Ferrera

This famous Italian make was produced by two brothers who gave their name to the marque from 1909 to 1948. One re-membered model is the 500cc ohc V-twin racer of 1922 with chain-driven camshafts with the chains exposed. It did well in minor events. Production models were mostly in large engine sizes from 500 right up to 996cc twins. Della Ferrera was also credited with one of the first machines with the sprung rear wheel, back in the 1920s.

Delta and Delta-Gnom

In spite of the similarity in name these two machines were not related. The first was of German origin, made in 1924; like the Della Ferrera it had rear suspension, but in this case by leaf springs. It used a two-stroke engine which was fully enclosed. The Delta-Gnom, although of the same period (1925 onward), was Austrian, also two-stroke in the smaller 250 machines, but with JAP engines in the bigger 350 to 1000cc models. From 1945 for about 10 years Delta-Gnom used bought-out two-stroke engines in smaller machines.

DEMM

DEMM, an Italian maker of small two-strokes, also sold engines to other makers from 1953 onward, and is still selling 50cc mopeds. The factory also made earlier small-engined ohv machines in the under-200cc class as well as one ohc racer of 173cc which offered very high performance.

Derbi

Derbi is a Spanish motorcycle that has been made near Barcelona by the Nacional Motor SA since 1951. The name comes from Derivados de Bicicletas (derived from bicycles) as the company had been making bicycles from 1922. It made off-road moto-cross machines and others for the army and was successful in the sporting sphere with small two-strokes. But the 50cc road racer was something else again, and Derbi won the World Championship in this class for four years from 1969. In 1970 it took the 125cc as well. The 125 twin turned over at 14,500rpm and had six speeds. The tiny machine could top 140mph, and its star rider was Angel Nieto. Derbi also built a plant in France at Perpignan to build machines for Common Market countries pending Spain's entry into the community.

De Tomaso

Alessandro de Tomaso, from the Argentine, raced cars from 1956 and then turned manufacturer, making various racing and sports cars including the Ford-engined Mangusta. In 1972 he took over the Italian Benelli factory, which had been successful in motorcycle racing, as well as the part of the Moto Guzzi organization which is not owned by the Italian government.

Deubel, Max

Max Deubel, a German sidecar racer, won the World Championship four times (1961-64) and the TT three times. His first full year as a racer was 1960 when he competed on BMW, as he always does. His passenger was mechanic Emil Horner. Deubel, a hotel owner, and Horner first competed in 1959 when they were third in the German Grand Prix. In 1961 they had BMW factory backing and a works engine. The team was second in the World Championship in 1965 and 1966 and then retired.

Devil

The Devil was an Italian machine which was manufactured for only five years and won a good name between 1953 and 1957. The factory was based at Bergamo and used both two-strokes and ohv singles in the smaller capacities up to 175cc, some with five-speed gearboxes. The engines were designed by the well-known Soncini.

Diamant

Diamant was a complicated company in Germany which began making three-wheelers in the early years of this century and also made some motorcycles. There was then a big gap until 1926 when it came back with 350 and 500cc machines, some with British JAP engines and some with Kuhne ohv units. Diamant merged with a car maker called Elite which went out of business, and Opel jointly used the factory for building Opel motorcycles up to 1933. After this 350 and 500cc Elite-Opel bikes were made under the marque name of EO. The last models before production ceased in 1939 were two-stroke mopeds.

Diamond

The English Diamond factory produced motorcycles from 1910 until it went into liquidation in the 1920s after making Villiers-engined two-strokes up to 350cc and bigger machines with several other makes of engine. The company came back as Diamond Motors in the 1930s, and built sidecars and bodies for three-wheelers and motorcycle frames until 1939. Between 1920 and 1930 there was a spell when Diamond belonged to Sunbeam who raced the Diamond label in the TT. There was another revival in 1969 when Sachs-engined lightweights were offered under the Diamond badge.

World Champion Roger de Coster (inset) and in action on his 500 Suzuki at Farleigh Castle in England.

1957 Volkswagen took over Auto Union and the DKW motorcycle company became part of Zweirad-Union AG along with Victoria and Express, and in 1966 Fichtel and Sachs bought Zweirad. Zweirad-Union already owned Hercules, and has tended to push this name at the expense of the DKW brand. The cars also disappeared in the 1960s. DKW developed a Wankel-engined motorcycle, the W2000, but it has not been a commercial success. The DKW name is still used on exports to England.

Dirt-track racing

In Britain dirt-track racing is another name for speedway; in the United States it is a separate sport for machines up to 750cc and capable of much higher speeds, and is an AMA Grand National Championship. Dirt track began in the 1920s and is now a big business in which the top riders can make $200,000 a year or more. Stars who have graduated from this form of the sport include Kenny Roberts, now a top international Grand Prix rider.

Ditchburn, Barry

Barry Ditchburn is a British road racer who began in 1965 and won his first race in 1968. He then rode Aermacchi, Norton, and Seeley bikes before achieving success on a Yamaha. In 1974 he joined the Kawasaki team riding 500 and 750 water-cooled three-cylinders with Mick Grant. He won places and the King of Brands title, and was second in the 1975 Superbike Championship.

Dixon, Freddie

Born in 1892 in Stockton-on-Tees, County Durham, this rider was the only man to win the Tourist Trophy on two, three, and four wheels and inspired more legends than any other six riders. He died in 1956. He first raced in the Isle of Man in 1912 on a Cleveland, made in his home town, and went back in 1920 to finish twelfth on an Indian. Freddie Dixon insisted on American equipment on his machines, footboards, foot clutch, and twist grip when others had levers. He was third in the 1923

TT and won the first sidecar TT with his banking sidecar which tilted over for the corners. He won the 1927 Junior on HRD and was sixth in the Senior. After driving officialdom mad in the bike world he turned to car racing with Rileys from 1929, and was equally successful using motorcycle Amal carburetors at the rate of one per cylinder.

DKW

This German machine's initials actually stand for *Dampf Kraft Wagen* (steam lorries), which the company was founded to build in 1920 in Zschopau, now in East Germany, by a Dane, Jorgen Skafte Rasmussen. He later used the initials to stand for *Das Kleine Wunder* (the little marvel) and made small-engined two-strokes until he merged DKW with Audi, Horsch, and Wanderer into Auto Union in 1932. The company began making cars as well in 1920, still using two-strokes to drive the front wheels. Auto Union began road racing in 1925 and achieved success with the split-single supercharged two-stroke layout in 250cc form which lasted until 1939, at the cost of enormous fuel consumption. It won the Lightweight TT in 1938 with Ewald Kluge riding, and he was second the following year. The postwar ban on supercharging ended DKW supremacy, but meanwhile it had supplied the German army with 350cc two-strokes. In 1945 the Zschopau factory became MZ (Motorradwerk Zschopau) in the Russian zone, and DKW moved to Ingoldstadt. After the war DKW raced a 350cc three-cylinder. In

Left: The incomparable Freddie Dixon with his eight-valve Harley-Davidson and sidecar at Brooklands in 1921.

Above: Barry Ditchburn on Kawasaki leading Pat Hennen on Suzuki at Brands Hatch, England.

The British 1925 Dot-JAP 350cc sports model.

DMW

DMW is a British make of motorcycle made from 1945 onward by Dawson Motor Works, owned by 'Smokey' Dawson. The first machines, made at Sedgley, Dudley, Worcestershire, were grass-track racers succeeded by trials machines after Dawson left and Mike Riley took over. A twin-cylinder Villiers engined two-stroke looking rather like a scooter called the Deemster, with twin headlights and optional electric start came in 1962, and was sold to the police. That was followed by the Hornet 250cc Villiers-engined racer, and finally a trials machine.

Donington Park

Donington Park is a British road-racing circuit on the grounds of the seventeenth-century hall, first used in 1931 for motor-cycle races. It was taken over by the Army during World War II but restored for racing in 1978 by the new owner-builder, Tom Wheatcroft, with a 2.5-mile circuit. Donington Park houses the only single-seater race-car museum, and the British Leyland historical collection of cars.

DOT

The English DOT was started in 1903 by racer Harry Reed, who later advertised his machines under the slogan 'Devoid of Trouble.' He won the twin-cylinder TT in 1908 with a machine using a V-twin Peugeot engine at 38.6mph. DOT continued to make appearances in the Isle of Man without repeating this success. The company made machines from 293cc up to a big 986cc V twin in the 1920s, always finished in cherry red. In the 1930s it limited itself to small economy machines, and during the war made a three-wheel delivery Rickshaw with a motorcycle back end and box-carrier front. In the 1950s DOT went in for lightweight two-stroke powered trials machines, and also won the Manufacturers Team Award in 1951 in the Isle of Man with 125cc racers. Later machines with foreign engines were included

Above: Italian design, the 350 Ducati of 1974 with desmodromic valves.

Below: Aces Ray Amm from Rhodesia and Britain's Geoff Duke in the Dutch TT 500 class in 1952.

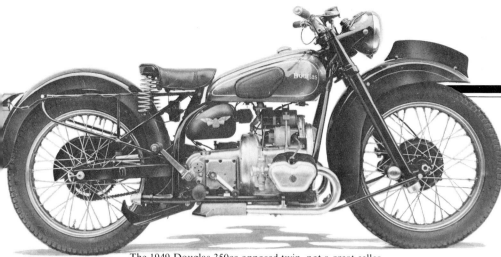

The 1949 Douglas 350cc opposed twin, not a great seller.

when Villiers stopped selling, but in the 1970s DOT was not selling many machines.

Douglas

This British machine was made from 1907 with opposed flat-twin engines of 350 and 500cc. The company produced a successful speedway racer from 1928. The original flat twins were set longitudinally in the frame but a later model (1949 on) placed them across the frame. The company's heyday was in the 1920s when its machines were favorites with British riders.

D-Rad

D-Rad was a German motorcycle made from 1921 to 1933 in Berlin at a former arms factory. The first model was a 400cc flat twin, followed by a 500 single, and these heavy models were successful in trials and endurance events. The company finished up with small two-stroke singles until it was taken over by NSU.

Drag racing

Drag racing is the modern name for sprinting over a short course, usually the quartermile. The competition began in California but there are also regular events in Britain and elsewhere for both cars and bikes.

Dresda

Dresda is a personalized motorcycle developed by David Degens from the manufacturer's standard product. He began making Tritons (Triumph-Nortons) but now uses mostly Japanese models as a base for his conversions.

Ducati

This Italian machine was made from 1950 onward, and was very successful in racing. The company began with small ohv machines under 250cc and developed desmodromic valve gear for racing. There were also production models and motocross versions, but from 1971 there have been much larger V twins in the 750 and upward categories. At the same time Ducati marketed Enduro bikes and a very fast 864cc twin said to reach 144mph. The company is partly owned by the Italian government.

DuHamel, Yvon

Yvon DuHamel is a French Canadian rider, born in 1939, who has a spectacular riding style and was successful in the Kawasaki team in between falls. He started racing at 20 years of age on a 250 Yamaha, won the Canadian Championship in 1968, and joined Kawasaki in 1971. He won the 1972 Canadian Grand Prix at Mosport and other events, and in 1973 scored four places including a win in the Anglo-American series as top United States scorer. Nicknamed 'Superfrog,' DuHamel went on to win places in long-distance events and 750 races until the factory pulled out of racing.

Duke, Geoff

A British racing champion born in 1925, Geoff Duke started in 1949 on Norton, after an apprenticeship in trials. He won both 350 and 500 classes of the Manx Grand Prix that year on Nortons and joined the works team. He won his first TT,

Below: Gilbert Smith of Norton (center) congratulates Geoff Duke on winning the Junior TT in the Isle of Man.

the Senior, in 1950 and was second in the Junior, and went on to win after win. He tried car racing and then moved to Gilera to win the Maker's Championship for them in 1953 and 1955, then won the Rider's Championship in 1954. When the Italian factories stopped racing in 1957 Duke rode a BMW the following year, then Norton again, and soon after formed his own Gilera team, which was not a success. He retired in 1959 with six World Championships behind him and lives near the TT course in the Isle of Man.

Dunelt

A British motorcycle made from 1919 to 1956, Dunelt began with a 500cc two-stroke with a simple form of supercharging by using a stepped piston. The company first raced with sidecars, finishing sixth in the 1925 TT and was placed in other races abroad. It introduced a 250cc model which proved a better seller than the big machine and consequently dropped the 500 in 1927. This model was followed by a 350 ohv and a 500 ohv in 1930, and finally a 250 ohc, but Dunelt closed in 1935. Twenty years later Dunelt came back with a 50cc moped, but this was not very successful.

Dunstall, Paul

British race-rider Paul Dunstall set out to modify other people's products to improve them for high-speed work, and developed a successful business, first with Nortons and now mostly machines with a Japanese base. His services included improving engines and frames, customizing, and supplying a range of bolt-on accessories.

Dürkopp

Dürkopp is a German pioneer machine produced from 1901 onward, originally as singles, twins, and even a straight four. The company went out of the motorcycle business after 1930 when it produced bicycles and motorized cycles, and reappeared after the War with small two-strokes and later a scooter. In 1959 Dürkopp stopped production of two-wheel machines to concentrate on the manufacture of bearings.

Dutch Grand Prix

This international race began in 1925 over a 17-mile road circuit near Assen, and has ranked in the world series from 1949. A new circuit was opened in 1955, only 4.78 miles long but much wider. The race average speed approaches 100mph.

Left: Paul Dunstall racing a Norton before he switched to the modification business.

Right: The EMC which was made in England to an Austrian design, this one a 350 of 1949.

Dutch Motorcycle Society (KNMV)

The Dutch Motorcycle Society is the ruling body of motorcycle sport in Holland which reports to the FIM as the national club. Their Grand Prix is held annually at Assen, where it has been since 1925 although not on the same circuit.

Dutch TT

The Assen race now known as the Grand Prix was known as the Dutch TT from its inception in 1925 and recognized by the FIM from 1930. The two titles are still used interchangeably for the same race, just as the Isle of Man TT used to be the ranking British race, and now the British Grand Prix.

E

Eastwood, Vic

Vic Eastwood is a British motocross rider born at Colne, Lancashire, in 1941 who has been active since the late 1950s. He started riding BSA/Matchless, moved to Husqvarna in 1968, and took sixth place at the end of the championships series that year. After breaking a leg in 1969, it was seven months before he rode again. He moved to CCM and was close to winning the British Motocross Championships in 1975 but his injury held him back.

Edwards, Rob

A British trials rider born in 1946, Rob Edwards rode for Montesa for many years and coached other riders for the company. He has won the British Experts (1971), was second in the Scottish Six Days (1972), was runner-up in the British Championship (1973), and won the three-day trials at Santigosa in Spain (1974). Before Montesa he rode Dot, Greeves, Matchless, AJS, Bultaco, Cotton.

Eichler

Eichler, a German make, produced two-strokes up to 175cc with various engines from 1920 for five years. It also made some of the first scooters, for much of the time under designer Ernst Eichler who gave his name to the marque which had a good reputation.

Elder, Sprouts

Sprouts Elder was a pioneer speedway rider who came from America by way of Australia in 1928 to introduce the new sport of dirt-track riding in England. He rode in the first night-time meeting at Stamford Bridge, London, in May 1928 and stayed on to be a star attraction in British Speedway for many years.

Elephant Rally

The Elephant Rally is probably the biggest motorcycling gathering anywhere, held annually in Germany, originally at the Nurburgring. The event originated with the crews of Zundapp sidecar outfits, called Green Elephants, and eventually drew riders from all over Europe to the winter celebrations which included a midnight procession round the 14-mile track in memory of those killed there. Many of the riders camp out. It was banned from Nurburgring because of hooliganism and is now held on different sites.

Elite

This German company amalgamated with Diamant in 1927 after being in business making cars from 1914. It manufactured motorcycles until Opel took over and made a machine called an EO (Elite-Opel) with bought-out engines.

EMC

EMC machines were made in England by Dr Josef Ehrlich who went to England from Vienna before World War II. He made some very fast two-strokes which did very well in 125cc racing and beat the works Honda. EMC was second in the World Championship in 1962. Riders included Mike Hailwood, Derek Minter, and Phil Read. There were also production models from 1946 onward which were full of ingenious ideas.

Enders, Klaus

Klaus Enders is a German sidecar ace who won the World Championship six times, always on a BMW. His last win was in 1974. He was born in 1937 near Frankfurt and began racing in 1960 on solos, then turned to sidecars. He began riding in the world sidecar events in 1966 and won the Championship in 1967, 1969, 1970, 1972,

Klaus Enders racing his BMW outfit in 1973, toward the end of his six-year world championship reign.

1973, and 1974. He won the sidecar TT in the Isle of Man in 1969, 1970 and 1973.

Endurance racing

This is a special form of motorcycle sport with races usually of 24 hours or at least 500 miles duration. Honda has been dominant in recent years. Classic events are the Bol d'Or at Le Mans in France, the Barcelona 24 hours, and the Thruxton 500 in England which began in 1955. The FIM formula operating from 1975 permits any engine size in the Endurance series, with races in Belgium, Britain, France, Italy, and Spain. Honda's RCB 750 is the one to beat.

Enduro

Enduro is a form of long-distance racing on loose surfaces which is an American specialty for which machines are purpose-built by many makers. American events may run for 400 miles or more, but elsewhere they tend to be shorter. In the best-known event, the Baja 1000, both cars and motorcycles compete.

Eso

The Eso factory in Czechoslovakia specializes in speedway engines and has now merged with Jawa. Jawa uses four valves in a 500cc single-cylinder configuration and is one of the principal makers of competitive machines, in business since 1949. The company also makes machines and engines for other branches of the sport such as ice racing.

European Grand Prix

Each year the FIM designates a different Grand Prix race to carry the title of Grand Prix of Europe, a practice which goes back more than 50 years. At that time the ruling body of the sport was the FICM which also began the forerunner of the World Championship series in 1938.

European Trials Champion

This championship was set up in 1968 and was won first by Sammy Miller, an English rider, who won again in 1970. The World Championship for trials was introduced in 1975 and was first won by British rider, Martin Lampkin, based on the best eight results out of 14 events.

Everts, Harry

Harry Everts is a Belgian motocross rider, born in 1952, who was 250cc World Motocross Champion in 1975. He was Junior National Champion at 15, having falsified his age since the lower limit is 16, and was in the National World Championship team by 1973.

Excelsior

Four different companies, American, British and German, have used the Excelsior name. The British one was the longest lived, manufacturing from 1896 to 1964 (they sold the first motorcycle in England). This company began by selling a small bicycle with a Belgian Minerva engine, and went on to build the Mechanical Marvel which won the 1933 Lightweight TT and other successful racers. The fortunes of its varied road machines went up and down, and the company finished making economy two-strokes. The first German company at Brandenburg began in 1901 and had no connection with the English firm, although it used English engines among other makes for its rather British-looking bikes. This company lasted until 1939, with no sporting history. The other German Excelsior, unconnected with the first one, lasted only one year (1923–24) in Munich where it produced a 250cc two-stroke which was not memorable. The fourth Excelsior, the American company, was based in Chicago from 1908 to 1931. It made small two-strokes and bigger singles and twins up to 1000cc and racing models with ohc. The American Excelsiors sold in England were called American to distinguish them from the Birmingham models. The American manufacturer also built the four-cylinder Henderson, a giant 1300cc motorcycle. The company was a part of the group run by Ignaz Schwinn which is still in the bicycle business.

Express

This German company based at Nuremberg began making small machines in 1903. After a long gap Express returned in the 1930s, disappeared again until the 1950s, and finally joined DKW and Victoria in the Zweirad-Union group and lost its own identity.

Eysink

Eysink was a prominent Dutch make manufactured from the start of the industry around 1899. The factory first used bought-out engines then made its own from 365 up to 750cc and sold many machines to the Dutch forces. After World War I Eysink produced small two-strokes with Villiers engines. English engines (JAP, Rudge, and Python) were used at one time, and then small two-strokes again from

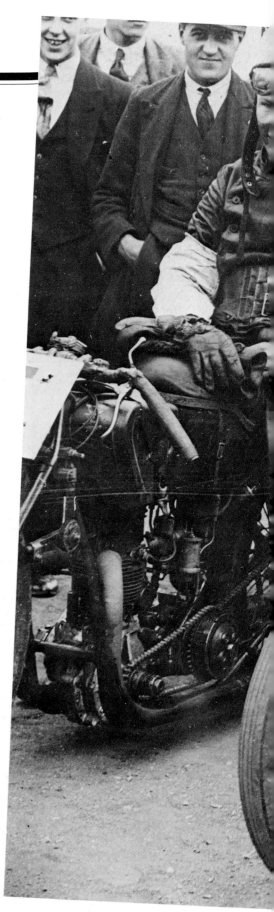

Chris Staniland (foreground) on his 1929 250cc Excelsior-JAP at Brooklands.

Sachs and Ilo. This company also made cars. Its founder, Dick Eysink, died during World War II and his son took over. The firm closed, then reopened briefly to make scooters, and was sold in 1975 but the name is no longer used.

F

Fadag

Fadag was a German motorcycle made from 1921 to 1925 by a company situated in Dusseldorf who also made cars. It began production with a bicycle with an engine attached, then 500cc single-cylinder machines, both ohv and side-valve; these were said to be of its own manufacture but some people thought they were imported. Fadag cars were considered to be better than most of the day.

Fafnir

A great German name in engines, Fafnir

Virginio Ferrari of Italy (inset) is seen in action (above right) at Silverstone in England riding Suzuki.

began production in 1900 but lasted only up to World War I, although it made cars up to 1926. Dozens of makes of motorcycles, both German and foreign, used the Fafnir engine from Aachen, which was actually the Werner design made under license. The firm also sold car engines and complete motorcycles.

FAM
The Federation of American Motorcyclists controlled the motorcycling sport and activities in the United States before 1924, when the American Motorcyclist Association took over. In the 1970s this organization became affiliated with the FIM.

Fantic
This Italian company which makes both sporting and utility models did not start production until 1968 when Henry Keppel and Mario Agrati joined forces to produce a new make. They have produced an enormous range of models, some aimed at the United States and some at the English market, which will rev up to 10,000rpm and have up to six-gear ratios. One of the most successful off-road bikes has been the Caballero.

Fath, Helmut
Helmut Fath is a German sidecar rider who has been twice World Champion. He began on BMW but later developed his own machine, the URS, named after his home town of Ursenback, which has also won the Championship for Horst Owesle. Fath first made his mark when he was third in the world title series in 1958, which he won in 1960. A crash killed his passenger and put him out for several years from 1961, but he came back with his own machine and won the 1968 Championship.

Favor
The Favor was a French motorcycle which

was popular for 40 years from 1919. The company made two-strokes up to 250cc and 350 machines with Jap engines, both sv and ohv. After 1945 it persisted with the two-strokes but also used British ohv engines up to 250cc.

FB and FB Mondial

There have been several FB marques, not connected. There was an English one (Fowler and Bingham) between 1913 and 1922 with a two-stroke engine, a German make which followed from 1923 to 1925 also making two-strokes and four-strokes, and the better-known Italian FB Mondial made from 1948 onward. Just to confuse matters there was also a Belgian Mondial, again unrelated. The Italian FB Mondial from Milan started making two-strokes and then produced successful ohc racers up to 250cc which were ridden by the world's top performers. This firm also makes utility and off-road machines which are successful in motocross.

Feilbach Limited

Feilbach Limited is an American machine —not the name of a company— which was in production from 1912 to 1915. The factory was based at Milwaukee, Wisconsin, where Harley-Davidsons were also made, and the products ranged from 500cc up to an 1100 V twin, some with shaft drive.

Fernihough, Eric

This British record breaker rode a supercharged Brough Superior with great success in the 1930s, challenging the German Ernst Henne and his blown BMW. They held a session in 1936 on the Frankfurt-Darmstadt autobahn at which time Henne did 169mph, and again at Gyon in Hungary the same year when Eric Fernihough topped this with almost 170mph for the flying mile.

Ferrari, Virginio

Virginio Ferrari is the young Italian idol of

the crowds who in 1979 was riding as team-mate to Britain's Barry Sheene in the Suzuki stable in the 500cc World Championship.

FFM

Fédération Française de Motocycliste is the French member of the national federation of motorcycle clubs (FMN) which controls the motorcycle sport in the various member countries.

FICM

Fédération Internationale des Clubs Motocycliste, the international controlling body of the motorcycle sport, was founded in Paris in 1904 and moved from Paris to London in 1912. It became the FIM in 1949.

FIM

The current controlling body of international motorcycling, Fédération Internationale Motocycliste is based in Geneva and has a membership consisting of the representatives of the clubs of 46 nations. There are 17 members from Western Europe, nine from South America, two from Asia, one from Africa, two from North America, and three from the British Commonwealth.

Finlay, Jack

The Australian road-racing star born in 1935, Jack Finlay won the 750cc Formula Championship in 1975 at the age of 40 and was still winning Grands Prix at 42. He finished high up in the placings in the 1960s after a bad start in 1958 when he left his job in a bank in Australia to race in Europe, and was fifth in the World Championship on his private Matchless in 1967. From

1973 he was in the Suzuki factory team and won the Senior TT. He rode for them again in 1974.

Finnish Grand Prix

Formerly run at Tampere, north of Helsinki, the Finnish Grand Prix moved in 1964 to the 3.74-mile track at Imatra near the Russian border. The event was first held in 1962 over a 2.75-mile circuit at Tampere, and was cut the following year to 2.25 miles. In 1964 the Grand Prix was moved to Imatra, although it had still ranked as a World Championship round at its previous venue.

Flottweg

Flottweg was a German make which was absorbed by BMW in 1937. The factory was near its headquarters in Munich and had been manufacturing since 1921, making powered bicycles initially and then machines up to 350cc some with British JAP engines. Later Flottweg made its own engines, but failed to survive as an independent.

Flying Merkel

The Flying Merkel was a famous American machine made from 1900 to 1915 in Middletown with some very advanced features, such as electric starting and spring frames. The firm made 500 singles and 980 V twins, finished in a distinctive banana-yellow color.

FMB

Fédération Motocycliste Belgique organizes motorcycle sport in Belgium as

national agent of the FIM, and is responsible for the annual Grand Prix on the wooded Spa-Francorchamps Circuit in the Ardennes.

FMN

The FMN (Fédération Motocycliste Nationale) is the national federation of motorcycle clubs, made up of representatives from each of the member countries, and responsible for deciding international policy.

FN

FN, the Belgian Fabrique Nationale d'Armes de Guerre at Liège, is a name famous in motoring and motorcycling history from 1901 onward. The maker used four cylinders and shaft drive in the early years of the century, and was copied as far away as the United States. After World War II FN was still in business with motocross machines, but eventually motorcycle production, like car production, came to an end around 1957. In its time FN had made many kinds of machine and was Belgium's leading maker in both the car and motorcycle field.

Foster, Bob

Bob Foster is a British rider best known as a road racer who won the 350cc World Championship title in 1950 and two TT races, but he was also a grass-track champion, motocross expert, and trials rider. He first won the Lightweight TT on a new Imperial in 1936, then rode AJS, Triumph, Moto Guzzi, and Velocette, winning the

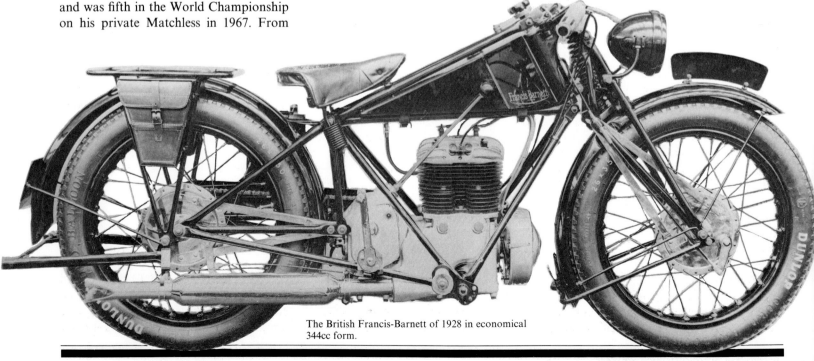

The British Francis-Barnett of 1928 in economical 344cc form.

Freddie Frith leading the 1949 Junior TT in the Isle of Man on his Velocette at Governor's Bridge.

1947 Junior on the works 350 Velo. He retired in 1949 after setting a record lap at 89.75mph in the Senior TT on a Moto Guzzi.

Fowler, Rem

This British rider won the very first TT in the twin-cylinder class in 1907, and was still watching the races more than 50 years later. He rode a Peugeot-engined Norton in that first race at a race average of 36.22mph on the short St John's course. He was credited with receiving the first pit signal ever when Mr James Norton himself hung out a board saying 'Oil' as he went by. Fowler rode Rex machines in 1909 and 1910 to finish sixteenth both times, then New Hudson in the 1911 Junior, and Ariel in the Senior.

Francis-Barnett

These British two-stroke machines known to generations of riders as the 'Fanny B,' came on the market first in 1920 and went on, although merged with James, until 1966. One of the model's features was a bolt-up frame in which damaged tubes could be quickly replaced. The firm used Villiers engines for most of its production life, and the most famous model was the 250cc Cruiser (1933–40). Another sold under the slogan 'Built like a bridge.' The company did not race, but private owners appeared in the TT and at Brooklands. Stunts included climbing both Snowdon in Wales and Ben Nevis in Scotland. Francis-Barnett became part of Associated Motor Cycles in 1947 and began to use AMC engines in place of Villiers.

French Grand Prix

The French Grand Prix is one of the oldest races, first held in 1920 at the Le Mans Circuit de la Sarthe over 22 laps of the 10.75 miles, and was first won by an Englishman, the only finisher. The French race did not come into the qualifying events for the world championships until 1951, two years after they were introduced. The race has been held at Albi, Reims, Rouen, Clermont-Ferrand, Ricard, and Nogaro. It has not been held every year and has not always qualified as a championship round.

Frera

The Frera is an Italian machine that was made for 50 years from 1906. The factory built singles and twins up to 1140cc and at one time a two-stroke, but the 350 and 500cc bikes were their mainstay until after 1945 when two-strokes came back. Frera was active in racing between the two world wars.

Frith, Freddie

Freddie Frith is a British road racer who retired after winning the 1949 350cc World Championship at the age of 40 on his Velocette. He won the Junior TT in 1936 and the Senior the following year, always on Nortons, and in 12 TT starts finished nine times, always in the first three. He came

British rider Mick Grant from Yorkshire, seen in action (inset) on his Kawasaki 250 in the Isle of Man.

back after the war riding a Velocette to win the 1948 Junior and make the fastest lap, and did the same in 1949.

Fundin, Ove

This Swedish speedway rider, born in 1933, was five times World Champion before he retired in 1976. Ove Fundin started riding at 19 and came to the British Club Norwich in 1955, remaining until 1964 when they closed. He won the Swedish and European Championships and went on to win his first world title in 1960 and his last in 1967. In between he won many other titles.

Fusi

Fusi is an Italian machine that was made from 1937 for 20 years. The company originally imported the Belgian FN. It made its own 250cc followed by British JAP-engined 175, 250, and 500cc bikes, with the engines made under license in Italy.

G

Galbusera

Galbusera is an Italian maker that produced machines from 173 up to 500cc with British Rudge ohv engines, which were raced by the chief engineer, an Egyptian named Adolf Marama. The factory started production in 1934 at Brescia, and in the last 10 years of its life from 1945, switched over to small economy machines with Sachs engines. At the annual Milan show in 1938 Galbusera displayed some unorthodox two-stroke machines with supercharged V8 engines, but these were never built.

Galloni

This Italian factory, active from 1920, was prominent until closure in 1931 and was successful in competition. The company started with 500cc singles and 750 sv V twins; it subsequently shifted to singles from 250 up to 500, finishing with a 175cc single with an imported British Blackburne engine.

Gamage

This famous British store, now out of business, at one time sold motorcycles under its own name (1904–24) which were made for them by a number of different companies. One of the well-known models was a lightweight 2.75 horsepower with pedals and belt drive, with an optional Sturmey-Archer three-speed cycle hub. Later they offered 250, 350, and 500cc motorcycles with single-cylinder side-valve engines and also two-strokes.

Ganna

Ganna is a well-known Italian maker which manufactured from 1923 for about 40 years. It used British engines, both Blackburne and JAP, made under license in Italy, in various sizes from 175 up to 500cc. After 1945 the firm mostly used small Italian two-strokes in sporty-looking machines, of which there were many makes on the market then.

Garabello

This pioneer Italian make came on the market in 1906 and lasted until 1929. The founder, Francesco Garabello, had some original ideas, including a design for a 175cc two-stroke single with a rotary valve and water-cooling, but this did not sell. Earlier he produced another water-cooled model, a 996cc four-cylinder in line with shaft drive, in addition to orthodox singles, but failed to make much financial impact.

Garazini

These machines were made for 10 years from 1921 by the Italian racer Oreste Garanzini, who raced them himself. He

Mike Hailwood with Rutter after his victory in the 1979 Senior TT in the Isle of Man.

An RGS 50 Garelli motocross machine from Italy.

used English JAP, Blackburne, and Villiers engines, and also imported an English bike known as the Verus for sale in Italy.

Garelli

Garelli has been a great Italian name since 1919, always famous for two-strokes and now making small economy ones and off-road models. Adalberto Garelli won a number of competitive events before he started production, and the company was in racing until 1924, taking many records. The firm was out of motorcycle production from 1935 to 1947 when it came back with the clip-on Mosquito 38cc for bicycles, and went on to make lightweight machines. Garelli merged with Agrati in 1972 to become one of the giants in the small-machine field.

GD

This Italian machine was made by Ghirardi and Dall-'Oglio for 15 years from 1923 and raced successfully in the 125 two-stroke class. These were flat single-cylinder 122cc machines, but GD also made a 98cc two-stroke, a 250cc vertical twin two-stroke, and a 175cc ohc single.

Geboers, Sylvain

Sylvain Geboers is a Belgian motocross champion who was born in 1945 and won his national 500cc title several times. He was twice runner-up in the world 250 title, and once third. He started off with scrambling in 1961 at 16, and rode BSA, Lito, Matchless Metisse, Maico Lindstrom, and finally CZ. Geboers gave up championship class events in 1975.

George, Alex

Alexander J S George was born in Glasgow, Scotland, in 1949 and is now a top road racer in the Honda team for 1979/80. He is a motor engineer who began riding at 14 and won the Manx Grand Prix at 20 years of age. He won the Scottish Championship in 1969 and the 250cc Manx Grand Prix the same year, the 350cc Dutch TT in 1975, and the Production TT in the Isle of Man the same year on a Triumph Trident. He has ridden Harley-Davidson, Triumph, Yamaha, and Suzuki before Honda, on which he won the 24-hour French Bol d'Or race at Le Mans in partnership with Jean Claude Chemarin in 1979.

Germaan

Germaan was a Dutch motorcycle made for 30 years from 1935 which finally merged with Holland's biggest makers, the Batavus group of manufacturers. The machines were originally lightweights with two-stroke engines, later including vertical twin two-strokes.

German Grand Prix

This event began in 1925 on the Berlin Avus Circuit of two parallel straights linked by banked turns, and then moved to the then new Nurburgring in 1927 in the Eiffel Mountains. In that year it was also the European Grand Prix on the 17.5-mile road circuit. It moved back to the Avus in 1933, and has also been at the Sachsenring, Chemnitz, later used for the East German Grand Prix, at Solitude near Stuttgart, Schotten, Hockenheim, and finally alternated between Nurburgring and Hockenheim.

Gilera

This classic Italian make started in 1909 and was taken over by Piaggio in 1970. Count Giuseppe Gilera founded the firm and made orthodox singles at first, then four-cylinder ohc fours for racing, which

Gilera dominated. This domination began in 1936 and in the 1950s it was still winning races and setting records until its retirement in 1957. Since the takeover Gilera has captured much of the market for the smaller machines and off-road bikes.

Gillet-Herstal

Gillet-Herstal is one of the few Belgian makes which began after World War I and produced a 350 two-stroke, 350 and 500 singles, and a 996 V twin. The factory was active in competition with ohc singles, and also went in for record breaking with these machines. From World War II to 1964 it made economy two-strokes and some bigger vertical twins.

Gnome & Rhône

A famous French name for aero engines, Gnome & Rhône entered the motorcycle field in 1919 and endured for 40 years. It first used the English ABC flat-twin designed by Granville Bradshaw, then made its own 350 and 500 singles and won races with them. Later the firm shifted to flat transverse twins in pressed-steel frames, and like many companies ended up in the post-1945 period making little economy bikes with two-stroke engines which deviated from its traditional product.

Goss, Bryan

Bryan Goss is a British motocross rider from Dorset, born in 1940. He began on grass tracks, and then turned to motocross, riding a number of makes on his way up, including Cotton, Husqvarna, Greeves, AJS, and finally the German Maico, for which he was the British importer. He won the British Championship on Maico in 1976 and 1977, and rode a Honda in 1978.

Goricke

This German motorcycle was made from the pioneer days of 1903, beginning with singles and big V twins. Later the firm produced Villiers-engined two-strokes in the 175 and 250 class alongside 350 and 500 bikes, with ioe for road machines and ohc for racing. In more recent times Goricke turned to the inevitable economy-size mopeds.

Gould, Rod

Rod Gould is a British road racer who retired in 1972 to run Yamaha's racing operation from Amsterdam. He began racing in the early 1960s and did well on Nortons before turning to a 250 Yamaha, on which he finished fourth in the World Championship, and third in the Grovewood Awards. In 1970 he won six of the 12 Grands Prix and the title, was runner-up in 1971, and third in 1972.

Grade

Grade is another German machine which always used two-stroke engines, from 1903 onward. The designer, Hans Grade, also produced cars and aircraft and the firm sold engines to other makers. It went on until 1925 with the 118 and 132cc bikes, and used two-stroke power in its planes and cars as well.

Graham, Les

This British road racer won the first World Championship in the 500cc class in 1949. A prewar rider, he came back after war service as an AJS team leader to win the title. In 1950 he was third in both the 250 and 500 Championships and second in 1951 on an MV Agusta and again in 1952. In 1953 he won the 125 TT on an MV Agusta, but was killed the following day in the Senior when lying second. His son Stuart followed in his footsteps in the 1960s, and in 1967 he won the 50cc TT after being placed in previous years and finishing third in the world title in the 125 Championship on a Suzuki.

Grand Prix

Grand Prix racing began in the 1920s, but the World Championship did not start until 1949. Originally races were 200 or 300 miles long, and the first European Championship in 1938 was based on eight races. There have been several different methods of scoring in Grands Prix, but current rules say there must be at least six starters and a minimum of 124 miles raced for 500s. The numbers of cylinders and gears are regulated, and there are also weight limits.

Grant, Mick

A British rider born in 1944 in Yorkshire, Mick Grant has been racing since 1967, previously riding BSA, Yamaha, and Norton, and more recently for Kawasaki and

British-Italian battle: Les Graham (MV Agusta) leading the ultimate winner, Reg Armstrong (Norton), in the 1952 Senior TT.

Dutch road racer, Wil Hartog (inset) and in action (above) at Donington, England, in 1978.

Right: American Pat Hennen from Arizona who was third in the 1977 World Championship.

now Honda. He has won many races including the production TT in 1974 and 14 international events that year, and signed for Kawasaki after that. In 1975 he won the MCN/Brut 33 series as well as the Senior TT and in 1977 set a new TT course lap record at 112.776mph.

Grass-track racing

This form of racing was popular in Australia and the United States before it was known in Britain, where hill climbs were popular until banned on public roads in 1925. Grass track as an organized sport started in England in 1927, and has gone on since, although other forms of motorcycle sport have become more popular and draw bigger crowds. Sidecar machines are limited to 1000cc but there are classes for the various engine sizes for solos. Speedway, trials, and motocross have largely taken over from grass track.

Greeves

The Greeves is a British trials machine made from 1953 by Bert Greeves. The firm specialized in scramblers and motocross bikes with Villiers two-stroke engines, but also made road racers. The bikes were originally made by the invalid car company run by Greeves before he retired. The original feature of the Greeves, a cast-alloy beam frame, was eventually dropped in favor of an orthodox tubular frame. Many famous off-road riders have made their way up the ladder on Greeves machines.

Grindlay-Peerless

The Grindlay-Peerless, a British motorcycle, was made from 1923 to 1934 with various engines, including JAP, Barr & Stroud, Villiers, and Rudge. The factory made 250, 500, and 996cc bikes, the big ones being twins. Various riders did well in hill climbs and races and broke many records, but the company was always a small producer.

Gritzner

This German machine came from a sewing-machine factory, using Fafnir engines, both single and twins. Gritzner was a pioneer in 1903, but in the postwar years came back with two-stroke engines in smaller sizes. When the company left the market in 1952 the current product was a sporting miniature bicycle with a rather Italian look.

Grizzly

The Grizzly was made in Czechoslovakia from 1925 to 1932 with a 250cc two-stroke engine. There were also 350 models with MAG engines, ridden in competition by local riders but not widely known outside their own country.

Grovewood Awards

This series of awards, given to the most promising three riders in road racing each season, is offered by Grovewood Securities, the owners of Brands Hatch, Oulton Park, Mallory Park, and Snetterton Circuits. The awards are cash prizes for non-assisted riders, presented since 1965. Famous riders who have won include Steve Parrish, Bill Ivy, Kel Carruthers, Ron Haslam, and Barry Sheene.

Gruhn

There were two different German machines under this name, made by two brothers, Hugo and Richard, and not connected at all. Richard operated in Berlin from 1909 to 1932 selling machines in various engine sizes up to 250cc which were strictly utilitarian, one, although only of 200cc, using shaft drive. Brother Hugo made a model with a 200cc single-cylinder side valve with an Alba engine, and was in business, also in Berlin, from 1920 for six years. He sold frames to other motorcycle makers as well.

Guazzoni

These Italian sporting machines, mostly for off-road work like motocross and trials, were produced by Aldo Guazzoni who used to work for Moto Morini. They are

mostly in the 50 or 125cc class, but there have also been 250 bikes, both two-stroke and ohv, since he started up in 1949.

Gutgemann, Johannes

Johannes Gutgemann was the founder of Veloce Limited, maker of the British Velocette motorcycle, who came from Germany to Birmingham and settled there in 1884. He changed his name to John Taylor and later to Goodman in 1917, and became naturalized. Taylor/Goodman originally set up as a pharmacist with a company making pills. The first Velocette was made in 1913.

Guthrie, Jimmy

Jimmy Guthrie was a Scottish rider born in Hawick in 1897 who became one of the great names of motorcycling. He was killed in the German 500cc race at Sachsenring when leading in 1937, at 40 years of age. He won his first TT on AJS in 1930, before moving to Norton, when he had a string of successes, including winning both Junior and Senior races in the Isle of Man in 1934. Guthrie won many other races and was European Champion in 1936. A memorial was erected on the TT course where he retired from his last TT.

H

Haas, Werner

Werner Haas was a German road racer who won three World Championships in two years and then retired, only to be killed

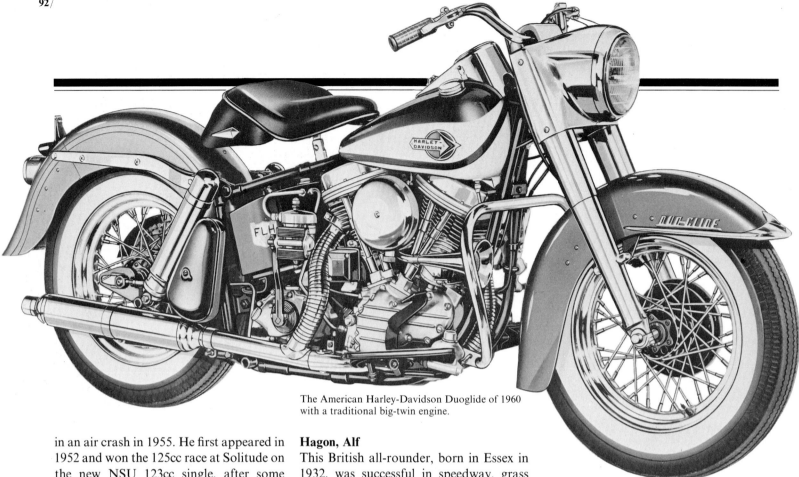

The American Harley-Davidson Duoglide of 1960 with a traditional big-twin engine.

in an air crash in 1955. He first appeared in 1952 and won the 125cc race at Solitude on the new NSU 123cc single, after some minor events on Puch. He was second in the 1953 TT in the 125 and 250cc events, and won two World Championships that year. His third title was in the 250 class in 1954 when he won five Grands Prix in a row. Haas retired when NSU gave up racing after a convincing demonstration of superiority.

Hägglund

Hägglund was one of the few Swedish makes produced from 1973 for the Swedish army with a 350 Rotax two-stroke motor in a monocoque frame, pressed-steel wheels, and shaft drive. It was later replaced by the Husqvarna.

Hagon, Alf

This British all-rounder, born in Essex in 1932, was successful in speedway, grass track, hill climbing, trials, scrambling, and finally drag racing or sprinting until he retired in 1970. He covered the quarter-mile at Santa Pod in 9.2 seconds with a terminal speed of 157mph on his 1260cc JAP V-twin engined bike in 1969 and reached 206mph to set a British record for a flying one-tenth of a mile at Honington, and also covered the standing kilometer in 19.1 seconds.

Hailwood, Mike

One of the greatest road racers of all time, Mike Hailwood earned nine World Championship titles and 13 TT victories. He was born in 1940 and first raced a 125cc MV.

His father was a wealthy motorcycle dealer, and 'Mike the Bike' did not lack backing; he proved to be a natural rider who won all kinds of events. He moved on to car racing in 1967 and was injured in a crash, but came back to the TT after a gap of 11 years to win once again. Hailwood planned to race again for the last time in 1979, but crashed in practice and was unable to ride on his last planned appearance.

Hallman, Torsten

Torsten Hallman is a Swedish motocross champion, born in 1946, who won 37 motocross Grands Prix and four World Championships, and led the two-stroke invasion of this branch of the sport. The Husqvarna which he helped design (he is an engineer) was the first two-stroke to win a championship in 1962; he also had a big hand in the 1977 machine on which Bengt Aberg won a Grand Prix, the first four-stroke to do so for seven years. Hallman began riding at 13 and was competitive at 16. He won the Swedish Championship on Husqvarna in 1961, and went on to the World Title for 250s in 1962, 1963, 1966, and 1967. He retired in 1968, but went on to develop the Yamaha motocross machine.

Handley, Wal

Wal Handley, a British rider born in 1904 in Birmingham, died flying in 1941 after a great career in the TT, where a corner is named after him on the Isle of Man course. He began racing in 1922 on OK Supreme,

Hailwood winning the 1978 Isle of Man Formula One race on the Sports Motor Cycles 900cc machine.

Harley-Davidson's racer sheds a good deal of the road machine's weight and gear.

moved to Rex-Acme, then Rudge, Husqvarna, Excelsior and Velocette, and finally BSA. He had many TT victories, both wins and places, including two classes in one year in 1925. He also did some car racing.

Hansford, Gregg

Gregg Hansford is an Australian rider on Kawasaki who has done well since coming to Europe. He finished fourth at Daytona in the United States in 1977 and won at Mosport Park, Canada, giving him seventh place in the FIM 750 World Championship.

Harlette

An Austrian machine made from 1925 to 1928, Harlette was sold in its home country as the Puch and in most other Continental countries as the Harlette. The double-piston two-strokes of 123 and 173cc were successful in competition, particularly in Italy where they were ridden by the champion, Umberto Faraglia.

Harley-Davidson

This famous American make was manufactured from 1903 in Milwaukee, Wisconsin, and was best known for its big twins, used by the police and the Army. In more recent times Harley-Davidson went in for fast singles as well and won the World Championship in the 250cc class with two-strokes in 1974, 1975, and 1976 and the 350 in 1976. In 1960 the company bought the Italian Aermacchi concern.

Hartle, John

John Hartle, a British rider, first rode in a major race in 1954 and was killed in 1968 at Oliver's Mount, Scarborough. In between he did well in the Isle of Man and in Continental races, riding for Norton in their last season (1956) to finish second in the Senior and third in the Junior. He was the first man to lap the TT circuit at more than 100mph, won the 1960 Junior, and was second in the Senior on MV Agusta. Hartle was out of action through injury, and later rode in the Geoff Duke Gilera team, then had a second spell of two years out of action from a crash. He won the production team TT in 1967 on Triumph and was third in the World Championship on Matchless.

Hartog, Will

Will Hartog is a Dutch road racer, a member of the Suzuki team, who has come to the top in the late 1970s.

In the drink: A Harley fails in the 1928 reliability trial organized by the Chelmsford motor club in England.

Haslam, Ron

This young British challenger on Yamaha came to prominence in the 1976 Anglo-American Challenge Cup series, which was won by the British team. He was a wild man from Langley Mill, Nottinghamshire, at 19 but he matured with experience. He was a Grovewood Award winner, and was TT Formula One World Champion in 1979.

Hawker

A name better known in the world of airplanes, Harry Hawker also made motorcycles from 1920 to 1923 and raced them himself. They were powered by their own make two-stroke of 300cc or Blackburne engines of either 350 or 550cc side-valve.

Hazlewood

Hazlewood is a British make manufactured from 1905 to 1923 for export to the then-existing empire and colonies. It was not sold in large numbers in England, but was well known abroad. The firm did not compete in the sporting field but had a good name for solid machines, made in 500cc and 1000cc V twins, singles of 250 and 500, plus V twins with JAP engines.

Hellyet

A French make which lasted 30 years from 1925, Hellyet produced a wide range of machines from 98cc midgets up to 1000cc V twins with British JAP engines. They also used JAP engines in racing models

British rider Ron Haslam (and inset). He was TT Formula One Champion in 1979.

The American Henderson four-cylinder machine of 1301cc here in 1929 form. It sold from 1911.

and in some models with transverse mounting and shaft drive. After World War II Hellyet switched to small economy lightweight two-strokes.

Henderson

This classic American make of a four-cylinder machine was on the market for 20 years from 1911, and was designed by Bill Henderson, who moved on to the Ace and was killed in 1922. Henderson machines are much sought after by American collectors and have a high reputation.

Henkel

Henkel, a German factory, built unit-construction, single-cylinder, shaft-drive machines of 500cc from 1927 to 1932. It inherited the former KG (Krieger Gnadig) which had been built in turn by Cito, then Allright, and finally by Henkel. After the KG design became rather old-fashioned, Henkel built a 200cc machine with an imported British Blackburne engine.

Henley

Henley was a British make produced from 1920 for 10 years, first in Birmingham and then in Oldham, Lancashire. The firm used in turn Villiers, Blackburne, and JAP engines up to 500cc and changed the name to New Henley in 1927. Finally Henley made twins of around 700cc.

Henne, Ernest

A German record breaker, Ernest Henne rode BMW and set the world motorcycle speed record at 134.6mph in 1929. On the same supercharged but improved 750, he put it up to 159.2mph in 1935. He used a streamlined shell and added a vestigial third wheel to take sidecar records.

Hennen, Pat

Pat Hennen is an American rider from Phoenix, Arizona, where he was born in April 1953, and who later moved to California. He began riding at 16 on a Honda in a scramble, and won the American Junior title in 1974 after he had been a professional road racer for one year. He won the Marlboro series in New Zealand in 1975, 1976, and 1977 and the 500cc Championship race at Imatra also in 1976. Suzuki gave him a works ride in 1977 and he was third in the World Championship and won the British Championship. He was also best scorer in the Anglo-American races in 1977 and 1978.

Hercules

Hercules has been the top German make going since 1904, although it was out of motorcycle production from the middle of World War I to 1924. It used bought-out engines (JAP, Villiers, and Sachs) in both two- and four-stroke models up to World War II, when the Nuremberg factory was bomb damaged and the machinery subsequently removed. Hercules resumed bike production in 1950 with a Sachs-engined 125cc and was very successful in off-road racing, trials, and motocross. In 1966 it bought the Zweirad-Union (Victoria, DKW, Express) and the machines are sold in the United States as DKW. Hercules also produced a Wankel-engined machine, the W2000, which appeared in the International Six Days Trial in 1975. It is now part of the Fichtel and Sachs group. There was also an English Hercules, more famous for bicycles, which is not related.

Suzuki rider Pat Hennen prepares in the paddock.

Hildebrand & Wolfmuller

These two Germans made the world's first production motorcycle in 1893/4. They were also the first to use the name Motorrad (motorcycle) for their machine, which had a four-stroke parallel twin engine with water cooling. It was an ingenious affair with many novelties and they sold many of them, including a big order for manufacture in France. However, it did not work too well with hot-tube ignition and a surface carburetor, and rubber bands to help return the connecting rods, which were coupled to the rear wheel; they went out of business in 1897. Young Maurice Schulte went to England with one of the bikes and stayed on to establish the Triumph motorcycle concern.

Hirth

Helmut Hirth, a World War I pilot and racing driver, produced these German motorcycles from 1923 to 1926 in the course of testing the alloy elektron. They were both singles and twins of 144 and 244cc respectively, and were raced successfully by his brother Wolf and others. The light weight aided high performance from the engines.

Hobart

Hobart was a British make which lasted 22 years from a pioneer start in 1901. The firm was Coventry based and made many different models, some with its own singles and V twins, others with four different makes of bought-out engines (Blackburne, JAP, Morris, Villiers). Lastly Hobart made a 250cc two-stroke, but they also sold parts to other motorcycle makers, from frames to engines.

Hockenheim Circuit

In southern Germany this 4.2-mile track is used both for cars and motorcycles, including Grands Prix races. It was opened in 1939 but rebuilt to its present shorter length in 1970. There is also a 1.64-mile short circuit on the same site, eight miles from Heidelberg.

Hocking, Gary

Gary Hocking was a Welsh rider who went to live in Rhodesia as a child and came back to race motorcycles in 1958 when he was 20. He rode a 350 Norton and then joined the East German MZ team, winning many events. He won the 250 TT in 1960, and both the 350 and 500 Championships in 1961. He was second in the 1962 Junior TT and won the Senior, and then retired. He was killed the same year practicing for a car race in South Africa.

Hodaka

This Japanese make was produced by an American, Henry Koepke, in the old Yamaguchi works in Nagoya, and mainly exported to the United States. Hodaka machines are mostly off-road two-strokes for motocross and enduro in sizes under 250cc.

Hoffman

Hoffman is a German company which made the Italian Vespa scooter from 1949 and also manufactured two-stroke machines under 250cc with German Sachs engines. The firm also made the Gouverneur, a machine with transverse engines and shaft drive of only 250 or 300cc, but they were too expensive and slow.

Holden

Colonel Henry Holden was a British pioneer who followed Hildebrand and Wolfmuller and made the first four-cylinder motorcycle in 1897. It was originally air-cooled but later modified to water cooling, and produced three horsepower at 400rpm. As in the Hildebrand the connecting rods went straight to the rear wheel without gearing.

Honda

Honda is a major Japanese motorcycle maker which began manufacturing in 1948. It was dominant in racing in the 1950s and 1960s, and has made a return in the late 1970s. Honda offers about 50 different

The Japanese Honda endurance racer of 1978 in action.

The breathtaking Vincent-HRD Rapide 998cc machine of 1948, one of a long line.

models from mopeds to the four-cylinder Gold Wing with electric start and 125mph top speed, and is the world's biggest producer.

Horex

These German machines were made from 1923 up to 1960. The name was derived from Bad Homburg where they were made and Rex, a brand of glassware made by the father of racing driver Fritz Kleeman who started the business. Horex originally used Columbus engines, but later had its own vertical twins with chain driven ohc in the 600 and 800cc class. It had racing successes in prewar days, and came back in 1945 with a 350cc ohv single. The postwar works racers were dohc twins. The company also made a small two-stroke and a scooter.

HRD

The HRD is a famous English machine made by H R Davies in small numbers before he sold out to Phil Vincent who produced the Vincent-HRD until he dropped the HRD part of the name. Davies won the 1925 Senior TT on one of his own machines, which were powered by various engines.

Humber

A famous English car maker which eventually became part of the American Chrysler concern, Humber also made motorcycles from 1900 to 1930. The factory first made a copy of the Phelon & Moore before creating its own designs, and raced at Brooklands in the early days. Humber won the first TT over the mountain course in 1911.

After various models production was concentrated on 350s and the company won a team prize in the 1923 Six Day Trials; eventually when money became difficult Humber ceased making two-wheelers and concentrated on cars.

Husqvarna

Husqvarna is Sweden's top maker, originally an armament factory. Motorcycles came on the scene in 1903, first using the Belgian FN engine, then an engine from the Swiss Moto-Reve. The first 'Husky' motor was the 550cc V twin which went on for years. The factory became involved in racing early on, and the Irish rider, Stanley Woods, won the 1935 Swedish Grand Prix for it. The following year Husqvarna gave up racing, and in 1937 dropped all its famous twins to concentrate on a lightweight 98cc moped called the 301. After the war the firm went into off-road machines and became a power in the motocross field from 1953. It won the 250 and 500cc Championships and finally abandoned road machines altogether for the off-road bikes with which it had done so well. After this Husqvarna produced a special machine for the army with automatic transmission, and continued to win more motocross championships.

Ice speedway

Ice speedway is a very specialized version of motorcycle racing which began in

Sweden in the 1920s and has spread, although a Swede has never won the World Championship. Riders use up to 200 long spikes up to 16mm long in each tire and lean over to 45 degrees. They wear a section of rubber tire on their left legs and a chain from wrist or waist to the machine so that they can cut the engine after a crash, as spinning wheels can cause serious injury. The Russian rider Gabdrakham Kadirov was the first European Champion in 1963, and Russians and Czechs seem to dominate the sport. The Russian Sergei Tarabanko was World Champion in 1975, 1976, and 1977. Speeds are around 65mph and in Russia the temperature can be 45 degrees below zero Fahrenheit. Machines have to be warmed up with blow lamps.

IFA

This East German motorcycle was made at the old DKW factory at Zschopau from 1945, and later became the MZ (Motorradwerke Zschopau). The firm made two-strokes mostly in small sizes, including twins, some with shaft drive. Originally the MZ was identical to the IFA.

Imatra Circuit

The Imatra Circuit is the home of the Finnish Grand Prix, two miles from the Russian border. This 3.74-mile circuit was first used in 1964; the race had formerly been held at Tampere. The circuit is almost square with four main corners plus some kinks. Lap speeds are in the 90s.

Imola 200

The Imola 200 is a European attempt to copy the American Daytona 200, run on the Italian Imola track from 1972. The Americans turned up to compete and in 1973 the race was run to the Formula 750 rules, but in 1974 it was free formula. The race is run on the 3.1-mile Autodrome Fine Ferrari, an artificial circuit with a lap record close to 100mph.

Imperia

This famous German make was on the market for just over 10 years from 1924. Imperia made machines from 250 up to 1000cc with Blackburne, JAP, and MAG engines from Switzerland, many of them twins. The Cologne factory changed hands in 1926 but production continued with engines from the same sources plus some others, until importing units into Germany became difficult. The firm then designed an unorthodox two-stroke but went out of business.

Indian

Indian is a Great American name from 1901 which finished up making small machines under English ownership, but the great days were those of the big twins of the 1920s. They did well in racing on the European side of the Atlantic both before and after World War I, and had both an electric starter and rear suspension before 1914. Great riders of the Indian included Freddie Dixon and Bert le Vack.

International Six Day Trials (ISDT)

Usually shortened to ISDT, this event began in 1903 in London and became a six-day event the following year. It started with standard road machines but has become highly specialized and a special province of the Germans and Czechs riding Enduro bikes. Usually only about one-third of the starters finish the rough course.

Irving, Phil

Phil Irving, the Australian designer, was involved in Velocette's shaft-drive 600cc Model O and with Phil Vincent in the Vincent-HRD, for which he is best known among his many projects.

Ish

This large Russian producer has been going since 1928, with the factory at Izevsk. Ish started with large motorcycles with 1200cc V-twin engines or 750 ohv singles, and moved on to smaller two-strokes of 200cc which it has tended to use, sometimes in twin-cylinder units. There are also sporting versions.

Isle of Man

This is the site of the famous British TT which has been in existence since 1907, and based on the mountain course of 37.75 miles around Snaefell since 1911. The island has its own parliament and laws, and can hold races on public roads, an activity which has been forbidden in mainland

Above: American police used the big Indian twin in this form in 1931. Top: New York police had been using the Indian since 1912 along with 59 other police departments.

An American Indian big-twin road machine enjoying a picnic in an English field a long time after it was built.

Britain since the 1920s. The TT no longer counts as the British round in the World Championship, which is now the British Grand Prix held on an artificial track and not a road circuit.

Itala

In 1933 Guiseppe Navone started making these Italian motorcycles which had no connection with the great motor cars which were produced from 1904 to 1923. Navone had the franchise to import the French machine called Train, and used that engine in the first bikes; later he turned to the Chaise and the English Python engine made by Rudge, in 250, 350, and 500cc machines.

Italian Grand Prix

The Italian Grand Prix, a classic race, dates back to 1922 when it was held on the then-new Monza circuit in a royal park near Milan over a 6.75-mile lap. The 500cc race was won by the Italian Gnesa on Garelli and the 1000 by Ruggeri on a Harley-Davidson. The race did not stay at Monza, and has been held at the Circuito del Littorio in Rome, the Circuito della Fiera in Milan, the Circuito di Faenza, Monza

again, and in 1969 at Imola. Since then it has been to Mugello, and has alternated between Monza and Imola.

Italjet

This Italian factory is renowned for off-road machines and schoolboy scramblers, operating since 1957. The maker, Leo Tartarini, was a successful road racer himself. Italjet also makes the frames for Ducati,

installs the Ducati engine, and makes snowmobiles. Its Mini Mini Bambino bike starts in sizes for three-year-olds upward, with a Franco Morini two-stroke engine and automatic clutch.

Ivy, Bill

Bill Ivy was a pint-size British road racer who was killed at the Sachsenring in East

Germany in 1969 at 26 years of age. Always a theatrical and abrasive personality, he started at 17 on an Italian 50cc Itom, and went on to win many honors. He won the World 125 Title on a Yamaha, for whom he was a factory rider from 1966. Ivy and the other Yamaha rider, Phil Read, did not agree and he left the team to try car racing. When he came back to motorcycling with Jawa he had his fatal crash.

J

James

James, a British factory in Birmingham, originally made pedal cycles and produced its first motorcycle in 1904 with a Belgian FN engine. The firm then offered some strange machines with hub-center steering and wheels attached to the frame on one side only, but these did not catch on. James made its name with small two-strokes, and continued with these after it had bought the Osborn Company and the Baker, using Villiers engines as well as its own make. In 1951 James became part of Associated Motor Cycles and used AMC engines; the company continued with some success in off-road competition with the Cotswold trials model and the Commando for scrambles. The factory also made an unsuccessful scooter. The last machine was the Cadet in 1955 and in 1964 the firm closed down.

JAP

The most famous British name in engines, J A Prestwich began making them in 1903 after producing cameras and scientific instruments. It sold engines to other people but made motorcycles as well until 1908, when it dropped the complete bikes in favor of engine making. Engines were made in sizes from 150cc up to big twins until 1957 when the company merged with the other big engine makers, Villiers. JAP powered machines of many different makes and nationalities as well as aircraft, Morgan three-wheelers, and speedway machines, and had a range of more than 50 models in its heyday.

Japanese Grand Prix

The Japanese Grand Prix is run at the £3 million Suzuka Circuit which was built in 1962 as a test track for Honda, designed by John Hugenholtz, the Dutchman who made the Zandvoort track. It is in hilly country 30 miles from Nagoya with a 3.73-mile lap in almost a figure eight. The first motorcycle Grand Prix was in 1963.

Jarama

This Spanish circuit near Madrid was first used for a World Championship motorcycle race—the Spanish Grand Prix—in 1969. It is a twisty manmade 2.2-mile lap, and was the site of the Grand Prix again in 1971, 1973, 1975, and 1977 although not popular with the riders. There has been no 500cc race since 1973 but there is usually a formula 750 event. Jarama is also used for the Formula One car Grand Prix.

Jawa

This Czech factory, now under state control similar to CZ, began in 1930 making the German Wanderer machine, a 500cc single. The Jawa name came from Frantisek Janecek, the arms maker behind the scheme, and Wanderer. Its success began in 1932 with two-strokes using the British Villiers engine; Jawa went on making these and four-strokes in addition, earning numerous racing successes. The firm was under German control during the war, and the Jawa/CZ link-up came in 1949. CZ had continued with two-strokes but Jawa had been making both types. Jawa/CZ have been very successful in motocross and in road racing too. Another member of the organization is ESO, which has been making a successful speedway machine called a Jawa 500 DT Type 680 since 1966.

Jonghi

Jonghi is a French motorcycle which was made from 1931 until 1956. The factory employed an Italian designer and first made 350cc side-valve singles, followed by an ohv racing version, and even ohc models as well as two-strokes. Jonghi merged with the Prester company in the 1930s; they survived the war and continued to make two-strokes.

Jonsson, Ake

Ake Jonsson is a Swedish motocross champion, born in 1942 at Vasteras, who has had two seconds, a third, and a fourth in the World Championships. In his first year in the series (1968) he led after eight rounds on a Husqvarna, but finished up third. He has ridden a works Yamaha and the German Maico, and is also an ice-skating champion.

Juno

This British make was produced in London from 1911 to 1923 using JAP, Precision, and Villiers engines or others to special order. The company made 150, 269, 600, and 770 models but had no competition history.

JV Special

The forerunner of the Triton, the JV Special is a racing machine using a Triumph speed twin-engine in a Norton frame, made by John Viccars. Several riders, including Frank Perris and Howard German, did well on them in the 1950s. The JV was followed by the Triton and the Dresda from David Degens.

K

Kanaye, Hideo

Hideo Kanaye is a Japanese road racer who won his first European race in 1972 when he was 27 years old. He is a Yamaha tester and development engineer who teamed up with Giacomo Agostini and won many Japanese titles and European races. He also had some bad crashes, including one in the Daytona 200 in 1974. Kanaye was third in the World 500cc Championship in 1975, and helped develop the racing Yamaha OW31 750cc two-stroke fours ridden by American aces Steve Baker and Kenny Roberts.

Karsmakers, Pierre

This Dutch motocross champion has ridden mostly in the United States and won the National Open Championship in 1973. He rode a Yamaha in 1973 and 1974 before moving to a Honda contract, then back to Yamaha in 1977.

Katayama, Takazumi

This Japanese rider, nicknamed 'Zooming Taxi,' won the World 350 Championship in 1977, the first rider from his country to do so. He was in fact born in Korea in 1950 and rides Yamaha, for whom he was a tester, and came to Europe in 1976. He was runner-up in the 250 World Championship in 1976, and has also made records as a pop singer.

Kawasaki

Kawasaki is the big Japanese maker which moved into motorcycles in 1949 after making steel, rail coaches and wagons, and other products. It was the aircraft side of the company which produced the motorbikes, in all sorts and sizes over the years. Kawasaki moved to racing in 1965 and

Above: The Czechoslovak Jawa CZ 250 Sports twin-cylinder two-stroke which is still very popular.

Below: Biggest of them all: Kawasaki's Z 1300 superbike which can outrun most.

won the 125cc World Title in 1969. Later successes were with the three-cylinder two-stroke 500cc H1, and the company claimed to race developed production machines rather than purpose-built racers. It has also been successful in the off-road market and in competition motocross. The company officially stopped racing in the United States in 1975 but has not been without success since, particularly in the 750cc endurance races. In 1977 Kawasaki took part in 250cc events with considerable success.

KG

The German KG machine was made from 1919 to 1932, its name coming from Krieger and Gnadig, the designers and producers. They started with shaft-drive 500s, and the firm had a complicated history as the bike was made by Cito, which was taken over by Allright, and finally by Henkel. The original company had some racing successes in the 1920s.

Koehler-Escoffier

The Koehler-Escoffier machines were produced in France for 45 years from 1912 starting with a 996cc twin with ohc, plus a more orthodox 350 and 500 single, which used bought-out engines. After World War II it made small machines with British Villiers two-stroke engines.

Kreidler

This was a German machine which dominated 50cc road racing and won the first championship race in 1962. The company started production in 1950 and retired from racing in 1966. Before restrictions were imposed Kreidler used a 14-speed gearbox; later the Dutch importer van Veen developed the Kreidler and it took the world 50cc title for manufacturers from 1971 to 1975. They also attacked speed records and registered 140.02mph in 1965 on the Utah flats from 50cc.

Krieger

The Krieger brothers originally made the KG in Germany which was taken over by Cito, Allright, and finally Henkel, and started up again making what looked suspiciously like the same machine under the title Original Krieger. It was a shaft-drive 500cc but was produced for only a year or so from 1925/6. They also offered a 350 with a British Blackburne engine.

Kring, Arne

Arne Kring is a Swedish motocross rider who, as an unknown at the age of 26 in 1969, won the Swedish 500 Grand Prix and went on to second place in the Swedish Championship in the 250 class in 1963. He secured support from the Husqvarna factory but failed to win the title in 1969, and in 1970, when he was in sight of victory in the final race to clinch the title, crashed sustaining serious injuries. The next year he broke a leg, and although he rode for five more years, Kring still missed the title and retired in 1976.

KTM

KTM is an Austrian company which started in 1951 with two-stroke machines under 150cc using Rotax, Sachs, and Puch engines. It specialized in off-road and trials mounts, and became supreme in competition. The name comes from the names of

The Italian Lambretta firm is known for scooters, but this is a 447cc twin five-speed racer.

the partners, Kronreif and Trunkenpolz, who met at Mattighofen. They won the 250 World Motocross Title in 1974 and in 1976, and continued making bicycles, mopeds, and small motorcycles.

Kuhn, Gus

Gus Kuhn, a veteran speedway rider, captained Stamford Bridge, a London club, around 1929 riding a 350 Calthorpe, and led it to the Southern Championship. Later he became a tuner and BMW dealer. He also won the 1919 Victory Trial run after World War I, riding a 2.5hp Levis, and the Evans Cup for the best performance by a service man.

L

Lackey, Brad

Brad Lackey is an American motocross rider who has risen quickly to the top; in 1979 he was contesting for top honors in the world title which was won in the 500cc class by Britain's 22-year-old Graham Noyce.

Ladetto

The Ladetto is an Italian product also known as the Ladetto and Blatto, made for 10 years from 1923. The company started with small two-strokes and advanced to both side and overhead valves up to 250cc achieving minor racing successes.

Lag

This Austrian machine was made at Lie-

sing near Vienna from 1921 to 1929. The firm made two-stroke engines as well as complete machines with British JAP engines and then shifted to a one-model policy with a 350cc two-stroke motor. An experimental 350 ohc of its own never really succeeded.

Lagonda

A famous name in the car world, Lagonda also made motorcycles in the pioneer days at the start of the century. The Staines factory was started by Wilbur Gunn from Springfield, Ohio, and the name meant 'swiftly flowing stream' in an Indian dialect. Gunn won the London-Edinburgh trial in 1905 on his V twin, but then went over to car making.

Lambretta

Lambretta is an Italian make of scooter produced from 1946 by Innocenti in enor-

American motocross champion Brad Lackey.

mous numbers with 125 to 198cc as a competitor to the small motorcycle. By 1972 the motorcycle had made a comeback while the scooter had declined, and the Lambretta disappeared. In Spain there was still a demand and a company was set up there which is still functioning and making three-wheelers. Lambretta has also gone into mopeds and motocross machines.

La Mondiale
La Mondiale, the Belgian motorcycle, was made from 1924 to 1934 and had no connection with the Italian Mondial in spite of the similarity of name. The Belgian firm used a pressed-steel frame and pressed forks, with two-strokes in the small machines and ohc engines in the bigger ones. There were also JAP-engined racing versions.

Lamont, Billy
Billy Lamont is the pioneer speedway rider who showed Britain what speedway (or dirt track) was all about in 1928. He rode an AJS although the Douglas was the popular mount.

Lamoreaux, Wilbur
This American speedway rider was runner-up in the 1937 and 1938 World Speedway Championship run in England, and was a dominating influence on the sport in pre-war days.

Lampkin Brothers
The three British Lampkin brothers from Yorkshire have all won the Scottish Six Days Trial and had other successes in trials and motocross. Arthur (born 1938) won in 1963, having been riding for four years. Alan, five years younger, won in 1966, and Martin (born 1950) won in 1975 and was European Trials Champion in 1973 and World Champion in 1975. Martin rides a Bultaco under contract.

Lancefield, Steve
Steve Lancefield is an excellent British tuner, particularly famed for his work on Nortons when they dominated motorcycle racing. He was in charge of the Norton team when it ran the ohc racers at Daytona for the first time in 1948.

Lansivuori, Teuvo
This Finnish road racer, born in 1945, was teammate to Barry Sheene on Suzuki. He won his first ice race at 16 and tried motocross, speedway, and sand racing before taking to road racing. He won the 1971 Spanish Grand Prix as an unknown and joined the Yamaha works team in 1973 to replace his friend Jarno Saarinen who had been killed. Lansivuori was runner-up in both 250 and 350 World Championships.

After moving to Suzuki, Tepi (his nickname) came third in the 500cc class in 1974 and 1975, and second in 1976. He is an undertaker by trade.

Laurin & Klement
Laurin & Klement is an Austrian name which became Czech when the frontiers moved. The firm was a pioneer from 1899 with singles, twins and fours and tried the engine in various locations on the machine. In 1908 the company decided to make cars instead, using the V-twin engine. Before that the bikes were also made in Germany under license. The Skoda firm bought the company.

Laverda
An Italian company, Laverda has a parallel with the Lamborghini car firm, which also began as a tractor maker and then went for the high-price luxury sporting market. Laverda began producing motorbikes in 1949 with an economy single-cylinder 75cc machine; but progressed to 750 twins and 1000cc triples of formidable performance. The firm has never been in racing, except with the early economy model, tuned to run at 13,000rpm and produce 10 horsepower. The first 750 appeared once in the 1968 Giro d'Italia long-distance race and

The Italian Laverda factory has left it to private owners to race its machine.

won. The company has left it to private owners to race, and continues to produce the fastest and best-finished road machines for the discriminating owner.

Lawwill, Mert
An American racer born in San Francisco, Mert Lawwill has been racing since 1960. He is a long-track, dirt-track specialist ('Mert the Dirt'), but surprised many people by scoring as many points as Barry Sheene when he stood in for Mark Brelsford in the 1973 Anglo-American Match Races. He won the AMA Grand National Championship in 1969 on his Harley-Davidson.

Lazzarini, Eugenio
This Italian road racer was prominent in 50cc events on the Dutch Van Veen version of the German Kreidler, and, among other events, won the 1977 Italian 50cc Grand Prix ahead of the Bultaco twins Angel Nieto and Ricardo Tormo at Imola.

Lea-Francis
The Lea-Francis was a much-loved British bike from 1911 to 1926. The company made both cars and motorcycles until it dropped the bikes and kept the cars. The two-wheelers had MAG engines, 500 singles, and 600 twins; they also used JAP V-twin engines.

Le Vack, Bert
Bert le Vack is a pioneer racer who rode Brough Superior, Zenith, Indian, and other machines. He won the 1921 Brooklands 500-Mile race on an Indian, and the year before on an Indian Powerplus 998cc twin took the 50-mile record at 75.85mph, 100, 150, and 200 miles, and the one, two, and three hours. He was also the first man to do a Brooklands lap at 100mph, on a Zenith in the rain. He also took world solo and sidecar records at 123 and 103mph on a Brough Superior SS100 with 980cc JAP twin engine in 1925. Le Vack also made his own machines with 350 JAP engines.

Levis
Levis was a famous English maker of two-strokes from 1912 until World War II. The Latin word Levis means 'light,' the basis on which the Butterfield brothers named their machine, with a 211cc engine. They finished 1-2-3 in the 250cc TT in 1920 and won a cup for the best 250 performance. They won again in 1922. In 1927 they introduced a four-stroke 350, but this did not catch on like the two-strokes at first, although it overtook them later. The com-

pany still exists under the name of Levis.

Ligier, Guy
French patron of the Formula One car team, Guy Ligier was a racing motorcyclist in the 1950s and among other triumphs was fourth on a Norton in the 1957 Automobile Club de France 500cc race at the sports car Grand Prix at the 4.06-mile Rouen-Les Essarts circuit. He was also third the following year on Norton in the 500cc race at the same place, the 'Coupe de Vitesse de la Ville,' where nine Nortons finished in the first nine places.

Lomas, Bill
This British road racer is best known for his successes with the Italian MV Agusta, for whom he won the Lightweight TT in 1955, the same year in which he won the Junior on a Moto Guzzi, at 92.33mph. He also rode Velocette in the works team and did well in the 1950s in the Ulster Grand Prix, an event in which he also took top honors for Moto Guzzi.

Lorenzetti, Enrico
An Italian road-racer who won among other events the 250cc race at the Italian Grand Prix of 1950 on Moto Guzzi, Lorenzetti also won the 500cc race on Guzzi at the Dutch Grand Prix of 1947 and was a top rider in his day.

Louis, John
John Louis is a British speedway champion who was formerly a top scrambler. He began riding for Ipswich in 1969, and won the second division Riders Championship in 1972. He was fourth in the 1974 World Final, British Champion in 1975, and third in the World Final in the same year. He was sixth in 1976 when his club won the Gulf British League.

Luchinelli, Marco
This Italian road racer, born in 1954, rode hill climbs in 1974 and started circuit racing in 1975 on Yamaha. In 1976 he switched to Suzuki on an RG500 and was third in the French Grand Prix, second in Germany and Austria, and fourth in the World Championship.

Lundin, Sten
Sten Lundin is a Swedish motocross star born in 1930 who won the World Championship in 1959, was second in 1960 and won again in 1961. He was also third six times in the 500cc Championship over the years. He started on BSA but mainly rode

Back in 1917 the British Levis (Latin for 'light') 211cc made camping transport.

Lito. Lundin also won the shortlived 750cc Motocross Championship in 1966 and 1967. He retired in 1969.

Luthringshauser, Heinz
This German sidecar ace lost a leg in 1961 but kept on racing. Heinz Luthringshauser began in speedway in 1949 and won the French Grand Prix in 1972; he was leading the World Championship when he crashed, killing his passenger. He finished second for the world title. He was still riding in 1977 at 46 years of age, using a sidecar mounted on the left in British style to suit his missing left leg and having both pedals on the right.

Lydden Hill
Located near Dover in Kent, this British off-road circuit came into being for car autocross to be staged for television presentation, but is also used for motorcycle

events in which the winner of the season gets the 'Lord of Lydden' title. Dave Croxford is one of those who have held it.

M

Mabeco
The Mabeco was a German motorcycle made from 1923 to 1927 which appeared to be a Chinese copy of the Indian Scout, except that it was green instead of red. Eventually Indian took the firm to court when the Germans changed their color to red too, but the bikes were still made, although under a new name and to a different design.

McCandless Brothers
These two brothers from Northern Ireland, Cromie and Rex, ran a Belfast motorcycle business as well as racing themselves, and

Cromie rode for Norton tuning specialist Francis Beart. Apart from their riding skills they are credited with developing the Featherbed frame which enabled Nortons to handle so well in their last years.

McEvoy
Perhaps the principal claim to fame of this English machine is that it was financed by Cecil Birkin, brother of 'Bentley Boy' Tim Birkin. Michael McEvoy ran the Derby factory, which made machines up to 1000 JAP twins, using Blackburne, Anzani, and Villiers engines. McEvoy was a name in supercharging, for cars as well as bikes. When Birkin was killed the company foundered.

McIntyre, Bob
Bob McIntyre was a Scottish rider born in 1928 in Glasgow who was killed on a Norton in 1962 after a successful road-racing career with Norton, AJS, Gilera,

and Honda. He did well in the Isle of Man TT races, but when Norton became passé he turned to Gilera in 1957 and Honda in 1962. He took the world one-hour record on a 350 Gilera at 141mph in 1957.

Maffeis
This Italian make lasted 30 years from early beginnings in 1903. It was built and raced by the Maffeis brothers, originally with a Belgian engine, then with their own singles and twins, and finally with British Blackburne engines of 250, 350, and 500cc.

Magnat-Debron
The Magnat-Debron French motorcycle was made for nearly 50 years from 1906 and was a popular machine. The firm started with V twins, but after World War I went to singles, two- and four-stroke, and finally joined the famous French firm of Terrot in the 1930s. Mopeds, scooters, and ohv singles were built after 1945.

Magni

An Italian product from 1928 which lasted only a couple of years, the Magni has interest because of one design by Luigi Magni which was a 350-ohc twin with both cylinders facing forward. There was also a 'normal' 500cc single.

Maico

This German company which is now famous for motocross machines has been going since 1934 making road-going bikes as well. The brothers Maisch started it and shortened Maisch Company to Maico, making two-strokes with bought-out engines. They had no success and dropped the bikes until after World War II, then came back with a 150 utility model, followed by bigger bikes and a scooter, then a baby car which failed. After these problems they won success in both off-road and road racing, but they finally settled on motocross as their field and have won honors in off-road sport. Maico is one of the leading contenders.

Majestic

There have been three machines under this name, English, Belgian and French, and all are unconnected. The English ones were 350 and 500cc bikes made from AJS

parts from 1931 to 1935. The Belgian models were of the same sizes but slightly earlier, 1928 to 1931, assembled from JAP engines and other English parts. The French were of the same period (1927-34) and up to 500cc, using either French engines or the British JAP.

Malaguti

Malaguti machines are Italian lightweights made since 1940 and are very popular with the young. Top-selling models made at Bologna are the Cavalcone, Ronchino Junior, and other motocross and moped designs with a sporting flavor. Most of them use Morini engines, and have done so since before World War II.

Mallory Park

This British racing circuit is situated between Hinckley and Leicester in the Midlands with one-mile and 1.35-mile laps depending on the track used. At least three motorcycle meetings a year are normally held. Although short, the circuit is in a picturesque lakeside setting with sweeping right and left bends.

Mammut

There were two German machines of this name but they had no connection. One

The young American Randy Mamola has come to the top fast in road racing.

was in existence from 1925 to 1933 with under 200cc two-stroke engines as well as JAP, Blackburne, Villiers, and Baumi. The company also used the British Coventry-Eagle frame under license. The other company (1953-56) had a shorter life, making small mopeds and lightweights with bought-out two-stroke engines. Similar machines were also sold under several other names.

Mamola, Randy

Randy Mamola is an American road racer who started riding as a child and by the age of 19 was in the world class of racers. He was well up in the ratings by 1979, challenging Roberts, Sheene, Ferrari, and other masters.

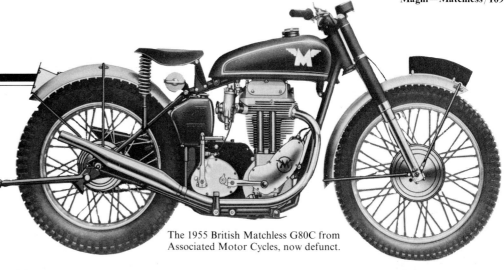

The 1955 British Matchless G80C from Associated Motor Cycles, now defunct.

Manx Grand Prix

A race for amateur riders on standard machines round the 37.75-mile Isle of Man TT course, the Manx Grand Prix has been held since 1923 except during the war years 1939 to 1945. The regulations have varied from time to time, but there is normally a four-lap 250cc race, then a six-lap Junior and Senior on 350 and 500 machines, just like the TT. Lap speeds are now over 100mph, and the races are run in September.

Mars

There have been three machines with this marque label, one German and two English. The German firm (1903–57) was the major one with a factory in Nuremberg, and made some unorthodox models. The famous one was the White Mars in the 1920s with an opposed flat-twin 956cc engine, a hand starter, and both tools and gear-change in the gasoline tank. The Germans made several other varieties and finished up with small two-strokes. One of the English companies ran only for three years from 1905, fitting German Fafnir and Belgian Minerva engines at its London factory. The second English company (1923–26) was Coventry-based and did not make anything bigger than 350cc, using engines from Bradshaw, Barr & Stroud, JAP, and Villiers.

Mas

Mas was an Italian company which was in production for 35 years from 1920. Some German two-strokes were made for a year or so (1923/4) under this name but were unconnected. The Italian Mas started with small engines and then grew to 500cc and continued to make both the ranges together. They too ended with small two-strokes.

Maserati

This famous Italian car factory run by a team of brothers also went in for motorcycles on a small scale for 10 years from 1953, but did not achieve the standing they did with racing cars. The bikes were all under 250cc, both two-strokes and vertical twin ohc with pleasing lines.

Masetti, Umberto

An Italian road racer dominant in the 1950s, Umberto Masetti was twice World Champion in the 500cc class on the four cylinder Gilera. He won most of the classic European Grand Prix in his victorious years. Earlier he had ridden Moto Morini.

Matchless

This famous British make familiarly known as 'the Matchbox' began production at the beginning of the century; it was eventually swallowed up by Associated Motor Cycles with so many others and died in 1969. The Collier brothers were behind Matchless and rode their own ma-

A period piece, the Matchless Model J of 1923 with JAP 976cc engine.

World Champion speedway superstar Ivan Mauger from New Zealand in full flight.

chines to win and be placed in the early TT races.

Mauger, Ivan

One of the superstars of speedway, Mauger from New Zealand has won five world finals after racing since 1957. He started in England with the Wimbledon Club, then for Newcastle, and won the European Championship in 1966. He moved to Belle Vue in 1968 and Exeter in 1973. In 1977 he won his fifth title and, including long-track speedway, has won seven individual world titles. He was awarded the MBE in 1975.

Maurer

Ludwig Maurer of Nuremberg first designed cars for Maurer-Union. He left and produced the Maurer after putting the company in the name of his wife Johanna, as his contract banned him from making cars when he left in 1908. Then after World War I he made motorcycles with strange water-cooled, twin, two-stroke engines, with outside 'bacon slicer' flywheels. They were produced until 1926.

Mauser

This famous German arms works began to make in 1922 what was really a single-track car, an Einspurauto, although it might be classed as a motorcycle. It had two running wheels with jockey wheels on either side, like a child's bicycle, and curious handlebars. Power was from a water-cooled 500cc sv with chain drive, but it did not sell well and ultimately another company took over production until 1932.

Megola

A most extraordinary machine made in Germany from 1921 to 1925, the Megola looked a little like the Ner-a-Car but had a radial five-cylinder, air-cooled engine inside the front wheel which it drove directly without clutch or gearbox. It was very low and thus handled well, and even won races with a more powerful engine than the standard 640cc version.

Meier, Georg, (Schorsch)

Georg Meier, a top-ranking German road racer on BMW, won the Belgian Grand Prix in 1939 after winning the German Grand Prix and being European 500 Champion in 1938. He also won the Senior TT in 1939 at 89.38mph on a supercharged BMW breaking the Norton chain of victories. Meier was an army sergeant and hid his machine in a barn during World War II, to come back and start to win again from 1947 to 1953. He was German 250 Champion in 1947, 1948, 1949, 1950, 1953, and other victories included the Dutch TT in 1938 and 1939.

Mellors, Ted

This British road-race rider did well on Velocette in the TT in the 1930s and also in European events, winning the 1936 Belgian Grand Prix among other events. He won the 1939 Lightweight TT after switching to an Italian Benelli 250cc machine to record his first TT outright win at 74.25 mph.

Meriden Motor Cycles

This co-operative, backed by British Government money, continued to make Triumph motorcycles at the Meriden factory in the Midlands after Norton-Villiers-Triumph had ceased production. It started operations in March 1975 and was fully operational, both making and selling machines, by 1977.

Metisse

Metisse machines were made by the Rickman brothers, Don and Derek, both riders themselves, by modifying production bikes for competition.

Michanek, Anders

Anders Michanek is a Swedish speedway rider who won the World Championship in 1974. He was born in 1943 and began riding in 1965, moving to England in 1967 to ride at Long Eaton. Later he was with Leicester, Reading, and finally Cradley in 1977, after a spell in 1974 when he was banned in England. He won three Swedish titles as well.

Michigan Motors Corporation

Michigan Motors Corporation produced the American four-cylinder motorcycle, the Ace, in 1926 after the original company had stopped production.

Milne, Jack

Jack Milne is an American speedway rider born in 1910 in Buffalo, New York, who with his brother Cordy made a great name in Britain, Australia, and the United States right up to 1950 when he retired. He first rode in the Los Angeles area, then moved to Australia where he won the Championship and then on to Britain. He rode for New Cross and his brother for Hackney. He also won the World Championship in 1937, when his brother finished third.

Another American, Wilbur Lamoreaux, was second.

Mikkola, Heikki

Heikki Mikkola is a Finnish motocross champion who was born in Sanjaniami in 1945 and began on Husqvarna in 1964. He was 500cc World Champion in 1974 and 250cc Champion in 1976. In his first season he won 14 out of 15 races, and has also been successful in ski jumping, ice speedway, and car rallies, like his namesake Hannu Mikkola. He also goes in for weightlifting when training for his riding. In 1977, then riding Yamaha, Mikkola won the world 500cc title for the second time, winning eight out of 10 races. He lives in Belgium.

Militaire

This American machine, later known as the Militor, had a four-cylinder car-type engine and outrigger wheels like a child's tricycle to hold it up when stationary. It was made before World War I.

Miller, Sammy

A top trials rider born in 1933 in Belfast, Northern Ireland, Sammy Miller began as a road racer, riding NSU, Ducati, Mondial, and CZ, and finished third in the 1957 World Championship. In trials he rode first 500 Ariel and then Bultaco, and was British Champion for 11 years and twice European Champion. He helped Honda to develop its trials machines. He was still riding in 1977 at 43 years of age.

Miller-Balsamo

Miller-Balsamo, an Italian make from 1921 to 1959, did well in racing and record breaking with 174cc ohv engines. The firm also made two-strokes and bigger bikes up to 500cc. In postwar times it concentrated on small two-strokes.

Minarelli

Minarelli is an Italian maker of two-stroke sporting engines used in Cimatti, Cotton, Fantic, Simonini, and other machines, producing 6.8 horsepower from 50cc at 8800rpm.

Minerva

Minerva is a famous Belgian car factory which began with motorcycles but gave them up before World War I. It began making bicycles in 1897 and its first motorcycle in 1900 was a bicycle with a bolt-on motor over the rear wheel. This unit was enlarged to 239cc and sold to many makers,

The Miller-Bolsame Jupiter of 1947, an Italian lightweight of 250cc ohv (above), and (below) another Italian, the Tecnomoto Minarelli off-road bike.

including the British Triumph. Eventually Minerva stopped selling engines and made its own complete motorcycles in three models, but stopped producing in 1909.

Minter, Derek

British road racer, the 'King of Brands Hatch,' Derek Minter rode many different machines with equal success. He started in 1948 and retired in 1967 after many wins and places in the Isle of Man and elsewhere. He did not take kindly to team discipline and mostly rode his own machines. He won the 1962 Lightweight 250cc TT on a nonworks Honda, beating the works machines.

Britain's Derek Minter (King of Brands) wearing the winner's laurel away from home at Silverstone.

Motocross star Gennady Moisseev leaps over Girling's Jump on his way to win the Girling Grand Prix at Hawkstone Park, England, in 1977.

MISCUS

The Motorcycling International Committee of the United States, formerly the International Motorcycling Board of the USA Inc was the American organization representing the country at the FIM, with headquarters at Daytona Speedway. They shared control of the sporting events with the American Motorcyclist Association (AMA).

Mival

This Italian firm built two-stroke machines up to 200cc from 1950 to 1966, and also single and double ohc machines, some for motocross, as well as trials bikes.

MM

There were three different makes under this name at different times—one in America, one Italian, and one English. The American firm, which ran from 1906 up to 1940, used bought-out engines from five different suppliers and produced both singles and twins. The Italian company lasted 40 years from 1924 and first made two-strokes which set world records, and then single-cylinder ohv models which also took records and races. The English company made a bike with a 269cc Villiers two-stroke engine in 1914.

Mobylette

The Mobylette is a moped produced in enormous numbers since 1949 by the French manufacturer Motobecane, founded in 1923. The machines are automatic with no clutch or gear change and 50cc engines made by Motobecane. They give 30mph with 120mpg, in a simple-to-ride step-through bicycle for the commuter or town rider.

Mohawk

This English motorcycle was made from 1903 to 1925, although there was a gap in production between the early versions and the later machines made with bought-out engines from three different suppliers. Some were two-strokes and some orthodox models from a company who also made bicycles.

Moisseev, Gennady

Gennady Moisseev is a Russian motocross expert who was World Champion in 1974 and 1977. He was born in Leningrad in February 1948 and began riding in 1964, winning the Soviet Championship in 1968, 1972, 1973, and 1976. He is one of three Russian works riders who ride Austrian KTM machines.

Molaroni

These Italian motorcycles were made from 1921 to 1927 at Pesaro, originally with two-stroke engines, later using an imported British 350cc Blackburne engine.

Monarch

Three different varieties of machines were sold under this name—one in America, one in England and one in Japan—but at different periods of time. The American machine ran for three years from 1912 with a 500cc single and a 990cc V twin, one of the first with a sprung frame. The English version was slightly later, 1919 to 1921, and no relation. It was in reality a cut-price edition of the Excelsior, a Birmingham product, with either side-valve JAP or Villiers two-stroke, both just under 300cc. The Japanese Monarch in 350 and 500 form bore a striking resemblance to the British Norton, and was made for seven years from 1955.

Monark

This Swedish bike made from 1920, originally under Esse label, was first of all a motorized bicycle. Later the firm used German 110 engines and then Husqvarna, finally turning to lightweights. Since World War II Monark has been successful with motocross mounts, winning the World 500cc Motocross Championship in 1959 and 1961. Monark is part of the MCB Group, and in recent years has had great success with its 175 Enduro and other off-road models.

Mondial

Mondials are Italian mini-racers which won the 125cc World Championship in 1949, four other manufacturers' titles and many others. The company began in 1929 but did not come upon the two-wheel scene until 1949. Its 123cc racer turned over at 11,000rpm using ohc. It took the first four places in the 1951 Lightweight TT and Mondial also took the first three places in the 250cc World Championship in 1957. By 1977 the company was making only small machines, mostly off-road two-strokes.

Monet Gyyon

Monet Gyyon was a successful French machine for 40 years from 1917. It began with Villiers-engined two-strokes and moved on to racers in the 350 and 500 classes with MAG engines from Switzerland. In postwar days the company mostly reverted to two-strokes, plus 350 singles, and a scooter.

Montesa

Montesa is a Spanish company founded by Francesco Bulto, later of Bultaco, and Pedro Permanyer in 1944. The Montesa 125s were very quick and in 1956 finished third and fourth in the Isle of Man Lightweight TT. Bulto left in 1958 when the company cut back on sport, but it went on to make successful trials machines and won the 1968 Spanish Championship with its 250cc. Montesa then concentrated on off-road bikes in various sizes up to 350cc.

Montgomery

An English make, the Montgomery lasted from the pioneer days at the turn of the century up to World War II. The machines were made in Coventry in all sizes from a baby Villiers up to big V twins. The company had some racing success with JAP-engined models.

Montjuich Park

This park in Barcelona houses the racing circuit where the car and motorcycle Grands Prix are held alternately with the new Madrid Jarama Circuit. The exhibition buildings used for motor shows are on the same site.

Montlhery

The Montlhery Racing Circuit near Paris has been in use since 1924 for car and motorcycle races and record attempts, and has a banked track part of the way around. There are various combinations of road and track to give different circuit lengths, ranging from 1.58 to 7.8 miles. The Bol d'Or has been held at this circuit.

Monza

This race circuit in the former Royal Park at Monza outside Milan opened in 1922 with a 3.4-mile road course and a 2.8-mile banked track. It was used for both car and motorcycle meetings until 1973 when, in a multiple pile-up in the Italian Grand Prix, Jarno Saarinen and Renzo Pasolini were killed and others injured. It has since been banned for two-wheelers.

Moore, Ronnie

Ronnie Moore is a top speedway rider born in Tasmania, Australia, in 1933. He won the New Zealand South Island Championship in 1949, and went to England to ride for Wimbledon in 1950, aged 17. He won

Chas Mortimer, racing son of a racing father, in action.

Above both: America's young racer, Randy Mamola.

his first world title in 1954, and again in 1959, and retired in 1971, after many injuries in the course of his career. In a one-time appearance in 1975 he suffered a fractured skull as well as other injuries.

Moped

The moped is a small motorcycle with pedals still attached. These machines have been in use since 1923, when they used to be called autocycles, and moped did not come as a name until about 1960. In Britain mopeds are no longer obliged to have pedals and may be operated by riders of 16 provided the machines cannot exceed 30 mph.

Morbidelli

These small Italian racers have been made since 1968 by Giancarlo Morbidelli. His 50cc model is capable of about 100mph at 14,500rpm and won the Czech Grand Prix in 1970. These machines won many other races and the firm had great success with its second-generation 125cc from 1975 with a machine said to do 130mph. Morbidelli took the first and second places in the World Championship, and has gone on to many successes, some with machines in private hands.

Morini

The Morini is an Italian racing machine that was first made in 1937 by Alphonso Morini. The modern style ones began in 1945 as two-strokes, but there have been good ohv and ohc designs as well. After Alphonso's death in 1969 the factory produced the 350cc V twins, made in both road-going Strada form and Sport with more power. Motor Morini which makes the Morini is not connected with Franco Morini which makes engines, although Franco is a cousin of Alphonso.

Morris

There were two English motorcycles of this name, one made with De Dion engines from 1902 to 1905 by William Morris who founded the car firm and became Lord Nuffield. The other (1913–22) was not connected with William Morris and made a 250cc two-stroke with its own engine.

Mortimer, Charles

An English racing rider born in 1949, Charles Mortimer was the son of a former rider. His first win was in 1966 on Greeves. He then rode a Yamaha until the private team was disbanded in 1970; following that he rode a works Yamaha, was runner-up in the 125cc 1972 World Championship, and third the next year. In 1976 he was runner-up in the 350cc World Championship, but has suffered from a number of crashes.

Moser

The Moser is a Swiss machine made for more than 30 years from 1905. In addition the firm sold engines to other companies. It was successful in racing with its ohv machines, which ranged up to 600cc, although most were in the 173cc version. There was also an Austrian Moser in the 1950s with a two-stroke engine, not linked with the Swiss firm.

Moskva

This Russian motorcycle was made for more than 20 years from 1940 with a V-twin engine and was used by the army. Later there were small two-strokes and a transverse flat twin with shaft drive.

Mosport

This racing circuit near Toronto, Canada, is a 2.59-mile circuit where the Canadian motorcycle Grand Prix has been run since 1967. The twisty circuit was built with financial aid from the Imperial Tobacco Company and is also used for car racing.

Motobecane

The French Motobecane factory has been going since 1922, making more recently the Mobylette moped as well as traditional machines. In the 1930s the company made big shaft-driven models as well as sporting singles. It also makes 123cc twins for production-bike races. Motobecane has a link with De Tomaso in Italy who owns Moto Guzzi and Benelli.

Motobi

Motobi is an Italian make from Giovani Benelli whose brothers make the machines of that name. It began in 1951 with two-strokes and went on to ohv singles up to 250 with pressed-steel frames and telescopic forks, eventually becoming part of the Benelli fold which now belongs to De Tomaso.

Moto-Borgo

This Italian product has been made from 1906 for 20 years. It was made by the Borgo brothers who also raced it in single-cylinder form up to 827cc. Later there were V twins in various sizes from 477 to 990cc. At one time there was a link with the British Rudge Company and the two firms' machines looked alike. In 1926 Borgo dropped bikes in favor of making pistons only.

Motoconfort

This French motorcycle maker is part of the Motobecane Group and makes motorcycles similar to Motobecane. Motoconfort started in 1925 but joined with the other company in 1930. A third firm, Polymecanique has been making engines for the others since 1928.

Motocross

Motocross is cross-country racing on motorcycles, originally known in England as scrambling or trials riding. Motocross is a combination of the two other sports with different scoring methods, and now has European and world championship races. They are perhaps wrongly called Grands Prix, which is really a road-racing term for the fastest kind of racing.

Moto Guzzi

Perhaps the most famous Italian make, Moto Guzzi has been going since 1921 when it was founded by Carlo Guzzi and Georgio Parodi, assuming the eagle badge of pilot Parodi's squadron. The company is now part of the De Tomaso empire after a huge success in racing with its idiosyncratic forward-facing cylinder. One of its milestones was the extraordinary 1956 V8 500cc racing machine.

Massed start of a motocross event at Britain's Hawkstone Park in 1979, with Andy Robertson (Yamaha) nearest camera.

Paul Harrison on his Maico blasting a trail at Deddington in 1978 in a motocross event.

Motom
Motom was an Italian maker of lightweight machines from 1947 up to 1964, mostly with two-stroke engines from Peugeot and others, or ohv units. It went in for off-road bikes as well as for motocross, some with automatic gearboxes.

Motosacoche
This great Swiss firm was founded in 1901 and made motorcycles until 1957, selling bikes under its own name and engines to many people under the MAG label. It was started by the Dufaux brothers in Geneva, originally with an engine to attach to a bicycle. They supplied many English firms, notably Royal Enfield and Matchless, and had factories in France, Germany, and Italy. They dabbled in racing from time to time, including the British TT. Famous models included ioe big twins and an 850 side-valve twin designed by Bert le Vack. Their final model before they switched to

industrial engines was a 250 with a shaft drive.

Mototrans
Mototrans is the Spanish factory which has been making the Italian Ducati machines since 1957. It produces the ohc singles up to 350cc and also its own designs in 50cc mopeds and runabouts.

Muller, Egon
This German speedway, grass-, and sand-track racer has won many titles. He was born in 1948 at Kiel and began to come to notice in 1972. In the next year he won the national long-track title, and the world 1000 meters sand-track title in 1974 and 1975, and the German Championship as well in 1975. He made brief appearances in British speedway—he was in the Rest of the World speedway side which beat Britain in 1977 and he was seventh in the world final. He also won the Strongbow British

Long Track Grand Prix grass meeting and set a world record on grass with a lap in Germany at 135.11kph. Muller also won the German Long Track Championship and set a world record speedway lap at 81.26kph. He is a pop singer who has made records.

Munch
Friedel Munch made the four-cylinder Munch Mammut to special order after an initial one-off for a customer on the basis of an NSU air-cooled car engine in 1958. He had backing from the late Floyd Clymer, an American publisher, then from Heinz Henke. A three-cylinder two-stroke was introduced and later dropped to concentrate on the four, and there was also a short-lived racing program with Helmut Fath and Horst Owesle. Munch himself finally left in 1977 to make parts for his own creation, the 1300cc TTS/E. All of his machines were hand built.

Left: George O'Dell, one of the great sidecar riders, leading at Silverstone. He was World Champion in 1977.

Right: Angel Nieto on his Minarelli-engined mount at Hockenheim in 1979.

MV Agusta

This Italian company which made helicopters came into motorcycle manufacture in 1946, and has had enormous success in racing and building production machines. In 1977 it had financial problems and made a link with another Italian maker, Ducati, who was building MV machines.

MZ

MZ is an East German make built in the old DKW works at Zschopau, which gave it the name, Motorradwerke Zschopau. The company makes two-strokes in various sizes up to 350cc and also motocross machines which have been very successful in competition. Water-cooled versions are used for road racing with twin two-stroke engines and the machines have been ridden by many different top riders over the years. An unusual feature is a gear drive in place of a primary chain. From 1946 the old DKW works made the IFA, and the MZ

came along in 1953, using rotary disk valves to feed the two-stroke engines.

N

Nacional Motor SA

Nacional Motor SA has been the Spanish maker of the Derbi motorcycle since 1951, a very successful lightweight racer. The company is located near Barcelona.

Neander

An extraordinary creation from Germany designed by Ernst Neumann-Neander and made for only five years from 1924, this machine had a frame of duralumin plated with cadmium which did not need protecting with paint. There were other oddities, too, such as a leaf-sprung front fork and a fuel tank inside the frame. Neander used

all sorts of engines from little 122cc two-strokes up to 996 twin JAPs, and even raced at Brooklands. The Opel car firm made some Neanders under licence.

Ner-a-Car

This is another eccentric design by the American J Neracher which used a bucket seat like a car and hub center steering on some models. It was built in England.

Neumayer, Dr Fritz

Dr Fritz Neumayer was the man behind the Zundapp motorcycle in Nuremberg, who started the company in 1917 and died in 1935. His son, Hans Friedrich, took over and became assistant managing director. The company made many models including the famous 750 flat twin used by the German army with sidecar.

Newbold, John

This British road racer was born in Derby-

The British 1924 Ner-a-Car designed by an American, with 2.75-horsepower Simplex two-stroke engine.

shire in 1952 and began racing in 1971. He was second in the Grovewood Awards in 1972, and was in the Suzuki team in 1975; he finished second in the Belgian Grand Prix, fourth in the Dutch, and seventh in the World Championship. He was also fourth in the Motor Cycle News 750 Super-bike Championship. In 1976 Newbold won the World Championship race at Brno and was fifth in the 500 title and third in the FIM 750 Formula Championship.

New Gerrard

The New Gerrard was a British machine made for 20 years from 1922 by race rider Jock Porter in Edinburgh, Scotland. He used Blackburne and JAP engines and won races with his own machines, including the 1923 Lightweight TT at 51.93mph.

New Hudson

This British machine was made in Birmingham from 1910 until 1952. The company was making bicycles before that and started with a clip-on engine. It went on to make a 500 which was raced successfully by Bert le Vack. New Hudson stopped making machines in 1933 but designed an autocycle which was made by BSA from 1941; after that it manufactured suspension units.

New Imperial

A British manufacturer which began in 1901, New Imperial failed to sell the first machines and retired until 1910. It had some later racing successes, winning the 250cc TT class in 1921, 1924 (plus the 350), 1925, 1932, and 1936. After that the company had money problems, was bought by Jack Sangster of Ariel and Triumph, but declined with World War II.

The 1921 New Hudson 211cc was so light you could pick it up and it would do 100mpg, they said.

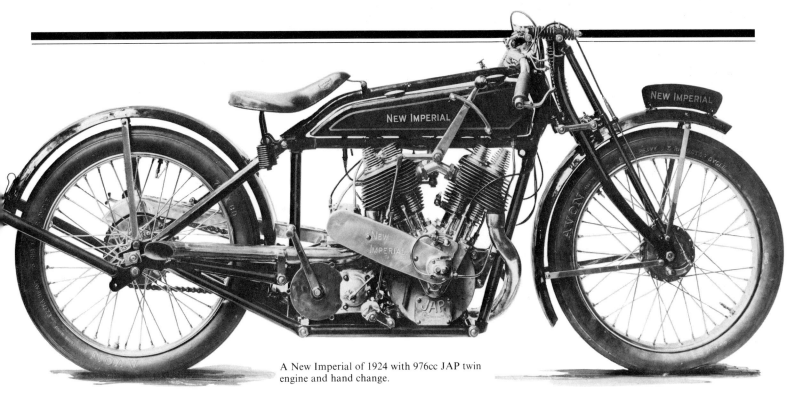

A New Imperial of 1924 with 976cc JAP twin engine and hand change.

New Map

This French machine was made for more than 30 years from 1920. It ran from under 100cc up to 1000 with 10 different makes of bought-out engines. In its later years the firm went in for two-strokes, mopeds, and even scooters.

New Scale

This English make from Harry Scale was made from 1909 for nearly 20 years. It used other people's engines and the machines were unremarkable; eventually it was bought out by the English Dot company.

Nieto, Angel

Angel Nieto is a Spanish road racer with eight world championships to his credit, all on small-engined machines. He was born in 1947 in Madrid, and first raced at 13 years of age. He came on the scene in 1968, was a Derbi works rider in 1969, and won the 50cc world title. He then rode Morbidelli, Van Veen Kreidler, and Bultaco. His wins have been in the 50 and 125 classes.

Nilsson, Bill

Bill Nilsson is a top Swedish motocross rider who was the first 500cc World Champion in 1957 and won again in 1960. He retired after a crash in 1965. He started on BSA, moved to AJS with the 7R racing engine, then rode Husqvarna. He was among the top stars for 10 years.

Nimbus

This Danish motorcycle was made for nearly 40 years from 1920 in Copenhagen, but always just the one model, a four-cylinder in-line 750cc air-cooled machine with a pressed-steel frame.

Nixon, Gary

An American road and dirt racer, Gary Nixon has had an appalling run of bad luck and injuries but still won the AMA National Title in 1967 and 1968. He was born in Anadarko, Oklahoma, in 1941 and has been a professional rider since 1962. He won the Daytona 200 on a Triumph in 1967, and was in the team for the Anglo-American races in 1971, when he crashed in practice. He rode Kawasaki in 1972 and Suzuki in 1973, then Yamaha.

NLG

These initials stood for North London Garage, a British motorcycle maker from 1905, which initially used Peugeot engines and then JAP. An NLG with a Peugeot twin engine of 944cc won the first Brooklands race in April 1909, ridden by W E Cook. Also in 1909 Cook did more than 90mph on an NLG with a JAP engine of 2713cc. The company had closed down by World War I.

Norman

This English make lasted 35 years from 1937. The first model was a Villiers-engined

A British lightweight of 1953, the 197cc Norman with Villiers two-stroke engine.

British road racer Steve Parrish (above and inset), a farmer and protégé of Barry Sheene.

lightweight called the Motobyk. Norman survived World War II and continued with small two-stroke machines and finally mopeds until the Norman brothers who ran the show retired and sold out to Raleigh.

Norton

The most famous make of English bike, the Norton reigned supreme in road racing for 30 years. The company began in 1902, originally with imported engines from the Continent, and went on to win the first TT in 1907. After that Norton never looked back and continued winning until the 1950s; it amalgamated into the Associated Motor Cycles Group in 1962.

Nott, Ernie

Ernie Nott is a British road racer who won fame with Rudge-Whitworth, riding in the works team in the 1930s. He was second in the Junior TT of 1930 at 70.89mph, third in 1931 with fastest lap at 71.73mph in the Lightweight, and third in the Lightweight in 1935. He also won the 350 class in the French Grand Prix at Montlhery in 1931 on Rudge, and rode for Husqvarna in 1935.

Noyce, Graham

Graham Noyce is a top British motocross rider who was British Champion in 1976 and 1977. He began riding at six years of age and was racing at 10 in schoolboy events, winning the Open Class Schoolboy Championship at 15. He rode Husqvarna, then Maico, and was fourth in the 500cc World Championship in 1976. In 1978 he was in the Honda works team. Graham Noyce won the World 500cc Motocross Championship in 1979, the first Briton to win the title in 14 years.

NSU

NSU was a great German maker which began in 1900 with a motorized bicycle in the town of Neckarsulm, which provided the name. The company made small machines and dabbled in racing before 1939; it took the world speed record in 1951 at 180mph on a supercharged 500 ridden by Wilhelm Herz. From 1953 onward NSU raced dohc 125 and 250cc machines which took the world title four times. In 1956 the firm abandoned racing and was making mostly economy machines like the NSU Quickly, although still taking world speed records with blown machines. Motorcycle production ceased in 1957, but cars went on until NSU was bought by Audi.

Above: The Norton Commando Fastback with 750cc engine made in 1969, almost the last of the line.

Below: Its vintage ancestor, the 1928 Norton with 490cc single-cylinder engine.

was lifted onto his machine. Nuvolari gave up motorcycle racing in 1930, and drove his last car race when he was 58, which he won. He died in 1953.

NV

One of the few Swedish makes, NV manufactured from 1926 and merged into the MCB-Monark group. The company originally made 250cc ohv singles, and after that small two-strokes with bought-out engines.

OD

This German motorbike was manufactured in Dresden from 1927 to 1937 ranging from 350s up to 1000, using British JAP and Swiss MAG power units. The firm also made some racers in the 500cc class and later smaller two-stroke models. The last efforts were three-wheelers.

O'Dell, George

A successful British sidecar rider who won a third-place Grovewood Award in 1972, George O'Dell has risen to the top of the field. He was second in the 500 Sidecar TT in 1974 riding a Konig at 86.21mph and has won many other events, including the World Sidecar Championship in 1977 on a four-cylinder Yamaha TZ 750. He also broke the 100mph barrier for sidecars on the TT course with a 1977 lap at 102.88 mph.

OEC

The Osborn Engineering Company was building motorcycles in the Isle of Wight, off England's southern coast, for Blackburne from 1914, but its own machine did not come until 1920. It made many odd machines, including a sidecar outfit/taxi with a steering wheel, and solo bikes with duplex steering. Production stopped in 1930, but OEC bounced back in a Portsmouth factory with more strange devices like the Atlantic Duo, from which it was said to be impossible to fall off. The works was destroyed in a wartime air raid, but the company moved to a new one, making lightweights and a speedway machine, but eventually faded away in the 1950s.

Ogar

Ogar was a Czech machine made from 1934 to about 1950, on a single-model policy of a 250 two-stroke, with a 500

Nurburgring

This motor-racing circuit was built in the Eifel Mountains of Germany in 1927 in two loops, the Southern 4.8 miles and the Northern 14.17 miles, which is the one mostly used. After changes the northern lap is now 17.91 miles. The German motorcycle Grand Prix has been on both southern and northern loops (on which there are 91 left-hand bends and 85 right-hand) and has alternated between Nurburgring and Hockenheim since 1970. Car drivers have banned the ring as too dangerous, and in 1974 the motorcyclists too refused to race.

NUT

This British machine was made from 1912 to 1933 at Newcastle-upon-Tyne, whose initials named the machine. The founder, Hugh Mason, won the 1913 Junior TT at 43.75mph, using a 350cc JAP V twin. He won other races and set records, and the firm could not meet the rush of orders. After World War I the company went bankrupt, but started again in 1921, closed again in 1922, and reopened in 1923. NUT gave up racing and made fewer sporting models, but the end came in 1933.

Nuvolari, Tazio

Generally regarded as the greatest motorracing driver of all time, Nuvolari also had a distinguished career on two wheels. He was born in 1892 near Mantua and was first a racing cyclist. He was nearly 30 when he started to race motorcycles in 1920, and his first win was in 1923. In 1924 he became Italian Champion on Norton. He won the Grand Prix des Nations in 1925 on Bianchi when bandaged up after a car crash, and

The British OK Supreme of 1927 with 250cc engine for the Lightweight TT, in which it finished third and twelfth.

speedway machine as extra. In postwar years a twin two-stroke was produced, which looked like a Jawa, under the nationalized industrial setup.

OK-Supreme

After two false starts this British machine came on the market in 1911 using Precision engines. After the war the firm came back with two-strokes. They were sold simply as OK until 1927 when the Supreme was added after a board-room split. The company won the Lightweight TT in 1928 with Frank Longman riding at 62.90mph, its only win. The best-known model for many years was the 'Lighthouse,' so-called from a glass inspection plate in the camshaft tower. OK-Supreme closed with the war, apart from some grass-track machines in 1946.

Oliver, Eric

Eric Oliver is a British sidecar champion who began riding solos before World War II and went into top sidecar racing after RAF service. He always rode Norton and was World Sidecar Champion in 1949, 1950, 1951, and 1953, and introduced the modern type of streamlined outfit. He retired in 1955.

Ollearo

This Italian factory was active for 30 years from 1923 making machines up to 500cc with shaft drive and some two-strokes with smaller engines. Ollearo did not engage in competition.

Olsen, Ole

Danish speedway rider Ole Olsen was born in 1946 at Hadersley and first rode in 1965.

He won the Danish Sand Track Championship in 1971, 1972, and 1973, then went to ride in England, first for Newcastle and then Wolverhampton. He won the World Championship in 1971 and 1975.

Opel

The Opel car factory, now part of the General Motors empire, made motorcycles from time to time from 1901 up to 1930. The company also made bicycles and early machines were bicycles with motors attached. The last models were the Motoclub with 500cc single-cylinder engines.

Ossa

This Spanish make has operated since 1951 with two-stroke engines, mostly in the moped and off-road market for motocross and trials. Its British works rider, Mick Andrews, has won the Scottish Six Days three times as well as the European title.

Oulton Park

Oulton Park is a British racing circuit in the north of England with two alternative laps, of 2.761 and 1.654 miles in a woodland setting with a lake used for the Anglo-American races.

Sidecar Champion George O'Dell with passenger Cliff Holland performing at Silverstone.

Bald slick and knees-out as American champion Kenny Roberts (top right) corners (above) and lays it down at Britain's Oulton Park (center).

The Don R in 1915 is using a P & M machine in which the engine took the place of the downtube of the frame.

Owesle, Horst

German engineer and racer Horst Owesle helped Helmut Fath produce the URS sidecar engine. He also rode the machine to win the 1971 World 500cc Sidecar Championship.

P

Pabatco

Pabatco was the United States importer of the Yamaguchi until it closed in 1963, and since then sold the Japanese-built Hodaka off-road bike. The company started with a 90cc two-stroke and a one model policy, but later diversified, choosing strange names like the Combat Wombat and the Dirt Squirt. It offered 100, 125, and 250cc machines and won the Canadian 100cc Motocross Championship.

Palomo, Victor

Victor Palomo is a Spanish road racer who won the FIM Formula 750 title in 1976, but has had more crashes than wins. He was formerly a water-skiing champion, tried motocross and hill climbs, and then road-racing on Norton and Yamaha.

P & M

This British maker of the Panther motorcycle was active from about 1904. The name came from the initials of partners Jonah Phelon and Richard Moore. A feature was that the engine also acted as the front down-tube connecting the steering head and bottom bracket. In the 1930s the cut-price Red Panther sold for less than £30 fully equipped. The big single 600cc was also distinctive, and even two-strokes were tried before the firm died in 1967. There were also two German Panthers (1903–07 and 1933–73) which were not

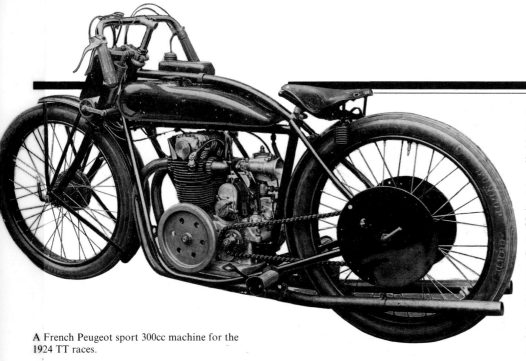

A French Peugeot sport 300cc machine for the 1924 TT races.

connected, and the later one sold in England as the Leopard.

P & P

P & P is a British motorcycle made by the partners Erling Poppe and Gilmour Packman from 1922 to 1930. They started with a very unorthodox design which was never produced, and followed with the Silent Three with a 350cc Barr and Stroude sleeve-valve engine. Then came a 976cc JAP twin and a 250 which finished fifth in the TT. The firm failed to sell many machines and closed during the Depression.

Parilla

Parilla was an Italian maker from 1946 to 1967, when it stopped making bikes to concentrate on engines. The firm started with sports and racing machines and finished with small two-stroke and single-cylinder ohv bikes and engines for kart racing.

Parker, Jack

British speedway rider who was born in 1908, Jack Parker retired in 1953 after a career which began in 1928. He was a trials rider before taking to the dirt track, and developed the BSA speedway machine. His wins included the Star Championship in 1934, a fourth in the World Championship in 1937, and a second in 1949.

Parrish, Steve

A farmer from Hertfordshire, England, Steve Parrish won the British Championship in 1976 and finished fifth in the World Championship on a works Suzuki in 1977. He was born in 1953 and began racing in 1973; he was a Grovewood Award winner in 1975.

Pasolini, Renzo

Renzo Pasolini was an Italian road racer who was in the Benelli works team in the 1960s and won many Grands Prix. He was killed in a multiple crash at the Italian Grand Prix at the Monza circuit near Milan in 1973, riding a 250cc Harley-Davidson.

Peugeot

Peugeot is one of the first motorcycle makers, producing from 1899 in France. It began with the usual motorized bicycle, and finished in 1956 making 50cc mopeds. In between it furnished the engine which won the first TT in 1907 for Norton, and became a great name in France. The motorcycle side was split away from the cars in 1933 and until 1956 made orthodox single-

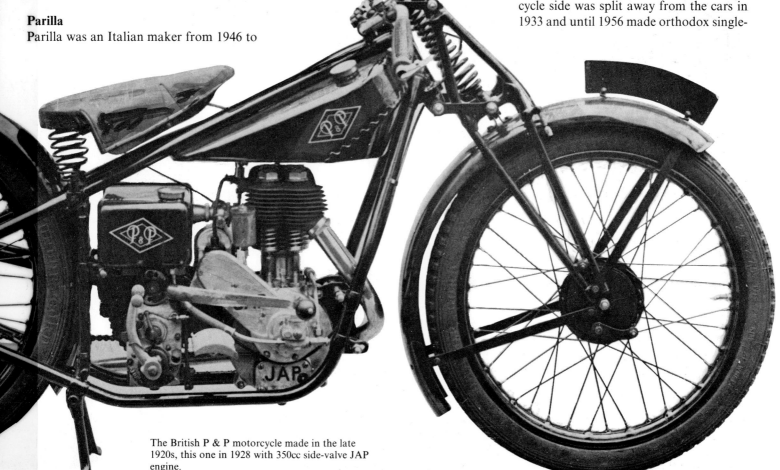

The British P & P motorcycle made in the late 1920s, this one in 1928 with 350cc side-valve JAP engine.

Top: A tussle between Baldwin and American Gene Romero, who has done well in AMA racing, at Oulton Park.

Above: Grazioano Rossie riding Morbidelli at Le Mans in 1947, and right, the late Cal Rayborn from the United States shows his paces on a 750 Harley.

French road racer, Patrick Pons, the 1979 Formula One 750 Champion.

cylinder machines which sold well. The Peugeots were successful in racing from 1913 to 1923 with an ohc design.

Phillis, Tom

Tom Phillis was an Australian road racer who was in the Honda works team from 1960 until he was killed in the Isle of Man in 1962. He came to Europe in 1958 and won the world 125cc title and was second in the 250 series.

Piaggio

This Italian firm has been making the Vespa scooter since 1946 with engines of various sizes, in addition to 50cc mopeds and lightweights.

Pickrell, Ray

A British road racer who was born in 1938, Ray Pickrell began racing in the 1960s and retired after a heavy crash in 1972. In between he had won four 750cc TTs and many other events on Norton, Triumph, and BSA. In 1971 he won three of the Anglo-American races and was joint top scorer.

Pierce Arrow

Pierce Arrow was the famous American car firm which also made motorcycles from 1909 to 1913. It made both singles and fours with shaft drive, with fuel held inside a frame tube.

Pileri, Paolo

Paolo Pileri is an Italian road racer who was born in 1944 and was best known in the Morbidelli works team for whom he won the 125cc World Championship in 1975. He has missed some races after crashes, and failed to win the 250 title.

Pons, Patrick

Patrick Pons was a French road racer born in December 1952 who began racing in 1971. His successes include a third in the 250 and 350 World Championships in 1974 and a second in the Formula 750. He was third in the 250, fifth in the 350 in 1975, and third in the 750, but crashes spoiled his record in 1976 and 1977.

Premier

There were three Premier firms—English, Czech, and German—and they were all related. The Czech company went on selling bikes 12 years after the English firm had closed down in 1921. The English firm, based in Coventry, made machines from 1908 up to World War I, both singles and twins which had an unsuccessful racing record. In 1914 the name changed to Coventry-Premier and in 1921 it was absorbed by Singer. The German branch opened in 1910 and moved in 1913 to Eger in Austria-Hungary which was incorporated in the new Czech state; it went on selling machines up to 1933.

Provini, Tarquinio

Tarquinio Provini, Italian road-racing star, was born in 1930 and won the Spanish Grand Prix of 1954 on a Mondial. He won the 125cc World Championship in 1957, both the 125 and 250 TTs in 1959, and 12 Italian championships before he retired in 1966.

Puch

This famous Austrian factory began making motorcycles in 1903. Originally Puch made single-cylinder four-strokes, then turned to the double-piston two-strokes for which it became famous and continued even after World War II. The company was successful with these in between the wars, but more recently has been making economy lightweights, although it still has competition success in the motocross field.

Q

Quadrant

Quadrant was an early English make from 1901 which ran from little two-strokes up to an 1130cc V twin. Ex-army officer Tom Silver rode them in stunts and endurance runs. He fell out with his partners and there were complexities of management. The company did not sell many bikes after the war, and came to an end in 1929.

R

Radior

This French manufacturer, active from 1904 to 1960, used Antoine and Peugeot engines in the early days and later made its own two-stroke power plants, although it used JAP as well. After World War II Radior used German NSU engines for lightweights while making its own 250cc units.

Rahier, Gaston

Gaston Rahier is the Belgian motocross expert who has won three 125cc World Championships. He began at 16 and won the Belgian 250cc Championships on CZ in 1970, and rode in the Suzuki team from 1972 onward, winning the title in 1975, 1976, and 1977.

Raleigh

Raleigh is the famous English make which now produces only bicycles but used to

Hugh Gibson on Raleigh after riding round Britain in 1928 in a gasoline company test run.

Britain's Barry Sheene (inset) at Donington in 1978 wearing his favorite Number 7 (right).

manufacture motorcycles in the pioneer days before 1906 and after World War I. It made singles and twins from 175 up to 800cc and did well in trials in the 1920s. After the motorcycle production ended it made three-wheel cars with one wheel at the front.

Rathmell, Malcolm

British trials and motocross rider, Malcolm Rathmell was born in 1949 and has won many events, including the British Experts. His first win was in 1967 on Bultaco. He then moved to Montesa and won the Scott Trial in 1975 and 1976, then to Suzuki, and is said to be one of the highest-paid riders.

Rayborn, Cal

This American road-racing star was born in 1940. He rode Harley-Davidson, then Suzuki, and won three of the 1972 Anglo-American races and was second in three. He was killed at Pukeohe, New Zealand, in 1973. He began as a dirt-track rider and switched to road racing later on.

Read, Phil

Phil Read is a British road racer, born in 1939, who entered his first road race at 16. He won the Junior TT in 1961 on a Norton then joined Yamaha and won the 250 World Championship in 1964 and 1965. In 1968 he won both the 125 and 250 Championships, and in 1973 and 1974 took the 500 title on MV Agusta. He came back to

the TT course, where he had refused to ride, in 1977 and won the 750 Formula One race for Honda, and then joined its team for 1978.

Redman, Jim

Jim Redman is a British racer who moved to Rhodesia and then came back to ride. He was born in 1931 and first raced in Rhodesia and South Africa, returning to England 1957. He returned to England in 1960 and won a ride with Honda, for whom he won the 250 and 350 World Championships in 1962, the 250 again in 1963, and the 350 in 1963, 1964, and 1965. He retired in 1966.

Rene-Gillet

This French machine was made from 1898 to 1957 and was much used by the police and the army. It comprised big V-twin engines and massive frames, some used with sidecars. The motorcycles were solid rather than sporting, but the company finished up making two-stroke lightweights like so many others.

Rex/Rex Acme

A famous British make from the early 1900s, Rex made singles and twins and had the peculiarity of a longer wheelbase for sidecar machines. Rex and Acme joined forces in 1922 to make the Rex Acme, which was raced by Wal Handley. They used all sorts, sizes, and makes of engines until concluding production in 1933.

Miss Muriel Hind (later Mrs Lord) with her 1911 six-horsepower Rex on which she had competition successes.

Ricard Circuit

This is a racing circuit in the south of France, officially called Ricard-Castellet, and built by Paul Ricard, maker of the French aperitif. It offers laps of 3.61 and 1.36 miles together with the most modern facilities and is issued for both car and motorcycle events.

Rickmann Brothers

The two British brothers, Derek and Don Rickmann, were scrambles riders who went on to build the Metisse, a machine based on various stock motorcycles with their own modifications or sometimes with their own frames. They made off-road bikes as well as road racers and ran a works team. The name Metisse is French for a mongrel bitch.

Former world champion Phil Read (inset) leading Mike Hailwood (Ducati) in the Isle of Man in 1978 at The Bungalow (above).

Robb, Tommy

A road racer from Northern Ireland, Tommy Robb was born in 1935 and by 1960 was riding for Bultaco. He was Irish 500cc Champion in 1961 and was third in the 350 Championship in 1962, when he had been signed up by Honda for whom he rode 50cc, 125, 250, and 350. He had many other places and his first TT win in the 125cc class of 1973 and then retired.

Robert, Joel

Joel Robert is a Belgian motocross champion who was born in November 1943 and began in motocross at 16. He was 250 World Champion at 20 and won six world titles in 1964, then from 1968 to 1972, riding first CZ and then Suzuki, before retiring.

Roberts, Kenny

This American road racer who was born in December 1951, was twice the American Dirt-Track Champion before going to Europe. In 1970 Kenny Roberts turned professional and won the American Junior Champion on Yamaha. He won four of the six 1977 Anglo-American races and the Imola 200. He was World Champion 500 racer in 1978 on Yamaha, and also won the Daytona 200, and was 500 Champion again in 1979.

Robertson, Andy

Andy Robertson is a British motocross rider who was born in 1948 and began riding at 15. He has ridden many makes and was second in the British Championship on Husqvarna, and won it on the same make the following year. He then moved to Montesa and was second in the 1977 Championship behind Graham Noyce.

Rokon

The Rokon is a most unusual American built motorcycle with both wheels driven. The company, set up in the 1960s in Wilmington, Vermont, called the machine the Trail-Breaker and have since produced sporting, trials, and motocross machines. The Trail-Breaker engine is a single-cylinder Chrysler two-stroke producing 10 horsepower from 134cc but the sporting Rokon has a 340cc Sachs with automatic transmission.

At the British Isle of Man TT in 1978 the Scot, Alex George, leads the pushing Chas Mortimer in the Senior TT.

Rider lies down to it in a bid for more speed from the 1959 Royal Enfield Crusader Sports.

Romero, Gene

An American road racer who was born in May 1947, Gene Romero began racing midget cars at 10 years of age and motorcycles in 1963, at first on dirt tracks. He won the Ontario 200 on Yamaha in 1974 and then the Daytona 200. He was in the American team which beat Britain in the 1974 Transatlantic series, riding Triumph, and then returned to Yamaha. He has done well in the AMA competition every year since 1968.

Rover

Rover is the British luxury-car concern, now part of Leyland Cars, which made motorcycles from 1903 to 1925. In fact their 1911 500cc lasted until almost the end of production. Rover went in for all sorts of competitions, with mixed results. The last models were a 250cc and a 350cc version of the same which did not sell.

Royal Enfield

Royal Enfield is a British make established in the pioneer days (1898) which continued until about 1970; the big Interceptor and the little two-stroke Crusader were the last models to be produced at a time when the British industry was declining. Some Royal Enfields are still made in India.

A Royal Enfield 1915 combination carrying a Vickers machine gun.

Close-up of the power plant of the Rudge 1925 model 500cc four-valve ohv machine.

Rudge-Whitworth Limited

This British company, founded in 1894, was a famous name in the motorcycle world right up to World War II. It did not make its own machine until 1910, but went on with famous models like the Rudge Multi, the Ulster which had a great racing record, and the four-valve racing machine.

Rumi

The Rumi is an Italian small-production machine made from 1950 with a 125cc flat-twin two-stroke with forward-facing cylinders. Rumi was the Italian champion in 1954, and went into scooter production with the Squirrel, the more successful Formichino (Little Ant), and the fast Bol d'Or model. There were also racing machines, but they all disappeared about 1957.

S

Saarinen, Jarno

Jarno Saarinen was a Finnish road racer who was born in December 1945 in Turku and killed in the Italian Grand Prix at Monza in 1973 in a multiple pile-up in which the Italian, Renzo Pasolini, also died. He began with ice racing and speedway and switched to road racing by 1964. Saarinen was fourth in the World Cham-

Former British Trials Champion, Rob Shepherd (1977), on a Honda tackling a rough trials section.

Above: Charlie Williams (Honda), the long-distance specialist, heeling it over at Donington, England, and (top) Williams with Alex George.

pionship 250cc series in 1970 and 1971, when he was also second in the 350. In 1972 he won the 250 world title on a works Yamaha. In 1973 he won the Imola 200 on his four-cylinder 500 Yamaha and won the French, Austrian, and German Grands Prix.

Sachs

The German industrial combine of Fichtel and Sachs started in 1895, but did not come into the business of building two-stroke motorcycle engines until 1930. Since then it has become a major supplier of very advanced units up to 175cc fitted in machines which have been dominant in off-road racing. The Nurberger-Hercules group and Rabeneick, both motorcycle builders, belong to the Fichtel & Sachs group.

Sachsenring

Sachsenring is a road-racing circuit in East Germany near Dresden with a 5.43-mile lap which has been in use since 1934, originally for the German Grand Prix before the country was divided. The East German Grand Prix has been held here since 1961 as a ranking world event, except when it was dropped to make way for the Japanese Grand Prix in the 50cc class. This did not affect the main classes up to 1972, when the race lost its world ranking.

Sandford, Cecil

This British road racer did well in the Isle of Man on various machines. He began on grass and turned to road circuits in 1950 on Velocette, and subsequently joined the MV Agusta factory team, winning the 1952 125cc TT (and the world title) and coming third in 1953 and 1954. In 1955 Cecil Sandford was second in the 250 on Moto Guzzi and third in the Junior. In 1956 he was fourth in the 350 Championship on DKW. He won the 250 TT on Mondial in 1957 as well as the Ulster Grand Prix and the world 250 title. He then retired.

Sand Racing

This branch of two-wheel activity has always been something of a Cinderella sport, although it has made a comeback recently. Races on sand have been going on since 1909 at Daytona Beach in the United States but came later in Britain, where Southport Sands in Lancashire was one of the favorite pre-World War II sites. There is now an Auto Cycle Union championship in Britain (since 1976) and most races are over a mile or more.

Sanglas

This Spanish factory has built machines with 350 or 500cc ohv singles since 1942, mostly for the Spanish and South American police. Earlier Sanglas made some smaller engines before adopting a one-model policy, although from 1962 to 1968 it also offered the two-stroke Rovena. There are more recent sporting versions of the 500 and a 400 for civilian use.

Schauzu, Siegfried

Siegfried Schauzu is a German sidecar rider who has been particularly successful

The famous Scott twin here in 1923 Senior Sidecar TT guise as ridden by Harry Langman.

in the Isle of Man TT on BMW, winning in 1967, 1968, 1969, 1970, and 1971. In 1972 he won both the 500 and 750, and 1974 and 1975 he won the 750. He turned from BMW to Aro, then Yamaha, and then Schmidt.

Scheidegger, Fritz
A Swiss sidecar rider, Fritz Scheidegger had a great success on BMW and won the world title in 1965 and 1966. He was second in the sidecar TT in the Isle of Man in 1965 and won in 1966 at 90.76mph. He was killed racing at Mallory Park in 1967.

Scott
This idiosyncratic British machine with water-cooled two-stroke engines was built from 1910 until the 1950s. It had a fanatical following and great success in competition. Famous models included the Squirrel and Flying Squirrel, which had a very individual exhaust note.

Scottish Six Days Trial
A famous event dating back to 1909, the Scottish Six Days Trial has achieved great status. Cars and sidecars were allowed in the early days until the going became too tough. It has become an international event attracting American and European entries, although a non-British entrant has yet to win the 1000-mile test with about 200 difficult rocky sections.

Seeley, Colin
Former British Sidecar Champion Colin Seeley turned to production of motorcycle frames after AMC went out of business, and fitted Matchless G50 engines after buying up the AMC racing department. He made the limited-production Condor and the Yamsel with a Yamaha engine, and finished up selling Honda kits to improve handling of the stock machines.

Serafini, Dorino
Dorino Serafini was the Italian road racer of prewar days who rode the four-cylinder 500cc water-cooled supercharged Gilera to win the 1939 German Grand Prix, beating the then-victorious BMWs. He won the Swedish Grand Prix in the same year and the Ulster Grand Prix at a record 97.82 mph. He took the 1939 European Championship after winning the most points in eight international races.

Sheene, Barry
Britain's most successful modern road-racing rider, Barry Sheene was born in

Idol of the fans, Barry Sheene, with a laurel wreath for yet another Suzuki win before he left the team and went freelance.

London in September 1950. He began racing in 1968 and has won many championships, including the world 500cc title in 1976 and 1977, riding a works Suzuki RGA 500. On the way up he won the British 125cc Championship in 1970 and was runner-up in the 1971 World Championship. He suffered a major crash at 170mph at Daytona in 1975 breaking several bones and suffering other injuries.

Shepherd, Rob
Rob Shepherd was British Trials Champion in 1977 and is a top performer in this field. He started trials in the 1960s and was given a works Montesa ride, winning the British Experts in 1976. In 1977 he rode for Honda.

Silk
George Silk manufactures a modern machine on the lines of the old water-cooled two-stroke twin Scott, having failed to buy the rights to make the Scott again. Production of the 700S with a 660cc engine began in 1976 and he plans to make two or three a week. He also planned a 350cc single and a three-cylinder 982cc unit.

Silverstone
Silverstone is a British racing circuit on an old airfield in the middle of England with a 2.9-mile lap that has been used since 1948 for car and motorcycle racing. There is also a short club circuit. The British motorcycle Grand Prix is held at Silverstone.

Simmons, Malcolm
This British speedway rider won the British Championship in 1976 and was second in the world final. Malcolm Simmons was born in 1946 and rode for Hackney Wick in 1963, then West Ham, Kings Lynn, and Poole.

The famous Jimmy Simpson on a Scott in 1922 at Mooragh Park, Ramsey, Isle of Man, where he rode so many times.

Simplex

There have been four machines under the Simplex name: English, Dutch, Italian, and American. The Dutch was the longest lived, from 1902 to 1968, and used seven different makes of bought-out engines from 60cc up to 500. The English one was a short-lived outfit lasting only three years, from 1919 to 1922, and making two-stroke engines to fit to bicycles. The Italian version was produced from 1921 to 1950, and mostly small machines with engines under 200cc, plus a 500 single, were built. The American company which ran from 1930 for 30 years made runabouts with 200cc four-stroke motors.

Simpson, Jimmy

A great British road racer in the 1920s, Jimmy Simpson began riding in 1922, first for AJS and later for Norton. He rode in 26 TT races but won only one, although he won many Continental events. In 1934 he won six Grands Prix plus the Lightweight TT on a 250 Rudge and was second in both Junior and Senior on Norton.

Singer

Better known as a car maker in England, the Singer company also made motorcycles from about 1900 in various shapes and sizes, and even tried racing, without much success. It was out of the motorcycle business by 1914.

Slippery Sam

A famous Triumph Trident machine so named because it spewed out so much oil, the Slippery Sam nevertheless was successful in racing. It was used by several well-known riders including Mick Grant, who won the Production TT with it in 1974.

Smart, Paul

Paul Smart is an English road racer who began around 1966 and was second in the 1967 Production TT on a Dunstall-Norton at 94.60mph. He rode a Triumph in Formula 750 for three years (1969–72) and had many wins; he then rode Yamahas, Ducati, Kawasaki, and finally Suzuki to wins in the American AMA series. Smart gave up in 1977 after accidents. He is married to Barry Sheene's sister.

Smith, Cyril

Cyril Smith was a British sidecar rider on Norton who was World Champion in 1952. He began riding after war service in 1949, first on grass. He raced in the Isle of Man TT from 1954 to 1959 but was never placed. In 1954 he was third in the World Championships and fifth in 1955 and 1958. He died in 1962 at 46.

Smith, Don

Don Smith is a British trials rider who was European Trials Champion twice. He won the European title in 1964 and 1967 on a Greeves and then joined Montesa, for whom he developed the Cota trials bike. After that he moved to Kawasaki and produced a machine for them. He did the same for Fantic and led their team in the 1978 Scottish Six Days Trial.

Smith, Jeff

Jeff Smith, British motocross rider, was nine times British Champion and twice World Champion riding BSA. He won his first title in 1955 and was still winning them 12 years later. He was born in 1935 in Lancashire and began riding for Norton, and then moved to BSA. After the company closed he moved to Canada in 1972 to develop a motocross machine for the Can-Am concern. He was awarded the MBE (Member of the British Empire) in 1970.

Smith, Tornado

Tornado Smith was the famed 'Wall of Death' rider who operated from 1929 in the Southend Kursaal, riding motorcycles, combinations and cars around the vertical cylinder to cover 110,000 miles by 1948. He used Indians, then switched to BSA. He retired in 1968 and went to South Africa, where he died in 1971.

Snetterton

Snetterton is a British road-racing circuit in Norfolk on an old airfield offering a 2.71-mile lap, or 1.917 miles plus a drag strip.

Several motorcycle meetings are held every year in this east-of-England setting.

Solitude

This German racing circuit was first used for motorcycles in 1922. It was near Stuttgart, offering a 7.1-mile lap on public roads, and was used more by motorcycles than cars because the roads were narrow. Eventually the circuit was abandoned owing to local opposition.

Spa-Francorchamps

The Spa-Francorchamps racing circuit in Belgium was used from 1924 but has been banned by some Grand Prix drivers as unsafe. The 8.76-mile circuit is used for the Belgian motorcycle Grand Prix and for long-distance car races. In 1979 a new 4.25-mile circuit was opened at Spa using part of the old track and the car Grand Prix may return.

Spanish Grand Prix

This race has been run since before World War I but won World Championship status only in 1951; it alternates between the Jarama Circuit near Madrid and the older one in Montjuich Park in Barcelona. Jarama is 2.2 miles and Montjuich 2.35 miles.

Speedway

Speedway racing takes place on short ovals with a shale surface, known in England as dirt track. (For the definition of dirt track in the United States, see the entry on Dirt-Track Racing.) It has been going in England since 1928 and longer in the United States and Australia. The motorcycles used in this race are special machines of 500cc with no brakes, or gears, usually JAP, Jawa, or Weslake.

Springsteen, Jay

Jay Springsteen is an American dirt and road racer who was born in 1957 and had won the AMA Championship by the time he was 19. In 1975 he was third in the Championship; he was signed up by Harley-Davidson in 1976 and won the AMA Championship, which he repeated in 1977.

Sprite

This British off-road machine was made from 1964 to 1978 in Birmingham by trials rider Frank Hipkin in various sizes for scrambles, trials, and motocross using various engines including a copy of the Husqvarna. Sprite sent a number of the machines to the United States to be sold as the American Eagle.

Standard

There were two different German companies using this name, one which sold a small two-stroke machine from 1922 to 1924. The other German company (1925–55) also had a Swiss factory and used Swiss MAG engines with 350 to 1000cc units and some JAP-engined twins for racing.

Steinhausen, Rolf

A German sidecar ace, Rolf Steinhausen was born in July 1943 and won the world

Above: Sidecar dicers in the Isle of Man: Rolf Steinhausen (No 10), twice World Champion, followed by Steve Sinnot at Waterworks in 1978.

Below: British road racer, Paul Smart, on a Suzuki racing in California.

Jack Stevens with his 1911 AJS TT racer of 298cc. He finished sixteenth after a fall.

title on Konig in 1975 and 1976. He started out on BMW after a serious solo accident at 18 and won the German Championship in 1970, then switched to the German two-stroke Konig.

Stevens

This British machine was made by the Stevens brothers who started the AJS firm, after they had sold this company to the Collier brothers in 1931. The machines were traditional ohv singles in 250, 350, and 500 form; Stevens engines also appeared in the AJW.

Sun

Sun was a British make which lasted for 50 years from 1911, and started from a former bicycle factory now part of the big Raleigh group. The firm made mostly two-strokes up to 1932, and came back with similar mounts in 1948.

Sunbeam

This British make was known for its quality product, made from 1912 to 1957. The 'Gentleman's Motor Bicycle' as it was called was all-black with the rear chain enclosed in the traditional 'Little Oil Bath.' The Model 90 won the 1928 Senior TT and the manufacturers' team award. In 1936 Sunbeam became part of Associated Motor Cycles who also had Matchless and AJS. After World War II it produced the shaft-drive 500 ohc vertical twin S7, but it did not sell.

Superbike Racing

The Superbike Championship began in 1971 with a capacity limit between 500 and 1000cc run by the British weekly *Motor Cycle News*. Two races were run at both Brands Hatch and Mallory Park, and one at Oulton Park and Snetterton. It is distinct from the Formula 750 series although some of the same people are involved.

Surtees, John

The only man to win both car and motorcycle World Champion titles, John Surtees was born in 1934 and won his first championship at 22 on MV Agusta. He won four more in three years, plus six TTs and in 1958–59 won each of 27 World Championship races he entered, to be both 350 and 500 Champion for the second year running. When he retired in 1960 he had taken seven World Championships and was awarded the MBE, and went on to be World Car Champion in 1964.

Suzuka Circuit

The Suzuka Circuit is a racing circuit built by Honda in 1962 with a 3.75-mile lap. It is used for the Japanese Grand Prix and for many motorcycle events.

World Champion John Surtees ('Big John'), the only man to be World Champion on both bikes and cars, on Norton.

Steve Beamish (Beamish Suzuki) in the British motocross Grand Prix at Farleigh Castle in 1979. He started racing at 14, winning all of the schoolboy championships, and moved on to grand prix racing with great success.

Suzuki

Suzuki is one of Japan's top makers which began producing two-wheelers in 1952. It won the 50cc World Championship when it was introduced in 1962, and has gone on to great glory in racing at the other end of the scale with the three-cylinder two-stroke 750 and the 500 RGA four-cylinder water-cooled racer. Apart from its racing activities the company makes road bikes in all sizes as well as successful off-road racing machinery. Although wedded to two-strokes in competition it favors dohc four-strokes for road machinery.

Swedish Grand Prix

The Swedish Grand Prix has been running since the 1930s on various circuits but moved to the new 2.5-mile Anderstorp track in 1971 and is officially the Swedish TT. It has had championship status since 1958. The tracks used before Anderstorp include Stockholm, Hedemora, and Kristianstad. Lap speeds are over 90mph for the 500s.

Swiss Grand Prix

The Swiss Grand Prix was first held in 1924 on a circuit near Geneva and last held on Swiss soil in 1954 at Berne's Bremgarten Circuit. After the French Le Mans disaster in 1955 when about 90 people died, all car and motorcycle racing was banned in Switzerland. The Berne Circuit of 4.52 miles was used from 1930, apart from 1938, 1948, and 1950 when it was on a street course in Geneva.

SWM

This Italian off-road machine has been made by Petro Sironi near Milan since 1971 with the German two-stroke Sachs engine. They won the 125cc class in the Italian Motocross Championships in 1972 and went on to other sporting successes, also adopting the Rotax engine for some models. SWM also makes trials machines.

Szczakiel, Jerzy

Jerzy Szczakiel was a Polish speedway rider, born in January 1949, who won the world title in 1973, the first Polish Champion. Apart from this one great success when he beat Ivan Mauger, not much has been heard of him outside his own country since.

T

Tait, Percy

This British road racer began in 1951 (he was born in 1929) and was still riding at 46 years of age, retiring in 1975. Percy Tait won the *Motor Cycle News* Superbike Championship in 1971, the Bol d'Or 24-hour race, the Thruxton 500-mile race (with Dave Croxford), and was second in the British Championship for the 750s that year. He was second in the 1975 1000cc Open Classic TT. He had many other wins and was in two British teams for the Anglo-American races.

Tandon

The Tandon is a lightweight British machine made near London from 1948 to 1955 with small two-stroke engines for the

The lightweight British Tandon 197cc two-stroke made near London around 1950.

economy market, using Villiers engines. There were also some trials models.

Taruffi, Piero

Piero Taruffi is an Italian racing driver who was born in 1906 and was a well-known racing motorcyclist and record breaker before he took to four wheels, riding AJS, Panther, Guzzi, and Norton. He last rode in 1937, but was racing manager to Gilera up to World War II. He set a record at 152mph in his 1935 four-cylinder Rondine on the Firenze-Mare Autostrada in 1937. In the same year he took the one-hour record at 121mph on another motor road in the 'Flying Pillarbox,' a tall, narrow, totally-enclosed, four-cylinder, 500cc, water-cooled supercharged Gilera. He also took the world record at 170.373mph in this device that year.

Taveri, Luigi

A Swiss road racing star, Luigi Taveri won three World Championships and many races. He began in 1954 and retired 1966, riding mostly the small-capacity machines. He rode for MV Agusta, MZ, Ducati, and finally Honda for whom he won the 125cc Championship in 1962, 1964, and 1966.

Terrot

Terrot was a famous French make from 1902 for more than 50 years, which made a great many machines and was involved in racing in the 1920s. The firm made a series of bikes ranging from small two-strokes to rather English-looking singles and some twins, in the Dijon factory. In 1950 it was taken over by Peugeot and closed down.

Thruxton

This British racing circuit on an old air-field near Andover, Hampshire, has been used for motorcycles since 1949. It was originally 1.89 miles but a later rearrangement made the lap 2.356 miles. At one time a 500-mile endurance event was run there which ranked in the FIM Coupe d'Endurance Championship.

Tiblin, Rolf

Rolf Tiblin is a Swedish motocross rider who won both the 250 and 500cc titles, the only man to do so. He rode Husqvarna, Hedlund, and finally CZ, winning the 250 European title in 1959 and the World 500 in 1962. He retired to California.

Tourist Trophy (TT)

The Isle of Man races began in 1907 and, although the honor of being the ranking British event in the championship passed to the British Grand Prix, they stand alone as perhaps the greatest test of a road rider with a tortuous 37.75-mile lap which includes climbing up and down a mountain. Famous riders have refused to ride in the Island on the grounds of safety, but the TT remains the pinnacle of achievement.

Triton

The Triton is a British machine made by inserting a Triumph engine in a Norton frame, carried out first by John Viccars and then David Degens, who makes them under the name Dresda.

Triumph

Triumph is the longest-lived British motorcycle which was first produced in 1902 and was still just about surviving in 1980. The firm began with the usual motorized bicycle and moved on to some famous models; the most lingering is perhaps the Speed Twin of 1937 which was a sensation in its day and was still being made very recently. It was an ohv vertical twin which went on to become the Tiger, the Thunderbird, and the Bonneville. Triumph was bought by BSA in 1951 and has had a checkered history since.

Twemlow Brothers

This British pair, Eddie and Ken, won three TT races between them in the early days of motorcycles. In 1924 Ken won the Junior and Eddie the Lightweight, both on New Imperial. Eddie won the Lightweight again in 1925. They were both placed again in 1928. Ken, at 19, won the 350cc class in the Manx Grand Prix.

U

Ubbiali, Carlo

This great Italian road racer was in action from 1947 until 1961 and won 39 classic races, nine world titles, nine Italian Championships, and five Isle of Man TTs. He was born in September 1929 in Bergamo near the Alps, and rode an MV Agusta at 19 in 1948. He moved to Mondial, then back to MV. His wins were in the 125 and 250cc categories.

Ulster Grand Prix

The Ulster Grand Prix was a classic race which began in 1925 on the 16.5-mile Clady Circuit in Northern Ireland and moved to the Dundrod Road Circuit in 1953. All classes from 500 down to 125cc were in action at the same time on the Clady Circuit after a massed start at one-minute class intervals, a stirring sight, with nearly 100 riders. Dundrod was shorter at 7.5 miles, and was used until 1973 (1972 excepted) although the event then lost its status as a World Championship event. In 1972 the race was moved to an airfield because of the political situation.

V

Van Praag, Lionel

Lionel van Praag was a pioneer speedway rider from Australia who went to England in 1928 and was the first World Champion

A 1940 Triumph 349cc Model 3TW which normally lives in the National Motor Museum at Beaulieu.

A nostalgic sight, a Velocette from the company in production from 1913 to 1971. This is the 350 MAC.

in 1936 when the series commenced. He defeated Eric Langton in the final.

Van Veen, Henk

Henk van Veen is the Dutch importer of the German Kreidler racer who took on development of the 50cc machine when the factory stopped racing in 1965. In 1969 he entered Aalt Toerson and Jan de Vries, the Dutch Champion, and the van Veen Kreidlers did well in international racing. Van Veen also produced the van Veen OCR 1000, the ultimate motorcycle with a Wankel engine and shaft drive costing about £5500 in 1977, with a 150mph top speed.

Van Velthoven, Jaak

Jaak van Velthoven is a Belgian Motocross Champion who was born in January 1951 and is six feet six inches tall. He was third in the World Championship in 1973 behind fellow countryman Roger de Coster and seventh in 1977 on his Austrian KTM, for which he was the Belgian agent. He rode Yamaha until a serious crash put him out in 1975.

Velocette

This famous British company with a French sounding name was founded by a German, Johannes Gutgemann. The first machine under the Velocette banner was offered for sale in 1913 and the firm went on to make classic models like the KIT which in 1930 took the first eight places in the amateur race, the Manx Grand Prix. It was a 350cc ohc engine. There was a shaft-drive model designed by Phil Irving, the Model O, the supercharged Roarer of 1939, and many models which made the name a lively legend which lasted until 1971, when their last venture, a scooter, proved to be a failure.

Venezuelan Grand Prix

The Venezuelan Grand Prix originated in 1977 at the San Carlos Circuit 160 miles from Caracas, the capital, with a lap of 2.75 miles and lap speeds approaching 100mph. Barry Sheene won the 1977 500cc event. The FIM 750 Championship race is staged on the same circuit.

Vesco, Don

This Californian record taker was born in 1940 in San Diego and put the world motorcycle land speed record to an ultimate 318.598mph in September 1978. He raced Yamahas and won the United States 500cc Grand Prix, a nonchampionship event, on a 250 rotary-valve, two-stroke, twin RD 56. Don Vesco became a Yamaha dealer and launched out on his spectacular record-breaking cigar-like machine which he runs on the Bonneville Salt Flats. The last one, Silver Bird, housed two 750cc Yamaha racing engines.

Vespa

Vespa is a leading make of Italian motor scooter which with Lambretta headed the scooter boom. The machines were made at

The 1950s Vespa scooter, made in Italy and in England to the tune of more than 125,000.

Comfort special: The 1910 Wilkinson Touring Auto Cycle with bucket seat and steering wheel. These machines did not last.

the Piaggo works at Pontedera from 1945 onward, the name being Italian for 'wasp' and the machines built by an aero company. They were also made in England by the Douglas motorcycle company from 1951 to 1963 in Bristol to the tune of more than 125,000. As well as the standard 125 and 150cc models there were sporting versions called the Gran Sport and the Super Sport.

Veteran and Vintage
Old motorcycles are catered for in many countries by special clubs. In England the Vintage Motor Cycle Club, formed in 1946, has more than 5000 members, and holds regular runs and races. There is also the Collectors Club, formed in 1954, and the much older Association of Pioneer Motor Cyclists dating from 1928. In the United States the appropriate club is the Antique Motor Cycle Club dating from 1954, and in South Africa the Veteran and Vintage Club. There are also clubs in Australia and many European countries.

Victoria
This famous German make dates from 1905 until it was taken over by Fichtel & Sachs in 1966. The company also tried its hand at cars from 1907 to 1909. It made machines from 74cc up to 600, but one of the famous models was the Bergmeister of 1951 with a 350cc four-stroke V-twin engine. In 1958 Victoria joined DKW and Express to form the Zweirad-Union, but this did not save the firm at a poor time for motorcycles. A Scottish Victoria was made from 1902 to 1926, unconnected with the German company. It used four makes of bought-out engines in machines from 125 up to 700cc.

Villa, Walter
Walter Villa is one of the greatest Italian riders who was 250cc World Champion in

1974, 1975, and 1976 on Harley-Davidson. He was born in 1943 in the great sporting town of Modena and raced Benelli and MV Agusta. Villa was Italian Champion in 1973 and 1974. He rode Harleys from 1974, but before that was involved in the 1973 Monza crash in which Saarinen and Passolini died, and was himself badly injured. He was also World 350cc Champion in 1976. Francesco Villa, brother of Walter, makes trials and motocross machines under his own name.

Villiers
Villiers was Britain's most famous maker of two-stroke engines from 1913 until it first merged with JAP, then became part of Norton-Villiers-Triumph, and ceased to sell engines in 1965. Two-stroke motorcycles all over the world were powered by Villiers engines for decades, and the engines are still being made in India.

Vincent
This prestigious English machine was made without regard for cost and sold under the slogan of 'the world's fastest.' Phil Vincent bought up the HRD name from H R Davies in 1928 and originally added it to his own name; he later dropped the HRD and simply called his machine the Vincent. It was always a big 998cc twin, apart from the 500cc Comet, and the company was usually in financial trouble even though its machines had such a high reputation; they were just too costly to build and in spite of their excellence eventually came to an end in 1955.

Vincent, Chris
Top British sidecar racer, Chris Vincent won many races at a time when the German BMW was dominant and he was riding an obsolete BSA. He was born in 1935 and began riding solos in 1954 on grass, and then won the Grass Sidecar Cham-

pionship. In 1962 he won the sidecar TT and the British Championship in 1969, 1970, and 1971. He held the lap record at most British tracks, and won the Finnish Grand Prix in 1972.

Vindec
Vindec models, made in England from 1902 to 1929 by the accessory makers, Brown Brothers, were produced as both two-strokes and JAP-engined machines. There was also a German Vindec sold in England (1903–14) which was an Allright in Germany and later called a VS (Vindec-Special) to avoid confusion with the other make.

Vink, Henk
Henk Vink is a Dutch drag racer who was successful in other forms of motorcycle sport before he turned to the drag strips with Kawasaki-engined machines he calls Big Spender. He set new records in 1977 for the 1000 and 1300cc classes and was timed at more than 210mph at the end of a kilometer. He ran a Kawasaki in 1978 with two supercharged engines, and even on his single-engined bikes was down to 8.1 seconds for the quarter mile with a terminal 180mph.

Voshkod
Voshkod machines are successful Russian two-strokes made from 1940 with 10bhp from 175cc at 5500rpm with engines along Jawa lines in design.

W

Walker, Graham
Graham Walker was a British motorcycle racer and editor of *Motor Cycling* from 1938 to 1953. He was a works rider and won the TT and was placed on Rudge in

1930–32. He won the Lightweight in 1931 at 68.98mph. His son Murray Walker is a commentator on motor and motorcycle racing for British television.

Wall of Death

The Wall of Death is a popular fun-fair entertainment which consists of riding motorcycles around an upright wooden cylinder. There are many variations, using sidecars, lion cubs, riding in opposite directions, hands-off riding, sitting backward, and all manner of stunts. Some speedway riders have graduated from this form of activity.

Walter

This Czech make of machine ran from 1900 for 50 years. The first ones were singles and twins, and joined later by some racing models which did well in competition in the 250 and 350 classes. Eventually the Jaroslav Walter designs were taken over by the CZ company. There was also a separate German Walter machine which ended before World War II. Jaroslav Walter died in 1975.

Wanderer

A great German make at one time, from 1902 onward, the Wanderer eventually became the Jawa in Czechoslovakia. Wanderer in Chemnitz (now Karl Marx Stadt in East Germany) supplied German army dispatch riders in World War I with big twin 500cc mounts, and went on to make twins and singles until the firm merged with NSU in 1930. Janecek in Prague was making the Wanderer under license, and ultimately was sole producer under the name Janecek-Wanderer, which was shortened to Jawa. The company now produces good sporting machines and speedway bikes.

Wankel engine

The Wankel engine, with few moving parts, has been tried in motorcycle form by several companies and Norton have one under development. One of the first was DKW or Hercules using a Fichtel & Sachs 250cc single-rotor design used in snowmobiles as well. It produces 32bhp at 6500 rpm in the model known as the W2000 with a 100mph maximum. Wankel engines have their own peculiar problems and tend to use a considerable amount of fuel.

Wasp

This British make of special outfits for sidecar cross near Salisbury in the west of England, has been producing since 1963. The frame is the heart of the machine, and it is fitted with Norton, BMW, or Yamaha engines. These machines have done well in competition all over Europe. Robin Rhind Tutt started the company.

Wassell

These British trials and motocross machines were made by Ted Wassell at Lichfield in the English Midlands from 1971 to 1975. They were also sold under the names Tyran (sold by Mitsubishi) and Penton in the United States.

Watsonian

Watsonian is a British make of sidecar produced by a company which originally made motorcycles. It is one of the oldest concerns and is still operating, making lightweight models now rather than the giant double-adult sidecars which were popular in the sidecar heyday before the popularization of the small car in the 1920s.

Werner

This pioneer French make was produced by two Russian emigre brothers in Paris from 1897. They were credited with being the first to put the motorcycle engine where the bicycle bottom bracket was in the 'Werner Position,' representing a milestone in history. The company was bought by an English concern, and the two brothers Eugene and Michel both died relatively young. The company stopped making motorcycles in 1908 and dabbled without success in cars up to 1914.

Weslake, Harry

Harry Weslake was the designer of a successful speedway machine and a tuning wizard who contributed much to the motor and motorcycle industries. He was born in Exeter in the west of England in 1897 and died in 1979. He worked on many famous engines and produced the Wex carburetor in the early days of motorcycling which was successful in various forms of competition. Harry Weslake was associated with Sunbeam, Bentley, Jaguar, Norton, Triumph, and others.

West, Jock

This British race rider was second in the Senior TT in 1939 when the BMW's made their first successful appearance there, behind Georg Meier on a similar machine, after Nortons had been dominant for many years. Jock West was sixth in 1937 on BMW's first visit and won the Ulster Grand Prix. He also set world records in an AJS team at Montlhery in 1938, and was a grass-track star before that.

Wilkinson

The Wilkinson company which now makes blades and garden tools was once in the

Jock West with his 1933 Junior TT AJS. He was second in the 1939 Senior on BMW.

motorcycle business, from 1909 to 1914. Its first motocycle was the TAC (Touring Auto Cycle), which became the TMC (Touring Motor Cycle) with a water-cooled four. The TAC was more unorthodox with a bucket seat and the option of a steering wheel, but none of the machines survived the First World War.

Williams, Charlie

Charlie Williams is a British road racer in the Honda long-distance team. He started on Matchless in 1969, and moving on had many successes in the TT. He did well on Yamaha in the 250 classes and rode Honda in endurance races, winning the Barcelona 24 Hours in 1976. He finished third in the Coupe d'Endurance series with Stan Woods. In 1977 the pair was second at the Nurburgring and won at Thruxton.

Williams, John

This British road racer began riding in 1964 and died after a crash at the 1978 Ulster Grand Prix. John Williams rode various makes until he switched to the two-stroke Yamaha in 1975, won the classic TT that year and the next, and was second in 1977 and 1978. He had won the 500cc Ulster event when he crashed. He had also had wins and places in the TT races.

Williams, Peter

A British road racer on Norton, Peter Williams retired after being injured in a 1974 crash. He started racing in 1963 and was placed in many events, including a second in the 1967 Senior TT, and won the 500cc British Championship in 1970. He won the formula 750 TT in 1973. He turned down many offers to ride foreign machines to stay with Norton.

Wilson, Ray

Ray Wilson is a British speedway rider who was born in March 1947 in London and won the British Championship in 1973. He led many English teams to wins in international events like the World Cup Team Final (1971), and four winning years in the World Team Cup for England. He also led the England team to win the Inter-Nations Tournament in 1972 and was second in the European Championship.

Peter Williams, the Norton ace, cornering in the Brands Hatch Easter Match Races on the track near London.

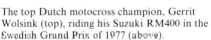

The top Dutch motocross champion, Gerrit Wolsink (top), riding his Suzuki RM400 in the Swedish Grand Prix of 1977 (above).

Wolsink, Gerrit
Gerrit Wolsink is a Dutch Motocross Champion who started full time in 1966. He was born in 1947. He rode Husqvarna until he joined Maico and was second in the Trans-Am series in the United States, then moved to Suzuki and was again Trans-Am runner-up. He was second in the 500 World Championship in 1976 and third in 1977.

Woods, Stanley
Stanley Woods is an Irish road racer with an unbeaten record of 10 TT wins and seven in the Ulster Grand Prix, apart from other events. He was born in Dublin and first rode in the TT in 1922 at 17, finishing fifth. He rode many makes before he joined Norton in 1926 and won the Senior, then both Junior and Senior in both 1932 and 1933 in an eight-year run of success. He moved to Moto Guzzi and won both major TTs again in 1935. He moved to Velocette

and won the Junior twice, but World War II ended his career.

Wooler
John Wooler produced strange machines at the annual motorcycle shows in London between 1911 and 1954, but few of them ever seem to have been manufactured. He bought the former P & P Company and made its designs up to 1930, but came back later with his unorthodox ideas right up to 1955.

World Championships
The World Championships in road racing began only in 1949, although there were international competitions dating back to the 1920s. There was a European Championship in 1938 with eight events in various countries, won by Georg Meier on BMW in the 500 class, Ewald Kluge, also of Germany, on the 250 DKW, and Ted Mellors of Britain on the 350 Velocette.

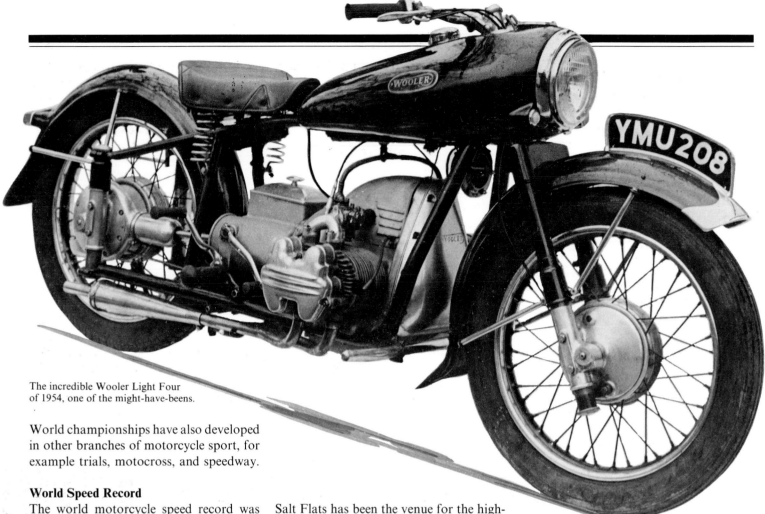

The incredible Wooler Light Four of 1954, one of the might-have-beens.

World championships have also developed in other branches of motorcycle sport, for example trials, motocross, and speedway.

World Speed Record

The world motorcycle speed record was first recognized in 1909 when W E Cook of England did 75.92mph over the flying kilometer at Brooklands on the NLG with a Peugeot twin engine. Many riders have specialized in record breaking right from the early days, notably Bert le Vack, Ernst Henne, Noel Pope, Piero Taruffi, Don Vesco, and many others, and the rate of progress has gone up to more than 300 mph. Brooklands was not used after 1923; riders looked for straight roads where speed trials were held, in France, Hungary, and notably the Italian and German motor roads. In more recent times the Bonneville Salt Flats has been the venue for the high-speed ventures.

Y

Yamaguchi

Yamaguchi was a popular Japanese make from 1941 to 1964 when Hodaka took over the factory. The firm made 50cc and 123cc two-strokes in both road-going and off-road sporting form before the now-famous names took over the whole Japanese industry.

Yamaha

This major famous Japanese maker with three motorcycle factories was founded in 1955, although the parent company is much older. The company began with a 125cc two-stroke and, after building its name on two-strokes, branched out into bigger Superbikes in the 750 four-stroke category and above. It now has a range of models in all the popular engine capacities. Yamaha has also had a successful racing history, winning the 350cc World Championship for four years running (1974–77), the 500cc in 1974, the 250 from 1971 to 1975, and the 125 in 1973 and 1974.

Yoshimura, Hideo

Hideo Yoshimura is a Japanese former racer known as 'Pops' who has built up a successful tuning business, now in the United States. He was born in 1922 and both rode in races himself and tuned machines for others in Japan before he moved to the United States, where his machines have been successful in road racing and record breaking. He prepared a Kawasaki 900cc four-cylinder 21 which Yvon Du Hamel rode to a record speed of 160.28 mph at Bonneville in 1973.

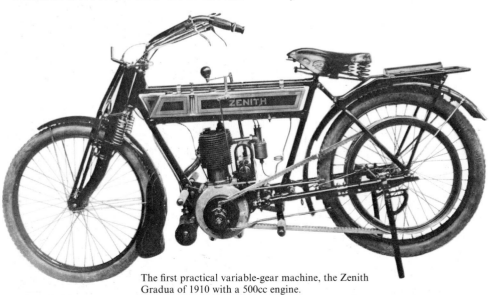

The first practical variable-gear machine, the Zenith Gradua of 1910 with a 500cc engine.

Young, Jack

Australian speedway rider Jack Young won the World Championship two years running in 1951 and 1952. He started riding in the 1940s and moved to England, later becoming captain of the Edinburgh team and winning the Scottish Riders Championship three years in a row. He retired and returned to Australia in the 1960s.

Yugoslav Grand Prix

Held until 1978 at the 3.7-mile Opatija Circuit at an Adriatic seaside resort, this event has had world championship status since 1969, when it covered a full program from 50 to 500cc. In 1973 the top riders and main entrants refused to accept safety standards and boycotted the circuit. There was no 500cc race the following year. Two riders were killed in 1977, after an attempt to organize a boycott in 1976 had failed. In 1978 a new circuit at Rejika with a 3-mile lap was opened.

Z

Zehnder

Zehnder was a Swiss make made from 1923 to 1939 which specialized in two-strokes in lightweight machines. Later it was owned by the German Standard company but production continued. Otto Zehnder himself rode water-cooled racing models successfully in the 125 and 250cc classes.

Zenith

This classic British bike existed for 50 years from 1905, although for practical purposes it ended with World War II. Its fame rested on the Gradua, a system for variable gearing by moving the two halves of the belt pulley in relation to each other and moving the back wheel to keep the belt taut. This was achieved by the 'coffee grinder' handle and put Zenith ahead before the invention of chain drive and gearbox.

Zundapp

This famous German factory was formed in 1917 in Nuremberg, backed by the Krupps armament firm. Motorcycle manufacture began in 1922 with a small 211cc machine, but the firm's name rests on the 750cc flat twins used by the German army with sidecars, the Green Elephants or KS750. This had a reverse gear, or in fact four reverse gears. Since World War II the factory has gone in for two-strokes and trials machines with success, winning the 125cc World Motocross Championship in 1973. In 1978 the factory, now in Munich, dropped the off-road bikes in favor of water-cooled, two-stroke road machines.

Sidecar racer Mick Boddice on Yamaha leading the action with the chair wheel off the ground.

MECHANICS AND CUSTOMIZING

The city man's bike, the Quasar, with all modern conveniences like a roof and heating, plus some of the motorcycle's fresh-air qualities.

Once upon a time the motorcycle was a simple, single-cylinder machine with side-valves, low compression, a separate gearbox, two chains to look after, and not much else. It was all well within the compass of the average rider to maintain, and motorcyclists built up a reputation for being self-reliant. They were also poor, so that garages were reluctant to do work on two-wheelers in case they did not get paid. From the combination of the two situations the image of the fellowship of motorcyclists, helping each other and seeking no other aid, grew up.

If a rider wanted slightly more performance than the man next door, there were a few simple and widely-known tricks. He could raise the performance by a higher-compression piston, a thinner gasket (if there was one), and he could change the valve or ignition timing, polish the ports, or use bigger jets, and that was about all he could do.

The manufacturers were unlikely to give support to any motorcyclist who played around with their products. A typical comment from a handbook of 1948 said: 'An enormous amount of money is spent by the motor-cycle trade every year on research, and some of the best brains in the country are engaged in the endless quest for more and more engine efficiency. The private owner may therefore rest assured that if the maker knew of a better timing for his engines he would most certainly use it.'

Another quote: 'The variation in cam design is enormous, and it may be said that there is no such thing as a standard cam formula. How then can the private owner hope to discover a better setting than the one adopted by the makers of his machine? To make the attempt is like playing with fire.'

But playing with fire or not, the riders did make the attempt. The easiest thing to alter was the ignition timing, yet the official word was: 'No improvement can be expected from an alteration to ignition timing. In fact, the reverse is almost invariably the case, too much advance producing roughness, without any speed increase, while a retarded spark causes sluggishness and overheating. . . .'

When it came to carburation, the owner 'is advised to leave his carburetor severely alone.' But of course he did not.

One of the first things the rider did if he was interested in competition rather than just going faster or making more noise on the road was to shed as much weight as possible. This could be achieved in drilled metal items all over the machine, sometimes making the frame flex so much that handling was lethal. The second course of action was to look for more power, and raising the compression was the obvious step, not always with good results.

The owner was looking for thermal efficiency, or better use of the energy in his fuel, and one way was to use special 'dope' fuels rather than straight gasoline. These special brews would stand any amount of compression ratio increase that the rider could produce, the limit being found through trial and error when the fuels ceased to produce more power. On the other hand the gasoline of 30 years ago, even mixed with benzol on a 50/50 basis, would not stand more than about eight-to-one compression.

Riders either planed the head, used a thinner gasket, or machined metal off the base of the barrel-block to lower the cylinder. It was all rather hit-and-miss except in specialist workshops. Other aids were larger valves, bigger jets, or a bigger carburetor altogether, cam changes, and playing with the exhaust pipe bore and length. Changes to flywheel assemblies were more technical for the everyday rider, and were tried more in racing practice. Thus, outside the fairly basic procedures mentioned, there was

The much-loved Duggie of long ago, the 1914 model 350 ohv which won the Brooklands Long Handicap, Les Bailey up.

not a lot the rider could do, and what he could do was straightforward and limited by the knowledge of the day.

But after the two invasions—Italian and Japanese—of Britain, Europe, and the United States, the whole picture changed; from a single-cylinder side-valve the British moved to four, six, and even eight cylinders in a V turning at 12,000rpm in a racing engine. Obviously the amateur was out of his depth. Also the racing machine was no longer a souped-up version of a ride-to-work bike, but something entirely different, perfect for its purpose but unrideable on the road as a utility machine.

The complexities were enormous: supercharging, water-cooling, desmodromic operation of valves (positive opening and closing without springs), front and rear suspension changes to very sophisticated specifications, electric starters and all the allied electronic gear, disk valves, rotary valves, and even automatic transmission.

The British motorcycle ruled the world, with the aid of the two American ones, Indian and Harley-Davidson, until the Italian invasion of the racing scene. The Italians began to appear as early as 1931, but only Gilera and Moto Guzzi had much success, the latter with a 500cc racer, first with four cylinders, then with three. The second model was more of a luxury tourer, although the four was a pure speed machine.

The British Isle of Man Tourist Trophy series of races was always a barometer of what was going on in the world of two-wheel speed, and the first foreign victory (apart from those Indians in 1911) was Moto Guzzi in the hands of former Norton rider Stanley Woods in 1935. The real invasion came much later, in 1955, when it began to read Gilera or MV at the top of the results table.

The Italian success lasted just about 10 years until Honda began to take an interest, and then the smaller capacity classes always read Suzuki or Yamaha at the top. Gilera, which was first on the scene, began making machines in 1909 under the rule of an aristocrat, Count Giuseppe Gilera, and won its Isle of Man laurels with the 500cc four-cylinder from 1955 onward.

The company had taken the world 500cc land speed record as early as 1937 with the incomparable Piero Taruffi inside the teardrop streamlining at 170-plus mph. The war put a stop to competition, but Gilera came back, only to face the ban on supercharging which had hit several other companies. While its designer sought a solution Gilera raced a single-cylinder Saturno, which even finished second in the 1949 World Championships.

The four was back in 1950, redesigned by Pietro Remor, and producing 55bhp without its former water-cooling. The firm signed up the great English rider Geoff Duke in 1953 and began its domination of the racing scene in the 500 class. The complexity of the design indicates how impossible it was for the amateur to tinker as he had been able to do in the days of bang-and-trundle machine. Gilera went on winning until MV Agusta moved up into the bigger classes. Later it ran into money troubles until taken over by Piaggo, who made mopeds and scooters, and moved into the 50cc and upward market in which it is still successful.

The other early Italian challenger, Moto Guzzi, might be called the Lancia of the motorcycle world, as the Italian car firm is famous for doing everything in a different way from everyone else and favoring complexity for its own sake. At the same time Lancia has sound engineers, or did until its products became Fiats with another badge.

So it was to some degree with Guzzi. The firm made its first machine soon after World War I in 1921 at Mandello del Lario on Lake Como. It was a 500 single with a forward-facing cylinder, which became something of a trademark, but was good enough to win races. On the TT scene success did not come until the 1926 Lightweight for 250 machines, when P Ghersi finished first but was disqualified for using a different kind of spark plug from that specified. It was a rather unsporting decision but his consolation prize was fastest lap.

The forward-facing cylinder and the 'bacon slicer' outside flywheel were trademarks of the Guzzi for many years and the model was known as the Falcone, a name used on successive models up to 1970 or later. Carlo Guzzi was not afraid of innovation, and tried many strange design quirks in his time, such as upside-down forks with the link at the bottom, a V8 engine, and semiautomatic transmission. His early racer had a bronze head and hairpin valve springs.

Success came with the big banger 500 ridden by Stanley Woods in the 1935 Senior, after his interim success in the Lightweight of the same year on the twin-cylinder Gambalunga. This was a 120-degree twin with one horizontal cylinder like the Falcone and the other leaning backward toward the rear wheel. Thus Guzzi had a TT double in one year.

Guzzi played with a three-cylinder with each cylinder horizontal and facing forward like the successful single, but this one —a touring machine— failed to sell. Later, after the TT wins, the company tried a similar layout for a racer, but once again World War II put a stop to a project. Guzzi came back in peacetime, reviving the 250 Albatros single of 1939, and won the first World Championship in its class in 1949, maintaining its record until 1952 when vanquished by NSU. Its former designer, Angelo Parodi, had died during the war, and Giulio Carcano was the new man.

Carcano developed a 350cc racer from the 250 which was really a modified version of the old 1938 Albatros with all sorts of novel design features, the key to many of which was weight saving. He also used a full fairing, and went on to win races from 1953 to 1957. In the same year, 1953, came the works 498cc in-line four water-cooled racers with shaft drive, then in 1956 the most complicated machine ever—the 498cc 90-degree V8 with four overhead camshafts.

This V8 used tiny pistons in 41mm bores with a 44mm stroke, and was housed in a double-cradle frame. This machine was developed and changed until it was giving 75bhp at 13,500rpm, but in 1957 Moto Guzzi retired from racing and production ceased.

The company was eventually bought by the Argentine Alessandro de Tomaso, who also owned Benelli and continued making relatively complex road-going machines with transverse twin engines of up to 1000cc with shaft drive. These were hardly the sort of fodder for DIY mechanics, especially when fitted with a torque converter and semiautomatic two-speed transmission. Small scooter-type machines continued to be made alongside the big monsters, which also had coupled brakes both worked from the pedal.

A machine as complex as the Moto Guzzi but even more successful in the competition field is the also-Italian MV Agusta, which was a postwar product of a helicopter maker run by an aristocratic family. Until his death Count Domenico Agusta ran the motorcycle side from a factory in the village of Verghera, and from the family and the village came the machine's name: Meccanica Verghera, or as the marque name MV Agusta.

It has been called the world's most successful motorcycle, with 37 World Championship titles and more than 4000 wins, an astonishing record for a firm which began only in 1945 in the two-wheel field. It started with mini two-strokes and began winning the Lightweight TT in 1952, taking the Senior in 1956 with John Surtees up. Carlo Ubbiali was the pilot on the race-winning two-strokes.

Arturo Magni ran the racing department, and the four-cylinder 497cc shaft-drive racer came from Pietro Remor, who had been with Gilera and had produced its winning four. Although running the company was almost a hobby for the Count, the racing side was professional and successful and had the benefit of the best riders in its prime.

The Four was announced in 1950 with torsion-bar suspension at both ends, but did not appear in the TT as it was not ready. Its first place was fifth in the Belgian Grand Prix, which started a run of successes. Two famous riders joined MV, Les Graham and Ray Amm, but both were killed in their first seasons, in 1953 and 1955 respectively.

The machines became more and more complex, running to three- and even six-cylinder racers, air cooled. They were winning the 125, 250, and 500cc world titles and were close to a 350 win also. They were helped in 1958 by the decision of their rivals—Gilera, Moto Guzzi, Mondial, and the British Norton company —to retire from racing because it was too expensive to win to be worthwhile. Companies just could not afford it any more.

Touring Italian-style on a Moto Guzzi superbike with every possible feature.

The heart of the matter, the Suzuki racing engine, a single-rotor Wankel used in the RE5 machine.

Sheene's Suzuki turns into a bucking bronco as he wheelies down the straight.

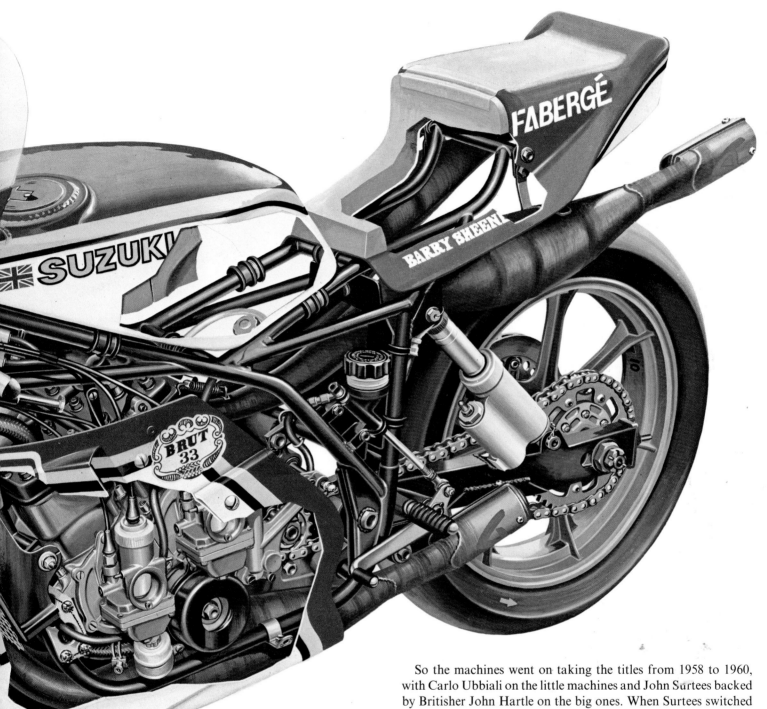

Sheene's 1977 Suzuki RGA 500 tops 180mph and was built at Hamamatsu, Japan. The four-in-line unit has a 494cc capacity and is a two-stroke with four disk valves, water-cooled, 54mm by 54mm. It uses four Mikuni carburetors fed from a seven-gallon tank, Champion plugs and Nippondense ignition. Transmission is by straight-cut primary gears and dog clutch to the rear sprocket by Renold chain. The frame is a Suzuki twin loop, and Barry's machine has special Suzuki front forks with air pressure. He also used Kayaba Golden Shock struts at the rear in place of the regular coil spring and damper. Wheels are Campagnalo cast alloy, braking by twin disks at the front and single ventilated rear disk, with Mintex linings.

So the machines went on taking the titles from 1958 to 1960, with Carlo Ubbiali on the little machines and John Surtees backed by Britisher John Hartle on the big ones. When Surtees switched to cars the Rhodesian Gary Hocking succeeded him and took the 350 and 500 titles. At this time MV decided to pretend they were not running works' entries and that Hocking was supposedly a lone ranger with 'MV Privat' lettered on the fairing; the ruse fooled no one and brought some brickbats from the fans.

The company continued selling its successful road-going machines in most capacity classes—singles, twins, fours—and after Gary Hocking left they had two more stars, Mike Hailwood and Giacomo Agostini. But by now (1965) the threat from the East was rising; Hailwood switched to Honda, but Agostini kept on winning in the 500 class with the three-cylinder machine up to 1972. When Honda pulled out of racing in 1958 Agostini went on winning the 350 class too.

With Honda gone Yamaha and Kawasaki had taken over and were the new threat. The tetchy Phil Read joined MV and won the 500 title for them, but Agostini moved over to Yamaha and won the 350 Championship. Suzuki had now also joined in, and eventually MV— with an enviable record behind it—retired from racing.

MV motorcycles were finally being made at the Ducati works at Bologna as the racing stopped and sales fell off. Ducati is a relative newcomer, having produced machines from 1950. Its early road-going machines were tiddlers of 50cc which looked like racers, but with the 125cc real racer with desmodromic valves it began to win.

Ducati profitted by the decision of the other Italian firms to stop racing in 1957, and began to dominate the 125cc class. It also secured Mike Hailwood, who won a British race on the 350cc desmodromic twin. The Japanese drive to the West swept Ducati away along with the others, although it continues to make road-going machines.

Benelli, now owned by de Tomaso like Moto Guzzi, started up at Pesaro in 1911 and was run by six brothers in the Italian fashion. Now, after all those years, it is one of the makers of a six-cylinder motorcycle, the Benelli Sei with its air-cooled engine across the frame and a 748cc capacity.

Benelli began with two-strokes, but one of the brothers Tonino, later killed on the road, began winning races with an ohc single of 173cc from 1927. In 1939 Benelli had a 1-2-3 victory at Monza and then won the Lightweight TT at 74.25mph with the Englishman Ted Mellors riding a 249cc dohc single. The camshafts were gear driven, the valves closed by hairpin springs, and there was an outside 'bacon slicer' flywheel as on Moto Guzzi. The engine turned at more than 8000rpm, which was phenomenal for those days.

The company came back with the same machine after the war, and in 1950 took the 250 World Championship. However, when its rider Dario Ambrosini was killed at Albi in France at the 1951 Grand Prix, the factory went out of racing for many years. Its comeback had been slow as their factory was destroyed during the war.

By 1959 Benelli was on the way back, but this was the year when Honda decided to investigate the international racing scene, and Benelli played a catch-as-catch-can racing policy, sometimes fielding a team and sometimes not, much to the disappointment of its followers. It used a four-cylinder which did well in the hands of Pasolini and beat Agostini on MV at Modena in 1967.

The Benelli firm had star names at times: Phil Read, Mike Hailwood, and Kel Carruthers. It was progressing well and planning a V8 like Moto Guzzi when the racing authorities banned machines in the under-250 class with more than two cylinders for 1970. In spite of much talk its last major placing in a ranking event was in 1970, and since then the production machines have been the news, especially the six-cylinder with a 112mph top speed.

Mondial started making motorcycles and an impact in the racing world in 1949, and retired from competition in 1957. In between it gained attention with its 125cc racer and a 1-2-3-4 finish in the first 125cc Lightweight TT. Those who scoffed at the idea of such tiny machines racing had to retract their words when Mondial finished with Cromie McCandless leading at 74.85mph.

Mondial won all sorts of races and titles, one of their later stars being Tarquinio Provini, who was very hard to catch and took two world titles. The winning power unit was a 123cc ohc single, originally a very unsophisticated affair with girder forks and tramline-thin wheels. The second-generation models after 1952 from designer Alfonso Drusiani were in a more modern mode,

with full fairings, sprung heel, and great lightness.

The Italian Morini company was another to make a considerable mark in the lightweight field of racing in the postwar years. It began manufacture in 1937 but the war cut short its career; the factory was destroyed in 1943 and did not produce another motorcycle until 1945. In between Morini produced airplane parts.

The firm made utility machines until the 123cc—a popular Italian size—ohc four-stroke single appeared which in 1948 would run up to 10,000rpm. Morini progressed through a 175cc and a 250cc which ultimately did 145mph. Agostini was one of those who began on Morini, and the company gave Honda stiff competition before the Japanese surpassed it.

After the lightweight racing era the Italian company concentrated on road machines, especially the 350 V twin known as the $3\frac{1}{2}$, produced in the 1970s. They are well made and kept simple in design for cost reasons, yet the Sport version will top 100mph and the touring Strada offers less performance with great economy and more comfort.

Aermacchi, an Italian maker which is now the Italian branch of the American Harley-Davidson, started production in 1948 but also made its mark in racing with a clever idea. The single forward-facing cylinder which it uses makes it possible to switch parts easily to produce a 250 or 350cc engine in the same frame, which is handy for the privateer. Now Aermacchi makes production machines, which Americans like for trials and speed events.

There have been many other lesser-known Italian makes (Fantic, Garelli, Itom, Italjet, Malaguti, Morbidelli, and so on) but enough has been said about the design of the major machines to illustrate their complexity and unsuitability for amateur tinkering. The fairly recent Laverda, the Ferrari of motorcycles, has not been used in competition officially, but is fast, advanced, and expensive.

Montesa has an Italian sound but is a Spanish machine which was born in 1945 by a partnership between the present owner, Pedro Permanyer, and Francesco Bulto who later left to form the Bultaco firm which makes such successful engines. The Barcelona factory produced small-engined machines up to 250cc which did well in competition, originally road-racing and later in off-road activities like trials and motocross.

The Montesa is really a Spanish intruder, but will do to separate the Italians who reigned for about 10 years from the Japanese who began to take over in 1960, the year after Honda previewed the European racing layout. As they developed, the Japanese machines illustrated even more perhaps than the Italian ones how the motorcycle had become too complicated a piece of machinery for the average amateur to tinker with. The other side of the coin is that reliability is of an order undreamed of in the days of frequent punctures, broken chains, blocked jets, failed electrics, broken valves, snapped control cables, and all the other mortifications of the early, but certainly not easy, rider.

The invasion was spearheaded by four major companies, Honda, Kawasaki, Suzuki, and Yamaha, but there had been perhaps 20 times as many domestic makers as this in Japan, most of them unknown outside the country, before they were all swallowed up by the giants or failed. It was in some ways a repetition of what had happened earlier in Britain and the Continent of Europe, where hundreds of makes dwindled down to a handful.

Honda was the forerunner, landing in the Isle of Man for the TT with a large team of mechanics, good riders including two Australians, Tom Phillis and Bob Brown, and both 125 and 250cc machines. In the first year they won some places and went on to

The Italian Laverda fast road machine, the 1000 triple-cylinder Jarama has everything, including good looks.

Kawasaki's Z250 single with ohc has rubber mounting to damp vibration as it runs at 10,000rpm.

compete in the ranking European events. When Tom Phillis was injured Honda took on Jim Redman from Rhodesia, and not long after Bob Brown was killed, not an auspicious start. But Phillis returned, and the team prospered. The sporting side was only one prong of the invasion force, and in the production machine field Honda was offering attractions like an electric starter on a 250cc machine.

The company was initially led solely by Soichiro Honda, who started with motorized bicycles and progressed until he was selling one of the world's largest and most luxurious machines, the Gold Wing. He was also making more machines than any other motorcycle factory. He began with a simple little two-stroke single in 1948 and went on to make twins, fours and some of the fastest racing machines. His first visit to the Isle of Man was in 1954, but he spent five years improving his machines before committing them to racing. This thoroughness has been the backbone of his success, and took him on to 16 World Championships and 137 Grand Prix wins in seven years' racing before he decided enough had been done and won.

The Honda story is the classic success epic of the determined man. He made 10 million machines in 20 years on his way to become the world's biggest producer, and his first success was based on a single-cylinder two-stroke model appropriately called the Dream. Honda himself bowed out in 1973 when he was 67 years of age, but until then was involved in the day-to-day problems of his one-man empire.

The empire was built on the small super-economy machine but later expanded to include some sophisticated designs. Many people feel that Soichiro Honda entered racing only to help sell his road machines, and in spite of his enormous success gave up without any qualms once he had made his point by beating the rest of the world numerous times. There were other considerations however. The company suffered a catastrophe around 1953–54 when it had made a huge investment in factory equipment just as a slump approached, forcing the company into very careful management to fend off take-over bids. Probably the company's only failure was in its attempt to capture the world's motorcycle land speed record, which lasted for several years, cost a lot of money, and produced 286mph in one direction, but never the mean of a two-way run which is what the rules require.

Kawasaki was the last of the Japanese Big Four to appear, in 1961, but is introduced alphabetically before Suzuki and Yamaha.

The parent company had long been in business in other engineering activities, and bought up a motorcycle firm (Meguro) to gain retail outlets. The company also used the name Meihatsu before Kawasaki was launched.

Like Honda it began small with a 123cc two-stroke and progressed until it entered the 1000cc field, although since Japan had a 750cc limit for domestic use the machines were exported. They sold well in the United States and the firm opened a factory there at Lincoln, Nebraska, in 1975. Famous models have included the three-cylinder two-stroke 500cc H1 and many off-road versions.

Kawasaki was also busy in racing, but always claimed that it did not produce special racers but modified road machines; it did in fact sell the H1R racing version of the 500 with a promised 150mph top speed. But also like Honda Kawasaki used racing as a marketing tool rather than an end in itself. The two-stroke H1 made the company famous, with outstanding performance from 60bhp although the handling was not in the same bracket.

The company did not enter the Grand Prix field but persevered with long-distance racing and the 750cc superbike class, and defied superstition by choosing green—regarded in motorsport as unlucky—as one of their colors. The big 'Kwackers' have certainly made their mark in the new motorcycling world of jazzy-colored leathers and handfuls of power on tap.

Suzuki, like Kawasaki, was established in another field of activity before moving into motorcycle making. The company was in the textile business from 1909 and looking for some other activity in 1952 when it moved into two-wheelers with a motorized bicycle. It went on to make outboard motors, boats, bicycles, cars, and vans as well as motorcycles, and also took most of the World Championships in the various capacity classes.

Suzuki began with small lightweights and finished making machines of up to 1000cc capacity in the superbike category, and with enormous success in all kinds of two-wheel competition. One of its distinctions was to have the only TT winner with a Japanese rider, Mitsuo Itoh, in the 50cc TT of 1963. Its ultimate 50cc racer had 14 gears and could approach 120mph when given time to wind up on a long straight. At the other end of the scale Suzuki was also on top in the 750 Superbike class, and in between had won world championships in 125, 500, and both the 250 and 500 motocross activity. Later success was tied in with Barry Sheene, who survived a very high speed crash at Daytona and came back to racing. Suzuki experimented with the Wankel

The trend to customize machines developed on the West Coast of the United States during the 1960s, and had less of an impact in the United Kingdom. Parts were constructed of lighter materials and unnecessary ones were discarded in order to make bikes as lightweight as possible. The result was slim, efficient machines of exceptional performance which were works of art in themselves.

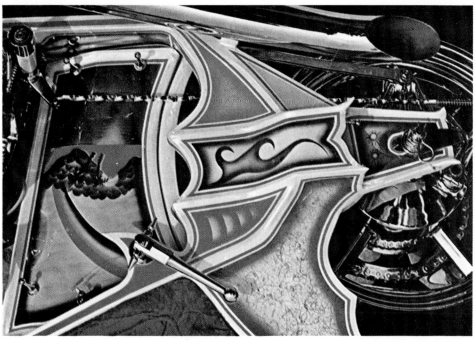

rotary, but the machine was not a great success, although in 1979 Norton was about to follow their lead.

The Yamaha story is very much like that of Honda and Suzuki. Yamaha diversified into motorcycles from another business, started with miniscule machines and ended up with superbikes, and did well in racing. Yamaha was a musical instrument maker under the name of Nippon Gakki (Japanese Musical Instruments) before entering the two-wheel world in 1954 to produce eventually one of the widest ranges of bikes of any company.

The motorcycle company began with a 125cc which was not unlike the BSA Bantam, and went into motorsport immediately, at first in domestic events, but by 1961 it was a part of the international scene. Its racers were superior in complexity with two-stroke engines with disk valves and water-cooling, in V4 formation but with only 125 or 250cc capacity. They peaked at 17,000/18,000rpm, and were not suitable for beginners. But the end came for these complicated machines when the governing body of racing, the FIM, banned more than two cylinders in machines of less than 250cc.

Yamaha persisted by racing near-production machines in 250 and 350cc form with two-stroke engines, and continued to be successful. As well as these mighty midgets the company made a 750cc superbike called the TZ750A or OW31 on which Steve Baker of the United States won the World Championship in the 750 class.

Like the other big Japanese makers Yamaha also has a super-

These Triumph Tridents are further examples of the American-style customized bike.

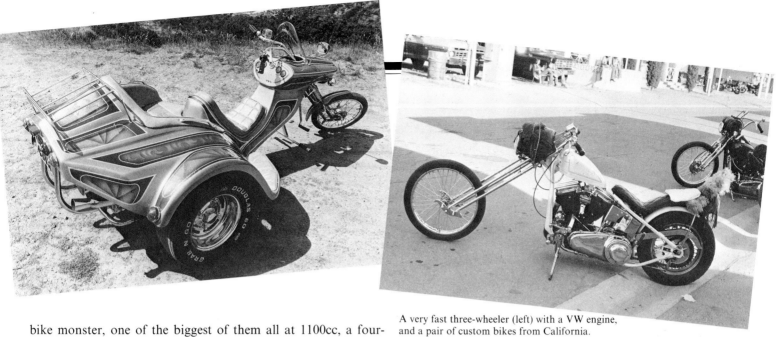

A very fast three-wheeler (left) with a VW engine,
and a pair of custom bikes from California.

bike monster, one of the biggest of them all at 1100cc, a four-cylinder with shaft drive called the XS1100 which matches the Honda Gold Wing for size, weight, and speed. Like the Gold Wing it is a tourer which excells in straight-line performance.

These brief histories of the Italian and Japanese companies illustrate how difficult it is for the amateur to play with the mechanics of a modern machine in search of more performance unless he has exceptional knowledge and skill. The emphasis has shifted with the modern machine so that anyone who is not satisfied with what he can buy can go to one of several super-experts who make changes to production machines and market them as an improved package which the DIY individual could not possibly produce himself.

The first man to produce and market a hybrid machine was Dave Degens, who put a Triumph engine in a Norton Featherbed frame and called it a Triton. He soon had people wanting him to make one for them to race. Previously a Norton engine in a Triumph frame had been tried, but that had proved unsuccessful.

In the 1960s Norton had the handling but not the straight-line performance, which was why people began to build Tritons even before Dave Degens. Degens had won the 1965 Barcelona 24-Hour race on one, although at that time he called it a Dresda or Dresda Triton with a fishtailed sea-God with horse's front legs on the badge. One of these people was John Viccars, who won a race at the London Crystal Palace Circuit on one, although he called it a JV Special. Others did the same thing, with varying degrees of skill, and thus the Triton was born.

At one time Manx Norton machines minus engines and gearboxes were available because drivers wishing to compete in the first postwar poor man's racing, the Formula Three or 500cc formula, could not buy Norton double-knocker engines because the company would not sell them. If they were rich enough they bought a complete machine and discarded what they did not want.

The Triumph Speed Twin, a prewar model now back on the market, offered the right power, even more so in its later forms as the Bonneville or Tiger, and that was the engine which went into the Featherbed frame. Sometimes riders made their own frames, but they were a variegated lot.

Three of the other specialists who sell (or sold) performance were Norton tuners, or to be precise two were Norton tuners and the third started as such but has since diversified into the modern Japanese makes as well. They are Francis Beart, Steve Lancefield, and Paul Dunstall.

Beart started as a rider himself and ended up as an entrant with other people riding machines he had prepared, very often for the works themselves. He was the high priest of the Norton and employed some of the best riders, as well as working on other makes of machine when it suited him.

Steve Lancefield was in some ways a rival, as he too was a Norton man, and prepared machines for events like the Daytona 200 which involved making them conform to American regulations. Beart also performed at Daytona, but in different years.

Paul Dunstall was also a racer who turned tuner, and then started a business selling bolt-on items and from Norton has expanded to Honda, Suzuki, Yamaha, and Kawasaki as each has taken over. He has also designed his own changes to machines, such as special exhaust systems and disk brakes, and sells them over the counter to the enthusiast. He also sells fairings or even complete machines modified to his own ideas.

Paul Dunstall might be called a customizer, although this has come to mean someone who sprays paint on a machine in strange patterns, and he is much more than that. We will come back to the custom scene after taking a brief look at a great person who died in 1979.

He was Harry Weslake, who was by no means exclusively confined to motorcycles in his work but as a wizard with cylinder heads did wonders for all kinds of engine. His father worked for a firm of gas engineers in the west of England, and Harry had the idea of borrowing a gas-meter tester to measure gas flow in and out of a cylinder head. From this simple basic idea his whole theory and practice of how to lay out a cylinder head and valves evolved, and his work was incorporated in many of the great motorcar engines. He worked on motorcycles too, and produced a special carburetor for them, the Wex, about 1920, and worked for Sunbeam and AJS as a consultant. He would never be anyone's employee. His greatest success in the two-wheel world was to produce the four-valve single-cylinder speedway engine which is now the one to beat, about 60 years after his first tuning experiments.

Customizing, the art or science of chopping bits off motorcycles, adding things on, and doing them up with a jazzy paint job, is largely an American preoccupation which has not caught on to the same extent in Britain. This applies in the car world, where it is very much a minority cult not known to the average driver unless he visits one of the annual shows or buys the magazine devoted to the subject.

But in the United States, particularly in California where the crazes always seem to originate, it is big business, with its own language, customs, meetings, dress, and workshops where the

Two drag racers ready to compete at Indianapolis in 1979.

transformation scenes take place on almost Cinderella lines, making a bicycle into a pumpkin or anything else the customer fancies. The 'chopper' craze did cross the Atlantic to put on the roads hardly-rideable motor bikes with extended front forks, high-rise 'ape' handlebars, and all the other gimmicks like leather fringes dangling. Perhaps the European or Japanese machine does not lend itself as well to the switch as the big Harleys and Indians.

The movement began as American motorcyclists tried to lighten their big machines to compete with the newly-imported British bikes which were much lighter and therefore faster. The first step was to discard as much as possible. At this time—the 1950s—the two types of machine, European and American, were poles apart. The American rider, if he wanted to save weight, could discard his footboards for footrests, dish the panniers, windshield, wide handlebars, crash bars and a few other nonessentials, fit a smaller fuel tank and wheels and seat, and cut down on the mud guarding.

'Chopping' or 'bobbing' produced its own pop art, the leader being David Manning (or Dave Mann) who worked for Ed 'Big Daddy' Roth, a leader in the 'funny-painting' business, first on cars and later on bikes. The more extreme machines were illegal on the road and used only for shows, and in the United States some states legislated to keep even more of them off the road by regulating seat and handlebar height and steering layouts.

The Harley-Davidson, which to a degree started the whole thing in competition with the imported European machines, gave way after a long reign to the Japanese superbikes and the second generation of 'café racers' which look the part but will not necessarily go farther than the next coffee-shop or transport café down the road. It is all show and no go compared with the serious riding world of the road racer or those involved in any form of motorcycle competition. Riders compete for the jazziest paint job, the most chrome, the most way-out look. Different types have their own names: bobbed-job, street digger, low rider, chopped hog.

Latest influence has been from the world of the dragster, and although the true drag bike could not be ridden legally on the road, there are derivatives which are legal but have near-racing performance. The whole movement is an American specialty. The British sprint racers, like the late George Brown with his Vincent 'Nero,' were interested only in how fast they could go, not the color of the paint. The climate may have an influence, as riding on a Californian-style chopper with no mudguards does not have much appeal in a European winter.

A more strongly-supported movement in Britain was behind the scooter-mounted gangs known as Mods, who fought street battles in seaside towns with Rockers or Greasers who were motorcycle mounted. Their scooters, vehicles regarded with contempt by bikers, were ornamented along the lines of the American customized motorcycles, and adorned with rows of spot lights. This parallels one Harley-Davidson in the United States which is said to carry 1000 lights of various kinds.

An aspect of the motorcycling scene which has affiliations with customizing is the world of drag racing, which began in America in the 1940s and crossed the Atlantic about 20 years later. This was another Californian fad which has spread, applied initially to cars and later to bikes as well. Some of the creations have to be seen to be believed, and they now reach terminal speeds at the end of the quarter-mile in the region of 200mph, achieved in just under eight seconds.

There are not many rules, although in the United States the rider may not use a car engine in a motorcycle except with a bike crankcase. In Europe this does not apply and MGB engines among others have been seen; in the United States there is a six-liter Chevrolet V8-engined bike, but it is not eligible to race and is used for demonstrations only by builder E J Potter, otherwise known as the Michigan Madman.

The idea is to cover 440 yards as fast as possible from a standing start, the riders running in pairs side by side against the clock. Nowadays there are even rules and classes, with a limit of 3500cc for unsupercharged machines and two liters for the blown jobs. There are further subdivisions into production machines in road trim and Pro Street (American terminology) or Pro Stock (European) which run on pump fuel but are tuned, and specials built for dragging, called competition bikes, which may run on dope or gasoline. This becomes confusing, as those running on nitromethane or some similar brew smelling like burnt boot polish are called 'fuel bikes' and those on gasoline are 'gassers.' There are also subdivisions by engine capacity.

All the dragsters tend to be long with a wheelbase of five feet or sometimes much more if they have two or three engines, and may put out 200 or 250 horsepower. They are also kept low and ground hugging with not too much in the way of creature comforts for the rider. All kinds of engines are used, and at one time the Norton motorcycle gearbox was popular. More recent developments call for a slipper clutch, which works like the old 'traffic clutch' with progressively less slip as speed rises from take-off, and a two-speed transmission, probably made from a car overdrive unit.

The field of drag racing is one of the few in which there is still scope for the amateur engineer to do his own thing, and he certainly does, experimenting with all kinds of options. Some riders do without gears and rely upon progressively less slip between tire and road to raise the gearing as the speed rises. The machine only has to hold together for less than 10 seconds, which leaves room for cutting down margins.

Rear tires which do the driving are treadless slicks up to 12 inches wide, and part of the entertainment for the spectators is watching the riders do a 'burn-out' to warm the tire and make the rubber sticky before the start of their run. They press the front wheel against the nearest truck or immovable object, engage gear, and spin the rear wheel, throwing out clouds of smoke. A refinement is a 'rolling burn-out' when the rear tire sits in a pool of water or fuel and is spun until it sets it alight if it is fuel. This is done on the start line just before take-off.

The two competing riders face a Christmas tree of colored lights on a pole one below the other, which light up in turn. When the green comes on it is 'go,' but if anyone jumps the start a red light comes on and the run is aborted. The Christmas tree sits between the two racing lanes and riders sit with gear engaged and clutch held out waiting for the green light.

In America it is a money-spinning business for the competitors, but much less so in England, where there are four major strips, at Santa Pod in Bedfordshire, on an old airfield, at Silverstone (another airfield), at Snetterton in Norfolk, and Huddersfield in Yorkshire. Santa Pod is the home of the British Drag Racing Association and the most popular venue.

At one time the aim was to beat 10 seconds, then nine and then eight. The Michigan Madman did 8.8 seconds elapsed time and 180mph, but this did not count and was a demonstration. Another American, Larry Welch, did 7.9 seconds and close to 200mph using hydrogen peroxide in a rocket-powered device. Russ Collins, a Los Angeles tuning wizard, used three Honda engines each of 1100cc in his $21,000 Atchison, Topeka and Santa Fe which did

Another competitor at Indianapolis, with the wide back slick and two big twins.

7.86 seconds and 178mph. In 1976 he went end-over-end and destroyed the projectile, but survived somewhat battered. In Britain times have generally been slower, except for Alf Hagon who ran his JAP V twin of 1300cc at 9.2 seconds in 1968, faster than the Americans at that time.

Tom Christenson from California used two Norton Commando engines with a slipper clutch and two-speed transmission in his Hogslayer in 1973 to record 7.93 and 176mph, and on another occasion 184mph. Another American, Danny Johnson from North Carolina, where he has a speed shop, visited England in 1973 and ran 9.28 at Santa Pod in a single-engined Harley, showing a terminal 160mph.

The English giant-killer is Brian Chapman, who runs a single-cylinder Vincent Comet dating back to 1951 and has shown 9.07 seconds and 154mph. His machine has semielliptic car-type leaf springs running back from the gearbox to small wheels behind the machine to prevent him from flipping on take-off. When he could not find a suitable cam for his engine he made one himself, not an easy job. His approach is typical of the English riders who have to make do. The American Danny Johnson can pick up $300 for running his standard-looking Harley in demonstrations, since this wolf in sheep's clothing has a racing engine and can get under nine seconds. He has a spare bike as standby, a luxury unknown to the British riders, even those in the bolt-on accessory business which they sell to others.

A popular British engine for dragging was the 750 Triumph Twin, now outclassed by some later power plants, but Keith Parnell's *Rouge Et Noir* with a blown Triumph running on dope put up some good times. Some people such as John Hobbs, one of Europe's fastest, have used two Triumph Twins in one frame. He later moved onto two Weslake engines, supercharged, and ran 8.47 seconds and 173mph. Another Briton, Keith Parnell, ran 8.93 seconds with a blown 750cc Triumph, the first to get under nine seconds with less than 1000cc.

This American sport has spread to many other countries, and one of the keenest scenes is in Holland, always a motorsport-oriented country. Henk Vink, the Kawasaki importer, rides his own machines and has shown 9.00 seconds and 160mph on a blown 975cc machine. In England John Cheadle ran a 350cc Yamaha—a midget by drag standards—to good times against the big monsters. No doubt times will go down even more as the riders think up new tricks, but machines are already much faster than anything one can buy to run over the quarter-mile, by more than one-third on elapsed time.

Although British and American dragsters do not meet very often, there is an annual event in which the road-racing stars of both countries come together. This is the Anglo-American Transatlantic Series which began in 1971 as a promotional idea for BSA-Triumph which was building three-cylinder bikes for the Formula 750 which was the newest thing.

The series began with five men on each side, six races to be run on three British circuits, Brands Hatch near London, Mallory Park, and Oulton Park, both farther north. All belong to Motor Circuit Developments, whose motorcycle racing manager, Chris Lowe, organized the events.

Initially the Americans had no experience of short-circuit racing on asphalt, but they learned fast and soon ceased to be a joke. Nowadays the problem is to beat the Americans with their very fast machines, which have progressed from the original BSAs and Triumphs to the world's fastest Suzukis, Yamahas, and Kawasakis.

Britain won for the first four years, and it was in 1974 that the new Japanese models began to overshadow the aging Nortons and BSA/Triumphs. But the new Americans, Kenny Roberts, Garry Nixon, Yvon du Hamel, Dave Aldana, and the others had opened a few eyes, even if they just failed to win the series.

In the fifth year—1975—the Americans took the trophy, in spite of riding in cold, wet weather which was not suited to their taste. Admittedly some British stars like Barry Sheene were out because of injury, but Kenny Roberts, Gene Romero, and Don

A trials expert picks his way up a tricky hillside staircase, where no bike was meant to go.

Roger de Coster, leading as usual in a European motocross event or over the normal rough-as-blazes circuit.

Castro on Yamaha, Dave Aldana, and Pat Hennen on Suzukis, supported by private entries by the up-and-coming star Steve Baker, Steven McClaughlin, and Phil McDonald all on Yamahas lead the British from start to finish.

The following year the Americans were suffering from men missing due to injuries, just as the British had the year before. They fielded Kenny Roberts, Steve Baker, Gene Romero, Garry Nixon, Pat Hennen, Ron Pierce, and Randy Cleek. But the British were in full cry with Phil Read, Dave Potter, Steven Parrish, Mick Grant, Barry Ditchburn, Barry Sheene, and John Williams, and Ron Haslam.

New boy Steve Baker won no less than four of the six races and was placed in the other two, but the British total in points was just high enough due to middle placings to take the John Player Trans-atlantic Trophy. In 1977 and 1978 Britain won again, but the United States took the 1979 trophy.

All branches of motorcycle sport have developed special machines for the one purpose, which has had a fascinating influence on overall design since features desirable for one aspect of the sport have spread to general use if applicable.

Road racing has played the biggest part in the development of the everyday machine, and the Isle of Man TT races over the past 70 years, as the longest races anywhere, have perhaps had the biggest influence. The short-circuit races, like the Anglo-American series, bring changes and development, but not as much as the long grind of the seven or eight laps of that twisting 37.75-mile TT course over the mountain.

One of the natural developments of the TT has been the rising lap speeds over the years, with riders aiming for the 60mph lap, then 70, 80, 90, and 100. The sidecars have always been one of the great spectacles, and we have seen the 100mph sidecar lap, although some people call the modern sidecar outfits three-wheel racing cars and there have been threats of bans and restrictions.

Apart from the TT, which existed almost from the start of motorcycle sport, the grass track was the first venue for competition, and is with us still although something of a Cinderella among the various kinds of events. Brands Hatch, now one of Britain's top circuits, started as a motorcycle grass track with very few facilities.

Grass machines have a close affinity with speedway bikes, except that they have brakes. Many riders learn their craft on grass and progress into speedway where they can become professionals, whereas grass racing remains the poor man's amusement without much in the way of prize money. In speedway all the machines are 500s; on grass riders can compete with 250, 350, and the bigger sizes too. Two-strokes are the winning wear under 500, and on grass the sidecars go for 1000cc big twins like the now-defunct Vincent.

Weight saving is one of the principal efforts of the sidecar grass men, who cut and trim their outfits to this end. The days of trailing out the old outfit and running a whole season without mechanical work are long gone, and the modern machine is stripped and tuned again after what amounts to not more than an hour's racing. It is an amateur sport, but hard work.

Grass racing began to be noticed from about 1920, and the first big meeting in Britain was in 1927, 10 years behind Australia. The length of tracks marked out around posts in farmers' fields ran from 400 yards up to more than a mile. Some events were even run under floodlights at night. Official control began in 1931 with machines divided into classes by engine size, but riders still arrived at the track on their racing machines, took off lights and mud-

guards, ran their races, then put them together again for the journey home. In the sidecar classes there were arguments about which way around they should go, since in Britain with left-mounted 'chairs' they ran clockwise, while in Europe with the passenger on the right they went the other way. Some people argued that it was better the other way round so that spectators could see more of the passenger at work. They did not win the point and both groups still go their own way. People used Matchless, Rudge, New Imperial, JAP, and BSA until the advent of the specialist machines, some imported from speedway which came to England from America by way of Australia in 1928.

Two famous names among sidecar men on grass were Stan Hailwood and Jack Surtees, the respective fathers of Mike the Bike and seven times World Champion John Surtees, who was also World Car Champion, usually known as Big John.

Close companions to grass-track racing are trials, scrambling, Enduro, motocross, and speedway, all variations of the same art, controlling a machine in rough conditions but with different rules and a different following. Scrambling is perhaps the closest to grass track, and is an earlier version of motocross, although still practiced and popular.

Scrambling was cross-country racing, as is motocross, whereas trials riding is more of a test of being able to cover a piece of country without falling off, losing points for putting a foot down in observed sections. Trials were not against the clock, until someone introduced the timing element which is now common. The International Six Days is the top event in this activity, in which teams from various countries compete against each other.

Favored machines in motocross are the Scandinavian Husqvarna, Monark, Lito and Hedlund, the Italian Saturno Cross, the Belgian FN and formerly the British Greeves. The Rickman brothers from Hampshire, England, made a special off-road racer called the Metisse (French for mongrel bitch) and still do, but have also moved on to road-racing machines. The Czechoslovak CZ is also in the running with the ESO from the same country.

Trials, which go back to the early days of motorcycling, have produced their own special variety of machines like all branches of the sport. The Spanish Bultaco and Ossa were long dominant, but challenged by Yamaha with a fuel-injected 250cc with cantilever rear suspension. The Scottish Six Days ranks after the International Six Days as a top event, and draw top stars like Mick Andrews (once said to be the highest-paid rider) and Malcolm Rathmell.

Many star riders come from Scandinavia, but the British, French, Belgian, and Spanish are also competitive. In England trials schools where hopefuls can practice are a useful forcing ground. Factories which have a leading rider on contract will not release him to ride other makes even in events in which they are not competing, and there have been law suits over this.

Apart from the contenders from Western Europe, the Eastern side is also active with riders and machines like the Jawa from Czechoslovakia, East Germany, Russia. Italy and West Germany are also involved in the international struggle, and the Japanese Honda company was at one time making more trials machines than anyone else. The trials fever has now spread to the point where schoolboys from eight years of age upward ride special 80cc scramblers in their own events.

The Scottish Six Days goes back to 1909, when it was only five days, and the International Six Days to 1910; foreign entries did not come until 1913 as it was originally a six-day trials run by the British Auto Cycle Union. In prewar days trials riding was strictly an amateur sport, but in the 1960s it became big business and the riders professionals.

One of the most amazing stars is Sammy Miller, who rode a 500cc Ariel from before 1960 right on up to 1964 when all the others had gone lightweight. He then developed a trials machine for Bultaco and went on riding for the company until he moved over to Honda and was still active in 1978, after leaving Honda for SWM (Speedy Working Motors), an Italian offshoot of Sironi.

Sidecars have always been an element in trials, with special high-clearance chairs developed for off-road use. There was resistance to the use of rear suspension for a long time as it was thought a rigid machine offered more grip, until the modern lightweight sprung-heel machines proved this to be nonsense. The original trials machines were straight roadsters with lights removed and upswept exhaust pipes, plus knobbly tires, until these were banned in 1938.

Trail riding is an offshoot of trials riding, but in noncompetitive gentler fashion done purely for fun. In Britain the Trail Riders Fellowship organizes local runs on off-road tracks and fights to preserve the right of motorcyclists to use tracks which farmers may try to close. They have come up against walkers, horse riders, and other interested parties but have been successful in keeping paths open.

Their machines tend to be homemade or adapted from road machines and the sport, generally known as 'green laning,' is quite divorced from the commercial competitive world of the big names and costly racers. In the United States and Australia there is more scope for off-road riding without the restrictions imposed in crowded Britain, although the Americans at one time tried to pass a law keeping riders off public land, which was defeated by lobbying by the Motorcycle Industry Council.

Motocross is more in the modern idiom than trials riding, and has produced special machines and riders who spend all their time on this one branch of the sport. It developed from scrambling and the cross-country car racing known as autocross, substituting part of the French name for motorcycle—*motocyclette*—for the 'auto' part of the name of the sport.

In the car version the drivers go off two at a time in a sort of match race, whereas all the bike riders start together in a mass start more like cycle racing. The bikes run over a course of 1.5 or two miles including climbs, descents, ditches, streams, and any other hazard the organizers can think up. The riders take a rough hammering and need a good sense of balance as well as a tough machine.

In foot-up trials riders were penalized for touching the ground with one foot or both, but scrambling, which developed from trials, allowed dirt-rack methods of using a foot. Motocross came even later and the winner is the fastest man, with no points lost

Trail riding in Wales, a noncompetitive and relatively gentle sport.

for 'footing.' Motocross began as a Continental European sport but Britain has been involved for a long time. The European title became a world title in 1963, and great names have been Briton Dave Bickers, Joel Robert from Belgium, Jeff Smith (Britain), Rolf Tibblin and Torsten Hallman (Sweden), and Paul Friedrichs from East Germany. He was three times World Champion (1966, 1967, 1968) like Roger de Coster from Belgium. Later Bengt Aberg from Sweden and Heikki Mikkola from Finland rose to the top, just as their countrymen have risen in motorcar rallying.

In motocross the machines are divided into classes by engine size as in road racing, and riders tend to stick to one-size machines, except the TT riders who may compete in several different classes. The old big-banger 500 single ruled by power and weight for many years until the lightweight two-stroke, at which the big-banger riders used to smile, proved that it could beat them in rough conditions. Now the courses have to be designed to beat the machines. The French, always a nation of rugged individualists, have different rules from everyone else, but motocross is a big spectator sport in France.

There is even one more variation of scrambling/trials/motocross known as Enduro, but it is perhaps a dying institution in face of the modern interest in ecology and the environment. There are special Enduro machines, offered largely by the Japanese makers, and the sport is like an extended motocross race going on for hundreds of miles.

America and Mexico are the home of this long-distance rough racing, and the event is the 1000-kilometer Baja 1000 from Ensenada to Tijuana and back. It originally ran 1000 miles from Tijuana to La Paz, but has been cut back to 600 miles in a loop. This event is open to all sorts of vehicles as well as motorcycles, but a 350cc Husqvarna ridden by Mitch Mayes and Larry Roeseler beat all the cars in 1976 in 11 hours 45 minutes. Enduro machines need a higher top speed than a motobike, and a bigger fuel tank in view of the distance to be covered. As they may be ridden partly on roads rather than private land they need to be equipped according to the legal requirements.

Some events are run in Britain on Forestry Commission land where the car rallies are held, but over distances of only about 150 miles compared with the really long-term endurance races held in the United States and Mexico. But the passage of a large number of bikes does destroy the flora, and how long this kind of event can last is in doubt.

So we come back to speedway, which was in some ways the father of all these other branches of motorcycle sport, except perhaps grass-track racing which is even older. The latest manifestation is long-track speedway, run in the United States, Australia, and elsewhere over a mile or more rather than the short tracks of quarter-mile or even less used for orthodox speedway.

In Britain speedway is said to be the second most popular spectator sport after football, which is Number One, and began in 1928. The machines are 500cc single-cylinders with no gears and no brakes, just a clutch and throttle by way of controls. Nowadays the Weslake is tops, but the older JAP and the Jawa are also used.

The JAP has been around a long time, and took over from the original favorite, the flat-twin Douglas. The modern machines run on dope (methanol) at around 15-to-1 compression ratio—about double that of a road machine—and produce perhaps 50 horsepower, burning their expensive fuel at the rate of six miles to the gallon. The power output compares with that of a road-racing machine, and so does the acceleration.

Airborne Neil Hudson, runner-up in the 1979 World 250cc Motocross Championship in 1979 at Bootle, here passing Steve Harrison.

The original speedway men used to ride with a trailing left leg, but the universal style now is with the left leg forward. There is no left footrest and the right leg in some cases goes under a hook which holds the man to the bike. The start, from horse-racing-style rising tapes, is the important bit, and races tend to be processions once the riders are away from the tapes.

Speedway began in the United States in the early part of this century, but on dirt and not the shale-on-concrete which is the modern surface. Riders also used half-mile tracks, twice as long as the stadium tracks today. The art of broadsiding, or keeping the machine in a slide all the way around the bends, began way back in those early days.

The Australians learned from the Americans, and then came to England, where the first track was at the Crystal Palace in London, a building erected in Hyde Park for the Great Exhibition of 1851 and then moved to this suburb. Within a short space of time there were eight tracks in London alone and others elsewhere in the country.

Early names among the riders were the American 'Sprouts' Elder and Stewart St George; girl riders appeared, but were banned within a year. Gus Kuhn and George Newton were also early stars, leading teams which were formed into leagues, and the sport boomed until the war in 1939. Speedway, or dirt track, as the public called it, was always divorced from the rest of the motorcycling world and looked down upon by the 'pukkha' racing fraternity. The sport came back in 1946 but by 1950 had lost popularity in Britain and many tracks closed down, until there came a second wind about 1970.

The World Championship has stimulated interest in speedway

in all countries, and Americans, Australians, Swedes, Danes, and many others are prominent in the four-lap clashes. Two New Zealanders, Barry Briggs and Ivan Mauger, have been at the top for many years. The dirt-track machine is of course a specialist tool good for nothing else and is another example of a sophisticated piece of machinery outside the competence of the amateur to maintain and tune.

The most refined pieces of machinery of all are the Grand Prix racers built regardless of cost by companies seeking the prestige of world titles. There are now seven classes ranging from 50cc up to 750 and each has its world champion, a title keenly fought for by both riders and manufacturers. The idea of a championship is comparatively modern; although most European countries held a Grand Prix by around 1930, there was no overall title for the man who won the most races.

The European Championship came first in 1938, based on the eight major races: British (the TT), Belgian, Dutch, French, German, Italian, Swiss, and Ulster in Northern Ireland. When racing came back after World War II in 1946 not all countries could run a Grand Prix, and the title did not re-emerge until 1949 when it had been upgraded to World Championship instead of just European. There were only six events, two of them British (the TT and Ulster), plus Belgian, Dutch, Italian, and Swiss, in 125, 250, 350, 500, and sidecar classes.

There have been several different methods of scoring, some very confusing, but nowadays it is a simple case of adding up points for each win or place throughout the season, running downwards from 15 for a win to 1 for being tenth, on the scale of 15, 12, 10, 8, 6, 5, 4, 3, 2, 1. One of the problems is that nonchampionship events may pay 10 times as much start money to a rider as the supposedly top-ranking Grand Prix, because the organizers know that the top contenders must appear in the point-scoring events.

The organizer, the Fédération Internationale Motorcycliste (FIM), insists on six starters for a race to count, and distances increase with the size of the machines. There are various controls on the specifications of machines, mostly in force for some years now. The 50cc machines must be singles, 125s not more than twins, similarly 250s, but 350s and 500s can be fours. Not more than six gears are allowed, a contrast with the eight cylinders and 14 gears of years ago. The 500cc class is still regarded as the top prize, although the 750 superbike category may be faster and more dramatic to watch.

It is an awe-inspiring thought that the bigger machines are approaching 200mph on the straights, yet are still so simple—apart from the mechanical complexities of the engines—and in direct descent from the powered bicycles of 80 years ago. The sidecars are an even more impressive sight to watch, weaving under braking and acceleration, and always apparently about to fly off the road.

The German BMW firm dominated sidecar racing for many years, sometimes with Swiss riders, until the advent of the slightly-disguised three-wheel cars which now pass for sidecar outfits, powered by various kinds of engine. The first Sidecar TT was in 1923 when 14 entrants turned up, and it ran until 1926, then disappeared right up until 1954.

In the Grand Prix world the 'chairs' were in right from the start of the World Championship in 1949. The great name from the prewar days was Eric Oliver on Norton, but in more recent times it has been BMW all the way since 1955 when it won its first TT. Oliver had his last TT victory the year before. BMW had 14 victories in a row in the World Championship.

The German riders were Wilhelm Noll in 1954, Wilhelm Faust in 1955, Fritz Hillebrand in 1957, Walter Schneider in 1958/59, and Helmut Fath in 1960, followed by Max Deubel from 1961 to 1964 inclusive. Fritz Scheidegger of Switzerland won in 1965, then Klaus Enders six times—all BMW mounted. The Germans won 20 times in 22 years, interrupted by George O'Dell of Britain in 1977. Another Swiss who was greatly respected although never champion was Florian Camathias who switched from BMW to Gilera. George O'Dell, the one-time British winner, used a Yamaha engine.

Sidecars allow more scope for the individual, as they are all independent entries even if backed in some way, and each design is different. Eric Oliver brought in the 'kneeler' in which the rider is kneeling rather than sitting, and others unified design of bike and chair into one unit. There are still many different ideas on engines, transmissions, and suspension, and room for experiment.

In the early days sidecars even ran on dirt tracks and always in trials, although they were rather a special breed of contraption, high and narrow and with minimum coachwork. Now they run in sidecar cross, with the chair attached to a motocross machine hammering across country, with riders risking life and limb. There is a European Moto Cross Sidecar Championship which the Swiss Robert Grogg won four times between 1972 and 1977.

So it seems that the keen individual who wants to modify his machine or build his own is limited to one of several fields: drag racing, which is recondite and expensive; trail riding, which is not necessarily expensive and where a simple machine will do; and sidecar racing, which costs more than solo activity, but is not too expensive if confined to sidecar cross or trials with a very primitive 'chair.'

Many of the people who have succeeded in various fields like road racing or other branches of the sport have a father-and-son history in the industry or business: John Surtees, Barry Sheene, and Mike Hailwood, for instance. Others who have built up a big name have been very skilled engineers: Rickman, Beart, Lancefield, Munch, Degens, Dunstall, and Weslake.

Room for improvement in the standard machine exists, but it is easier, cheaper, and simpler today either to buy a machine with the desired specification or to go to a specialist who has already refined it, like Rickman for instance. There is such a range of machines from 50cc to 1100 with every kind of engine, transmission by chain or shaft, all sorts of fairings, and all possible equipment that it must be a difficult customer who cannot be satisfied over the counter or with options from the maker.

It may not be as much fun to buy it ready-made as to 'do your own thing,' but without extensive mechanical knowledge and manual skill plus an engineering workshop with all the right facilities and tools, it is not so easy to beat the advanced manufacturers at their own game, which is providing performance, roadholding, handling, comfort, and economy in whatever kind of combination the customer wants.

One field in which simple modification or tuning does go on is in the comparatively new variety of moped sold in Britain for 16-year-olds, which must not be able to exceed 30mph. Norton-Villiers-Triumph marketed two models in 1979 under the revived BSA label which have a 50cc engine and a four-speed gearbox, deliberately restricted to keep them under the legal 30mph. As soon as the rider is 17 he may legally fit a bigger carburetor and recover the performance which the makers have been forced to throw away, and start himself on the DIY road to bigger and better things. Perhaps it is not so dull after all.

GLOSSARY

Absolute Track Record Fastest lap of a circuit, on two wheels or four, by any driver in any size of machine.

Absorption silencer A type of silencer which functions by the use of sound-absorbing material in an expansion chamber with a perforated tube running through it.

Abutment A stop to limit wheel lock, or, on the end of a control cable, to locate the outer covering.

AC Alternating Current as produced by an alternator, as opposed to Direct Current from a dynamo.

Accelerator Either (1) the throttle pedal of a car whose function is taken over by the twist-grip of a motorcycle, or (2) a chemical added to the resin in making fiberglass to speed up setting.

Accelerator pump A device in a carburetor which squirts neat fuel when the throttle is opened to richen the mixture temporarily.

Acetylene A gas formerly used for motorcycle lighting, produced by pouring water on calcium carbide. Also used in cylinders mixed with oxygen for welding.

Acoustic pillar A pillar linking cooling fins on the cylinder head or barrel to damp down ringing noises.

ACU Auto Cycle Union, which controls most types of motorcycle sport in Britain.

Additive A chemical mixed with lubricating oil in manufacture to prevent foaming, sludging, corrosion, or other ill effect.

Adjustable engine pulley The first method of varying gear ratios, by changing belts on a movable pulley whose diameter could be changed.

Advanced ignition Ignition timing set so that firing occurs before the piston reaches top dead center. Variation, once by hand lever, is now automatic.

Air bottle Compressed air in a cylinder used by trials riders to reinflate tires after a climb or muddy section.

Air cooling Most motorcycles rely on air cooling to the atmosphere rather than water-cooling as in car practice.

Air filter A filter to prevent abrasive particles entering the carburetor, which can be of fabric, felt, gauze, or paper.

Air intake The carburetor port which admits air to be mixed with fuel from the float chamber.

Air lever Replaces the choke for cold starting used on car engines, and cuts down the air supply until an engine is warm.

Air-line A hose supplying compressed air from a compressor used to inflate tires or for cleaning parts in a workshop.

Alloy A metal which is a mixture of more than one metal, usually aluminum and something else.

Alternator The alternator has replaced the dynamo on modern engines, and produces alternating current to recharge the battery.

Amal A British make of carburetor.

AMCA Amateur Motor Cycle Association, which promotes off-road events in England.

Apehanger Handlebars with an exaggerated rise as on chopper machines.

APMC The Association of Pioneer Motor Cyclists which was formed in 1928.

Aquaplaning A condition in which a film of water lifts a wheel from the road and control of braking and steering are lost.

Armature The central core of a magneto, dynamo, or other device which rotates in a magnetic field to produce current.

Armco Crash barriers made by an American company, much used around motor-racing circuits.

Artillery wheel Originally a wooden wheel as on guns, used also to describe some car and motorcycle wheels with heavy spoking.

Aspect ratio In a tire, the ratio of the height of the wall to the width of the tread expressed as a percentage.

ATD Automatic timing device consisting of weights and springs acting like a gramo-

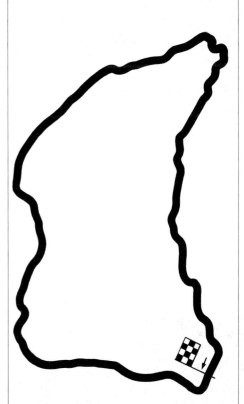

Isle of Man, England
Tourist Trophy
Mountain Circuit 37.75 miles
First held 1907

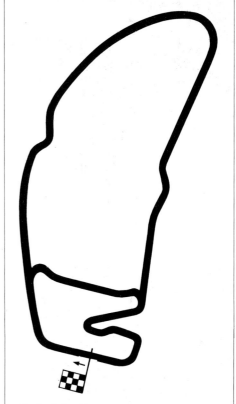

Hockenheim, Germany
German Grand Prix
Opened 1939, rebuilt 1970
4.22 miles
First held 1925 on Avus Circuit
Circuits vary

phone governor to adjust ignition advance to speed.

Auto Cycle Club The original governing body of motorcycle sport which became the Auto Cycle Union in 1907. It began in 1903.

Automatic inlet valve Forerunner of the mechanically operated valve, worked by the suction of the engine.

Autowheel A self-contained unit of engine and wheel which clipped onto a pedal cycle at the back.

BA British Association, a fine thread used on very small screws mostly in electrical or instrument work, with sizes denoted by numbers.

Back marker A rider who has fallen behind the rest of the field and has to be overtaken by the faster riders in a motorcycle race.

Back plate The plate on which brake operating gear is mounted in a drum brake.

Back pressure Pressure which builds up in a silencing system and absorbs engine power.

Baffle Plate in a silencer or fuel tank to reduce noise in the first case and movement of fuel in the second.

Ball joint A joint with a ball moving in a socket (like a human joint) to give wide degree of articulation.

Balloon tires Soft-running tires of wide section and low pressure used for comfort on tourers.

Bank A row of cylinders as those in a V engine.

BDC Bottom dead center, when the piston is at the bottom of its stroke in an engine.

Bead The edge of a tire, reinforced by wire, which locates it on the rim and forms a seal.

Beaded-edge tire Used before the wired-edge tire came in, with a rubber bead formed in the casing which located onto a channel on the wheel rim.

Bellmouth A bell-shaped end to a pipe, either on the carburetor intake or the exhaust pipe.

Belt drive The way motorcycles were driven before chains arrived, by a belt of fabric or leather from engine or gearbox to rear wheel.

Belt fastener Method of linking the ends of driving belts on early machines with steel hooks and other patent contrivances.

Belt rim brake These brakes used the belt pulley or a dummy one, pressing a shoe down in the V.

Bendix drive Method of operating a self-starter by flinging a pinion down a shaft, to engage with the toothed flywheel edge.

Benzole Fuel refined from coal and mixed with gasoline to allow a higher compression ratio, usually on a 50-50 basis.

Bevel gear Bevel drive through bevel gears which turn the motion through 90 degrees is used for camshaft, magnetos, or shaft drive to the rear wheel.

BHP Brake horsepower, a measure of the output of an engine. One horsepower is needed to lift 33,000lb one foot in one minute.

Big end The bearing at the lower end of the connecting rod where it joins the crank-pin.

Bing A German make of carburetor, used by BMW among others.

Binks An early make of carburetor designed by C Binks around 1903, who also built motorcycles.

Black flag Used to signal to a competitor in a race that he must retire, usually due to a dangerous fault in his machine.

Black ice Invisible ice on a black-top road.

Blip A burst of throttle, usually when gear-changing. Came from early aviation usage.

Blow-by Compression escaping past the rings in a worn engine.

Blower A supercharger, or pump giving forced induction; a compressor.

Blow-off valve A valve set to open at a predetermined pressure, usually in a supercharged engine.

BMCRC British Motor Cycle Racing Club, founded in 1909 and still going strong.

BMEP Brake mean effective pressure, a way of measuring the power pushing the piston.

BMF British Motorcycle Federation, a group of nonsporting clubs.

Bobweight Attached to the crankshaft to balance out the forces of the piston and con-rod.

Boost The amount of pressure applied by a supercharger, expressed in pounds.

Bore The diameter of a cylinder, usually in millimeters.

Bore/stroke ratio The ratio of cylinder diameter to stroke, square if they are equal, oversquare if the bore exceeds the stroke.

Bowden cable A control cable enclosed in an outer casing, used for throttle, air-slide, clutch, front brake, and so on.

Box spanner (wrench) A tubular wrench with a hexagonal end or ends with holes for a Tommy bar. Now largely superseded by the socket set.

Brazing A form of welding used on brass and similar metals.

Breather Orifice or pipe for the escape of fumes from the crankcase or gearbox.

Bridge Metal barriers across the window of a two-stroke port to prevent the piston rings catching as they pass.

Bridleway A track open only to horses.

Broach Cutting tool for making holes, not by drilling but by a thrusting action.

Brooklands Motor Course The world's first purpose-built motor speedway with a banked circuit. Opened near London 1907. Closed 1939.

Brooklands silencer More commonly

called the Brooklands can, this was obligatory to silence a racing engine at the Surrey track.

Brush A current pick-up made of carbon, usually oblong, rubbing on an armature.

Brush gear The carbon brushes and their holders plus electrical connections which pick up current from a commutator.

BSF British Standard Fine, a thread formerly widely used before international standards were agreed.

BTH British Thermal Unit, a heat unit enough to raise one pound of water one degree Farenheit.

Burn-out Dragster's trick to heat up a tire before making a timed run. Achieved by pressing the machine against a solid object while driving the rear wheel.

Bush A plain bearing usually pressed in place, without rollers or balls.

Butterfly A throttle control which varies the amount of gas passing by pivoting in the passage.

Button stick Application of the army button-cleaning tool shaped like a U used to support a piston while the barrel is lowered over it.

Calipers Fork bridging a brake disk and carrying pads and pistons. Also a measuring instrument.

Cam A kidney-shaped device for opening and closing a valve.

Cam follower As its name implies is in contact with the cam to transmit motion to the valve.

Camshaft The shaft upon which the cam is mounted. May be low down, high, or overhead.

Capacitator A large-capacity condenser used in various applications in the electrical system.

Capacity Motorcycles are classified by the cubic capacity of the engine, for example 500cc.

Carburetor Device for producing the air/fuel mixture of about 16:1 which is re-

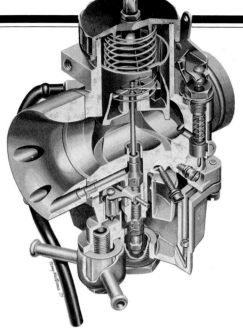

The Amal Mark 2 carburetor which is much used on motorcycles.

quired by internal combustion engines.

Cardan shaft A shaft to replace the secondary chain driving the rear wheel from the gearbox.

Cat's eyes Reflective studs buried in the center of the roadway or in the curbs to guide the driver/rider. May be various colors.

CB Either (1) contact breaker in the distributor, or (2) in the United States Citizens Band radio which is illegal in Britain.

CC Cubic centimeter, a unit of measurement.

Chain case Covering protecting a chain from the weather.

Chain drive Commonest form of drive from engine to gearbox (primary) and gearbox to rear wheel (secondary).

Chain-link belt Used before chains in motorcycle drive with pulleys, and in other applications.

Chain guide A guide to keep a slack chain in line with the sprockets.

Chair A racing sidecar.

Charge (1) The fuel/air mixture sucked into a cylinder, or (2) current applied to a battery from a dynamo or alternator.

Checkered flag A black-and-white chessboard flag which denotes the end of a race.

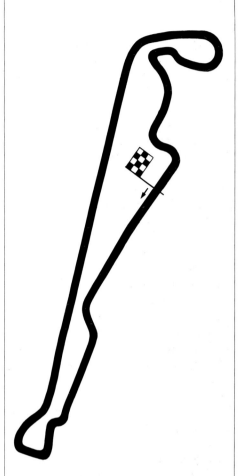

Le Castellet, France
French Grand Prix
Designed by Paul Ricard
3.61 miles
First held 1920 at Le Mans
Circuits vary

Assen, Holland
Dutch Grand Prix
Van Drenthe Circuit
Rebuilt 1955
4.796 miles
First held 1925

Cheesehead   A type of screw with a cylindrical head.

Chopper   A motorcycle with extended front forks, fancy paint and plating, and Apehanger handlebars.

Circlip   A circular clip to hold a component, for example a gudgeon pin, in position by slotting into grooves.

Clevis   A forked yoke with a pin through used to couple rods, often in brake systems.

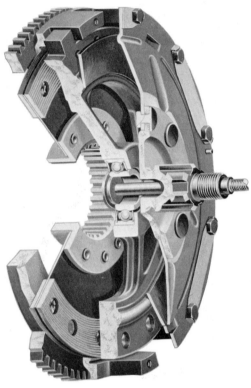

Cutaway Triumph single-clutch.

Clutch   A friction connection between engine and gearbox allowing progressive take-up and controlled by a handlebar lever.

C of G   Center of gravity.

Collet   Alternative to a circlip for securing one component to another, sometimes made in two halves, used in valve gear.

Combustion chamber   The area between piston and cylinder head where the fuel/air mixture is compressed and fired.

Commutator   The pick-up area of an armature, consisting of copper segments insulated from each other.

Compression ratio   The degree of compression of the fuel/air mixture, that is the sum of the cubic capacity (swept volume) and the cylinder head space related to the latter alone.

Compressor   Another name for a supercharger which forces the charge into the engine.

Concours d'Elégance   A contest for the best-looking machine.

Connecting rod   The rod clamped to the crankshaft at one end and the piston at the other.

Contact breaker   A contact set which breaks the low-tension circuit and induces a high-tension current to the spark plug.

Crankcase   The casing which encloses the crankshaft and its attachments.

Cranked link   Enables a chain to be shortened by half a link owing to its construction.

Crankpin   The shaft which carries the big-end bearing.

Crankshaft   The shaft which converts the up-and-down motion of the piston into rotary motion.

Crimping   Clamping an electrical joint by squashing.

Cross valve   A rotary valve which doubles as both inlet and exhaust in a four-stroke engine.

Crown   The roof of the piston.

Crown wheel   Meshes with the smaller pinion to make up the final drive in a shaft-driven motorcycle. Both are bevel gears.

Cubic capacity   The volume of an engine measured by multiplying bore and stroke.

Cubic centimeter (cc)   Metric measure used in expressing the volume of an engine.

Cubic inch   Alternative unit of measurement of engine capacity used in the United States.

Customize   To change or modify a machine with paint, plating, and gee-gaws.

Cycle thread   A fine thread used in the manufacture of cycles and motorcycles.

Cylinder   Contains the piston, is capped by the cylinder head and is the site of the explosion which provides power.

Cylinder head   Caps off the cylinder at the top end (in a vertical engine) and carries the valves in a four-stroke engine.

Damper   Device for slowing down movement, either in a suspension system or to balance a crankshaft.

DC   Direct Current, as produced by a dynamo and used to charge a battery.

Decarbonize   To remove carbon formed by burning of fuel from the top end of an engine.

Dell' Orto   An Italian make of carburetor.

Desaxé   An engine with the cylinder axis offset to slow down piston speed at top dead center and lengthen the stroke.

Desmodromic   Positive opening and closing of valves without relying on springs for the closing.

Diesel   A compression-ignition engine in which the charge is fired without a spark by heat generated by high compression around 20:1. Invented by Dr Rudolph Diesel in 1892.

Displacement   The capacity of an engine or amount of volume displaced by the movement of the piston from BDC to TDC.

Distributor   A gear-driven contact set inside a housing (the cap) which sends high-tension current to a number of spark plugs.

Dog   A simple device for mating components by slotting a projection into a space, used in gearboxes with sliding pinions.

DOHC   Double overhead camshaft.

Dope   Fuel other than gasoline, made up of chemicals like methanol or methyl alcohol.

Double knocker   A double overhead camshaft engine as distinct from a single knocker with one camshaft for all valves.

Dragster   Motorcycle (or car) specially built for short sprints against the clock.

Drift   Either (1) to slide a corner, or (2) a metal tool hit with a hammer.

Druid forks   An early type of motorcycle front forks, with coil springs and a top link.

Dry sump   A lubrication system using two oil pumps, one to supply oil to the bearings from a tank, the other to return it to the tank.

Duralumin   An alloy of aluminum, copper, magnesium, and manganese used in small-end bushes.

Dykes ring   A special type of piston ring which is L-shaped and fits close to the top of the piston.

Dynamo   A device to generate direct current to charge the battery. Superseded by the alternator.

Dynamometer   An engine brake for measuring power output.

Earles forks   An unusual front-fork design of many years ago with a long leading link and a rigid pivot through both links behind the wheel.

Electrolyte   The fluid content of a battery, usually acid plus distilled water.

End float   Endwise movement of a shaft between bearings.

Exhaust   The system which carries burned gases away from the cylinder.

Exhaust valve   Valve which opens once every two revolutions to allow gases to escape.

Expansion   Increase in volume due to heat, as in the fuel/air mixture in the combustion chamber.

Extractor   Special tool for removing components mounted on a taper or keyway.

Face joint   A joint in which the parts meet metal-to-metal without the use of a gasket.

Fade   Brakes which have been hard used will fade, or cease to be effective, due to heat build-up.

Feeler gauge   Metal strip marked in thousandths of an inch for measuring gaps in valve gear and plugs.

Fifth wheel   A bicycle-type wheel towed behind a vehicle on test to measure distance and speed.

FIM   Fédération Internationale Motorcycliste, which controls motorcycle sport worldwide.

Fins   Ribs added to a cylinder barrel in an air-cooled engine to aid heat dissipation.

Fishtail   Either (1) a wide slotted end to an exhaust system, or (2) sliding from side to side.

Flame trap   A bowl of gauze over an air intake to prevent a backfire spreading flames.

Flat head   A cylinder head with a flat surface.

Flat twin   An engine with two horizontally-opposed cylinders, or four to make a Flat Four.

Float   A box of brass or plastic which floats upon the fuel in a float-chamber and operates the needle-valve controlling the fuel.

Float chamber   That part of the carburetor which houses the float and the fuel awaiting use.

Floating gudgeon pin   A pin free to turn in the piston.

Flowmeter   A device for measuring the rate at which fuel is consumed by an engine.

Flywheel   A heavy wheel attached to the crankshaft which smooths out the intermittent firing impulses and aids slow running.

Footprint   The impression which a tire makes upon the road through its contact patch.

Footrest   A rest for a rider's foot, now often called a peg.

Four-stroke   An engine operating on the Otto cycle as opposed to a two-stroke.

Friction drive   An early form of drive involving disks in contact in place of chains and gears.

Full-flow filter   A filter in the main stream

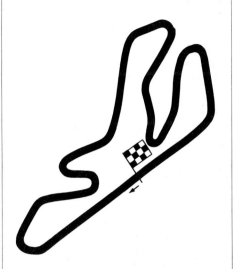

Jarama, Spain
Spanish Grand Prix
Artificial circuit
2.16 miles
First held before World War I
at Montjuich Park
Circuits alternate

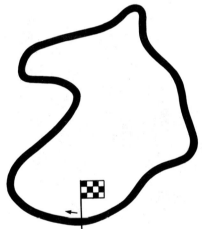

Mosport, Canada
Canadian Grand Prix
Artificial circuit
2.59 miles
First held 1967

Salzburgring, Austria
Austrian Grand Prix
Artificial circuit
2.64 miles
First held 1971

of the oil flow as opposed to a by-pass filter.

Fume valve A way of scavenging the crankcase of a four-stroke with induction suction.

Gaiter Formerly used for tire-repair, now more commonly a sleeve to cover moving parts.

Gasket A washer of paper, oiled fabric or rubber, or copper and asbestos put between two metal faces, to provide a gas-tight seal.

Gas seals Used in two-stroke engines to seal the crankcase around the main bearings.

Gear Either (1) a toothed wheel or pinion, or (2) riding clothing.

Gearbox A casing containing trains of pinion wheels which can be moved to provide alternative ratios; gearcase.

Gear ratios Differential rates of speed between sets of pinions to provide higher or lower rotation rates of the rear wheel in relation to the engine.

Girder forks Early form of front suspension with a single spring and links at the top.

GP Grand Prix, an international motorcycle (or car) race to a fixed formula.

Grinding paste A paste of carborundum used to grind-in valves on their seats.

Grommet A rubber bung to fill up an unwanted hole, perhaps hollow to contain a cable or wire.

Guarantee Also called a warranty, it is issued by a manufacturer backing his product against faults for a specified time or mileage.

Gudgeon pin A steel shaft which joins the piston to the connecting rod at its little end.

Hairpin spring A variety of valve spring shaped like a hairpin.

Half-elliptic A spring forming half of an ellipse.

Halftime pinion Pinion driving the cam-

shaft from the crankshaft at half speed.

Headlug Mounting of the steering column to the frame tubes by a forging or casting.

Head steady Bar from cylinder head to frame to steady the engine against vibration and torque.

Herringbone gears Gears formed in a herringbone pattern to make them quieter running.

High camshaft A camshaft mounted high up on the engine to shorten the pushrods in an ohv formation.

Horizontal engine An engine with horizontal cylinders, which may be opposed.

Horsepower A measure of engine power, enough to raise 33,000lb one foot in one minute.

Hot-tube ignition Used before electricity, it consisted of a tube projecting into the cylinder and externally heated to fire the charge.

Hub-center steering Steering from either end of the axle as on the Ner-a-Car.

Hundredweight Imperial weight measure of 112lb, shortened to cwt.

Hunting tooth A way of avoiding wear in gears by adding a tooth to one wheel so that the same ones are not constantly meshing with each other.

Hydrometer An instrument for measuring the specific gravity of battery acid to determine state of charge.

Idler gear One gear put between two others to transmit drive without affecting the ratio.

Impeller A pump to assist water circulation in an engine.

Indicated horsepower Power measured at the piston which does not allow for losses in an engine.

Induction The sucking-in of fuel/air mixture by an engine.

Inverted tooth A chain with projecting teeth which fit into recesses in the sprocket.

IOE Inlet over exhaust, a common arrangement with an overhead inlet and side exhaust.

ISDT The International Six Days Trial, an annual event of long standing.

Keihin A Japanese make of carburetor.

Kneeler A sidecar outfit on which the rider kneels in troughs rather than sitting on a saddle.

Land The face of a piston between the grooves for the rings.

Layshaft The secondary shaft of a gearbox, parallel with the main shaft, and carrying some of the gears.

Leading link Variety of front suspension with the pivot behind the axle.

Leading shoe A brake shoe with the pivot end ahead of the cam end in terms of drum rotation.

Leaf spring Spring consisting of metal blades clamped and bolted together, used years ago in suspension.

Lean-out A way of setting up a sidecar with the machine leaning out of the vertical.

Liner A sleeve inserted inside a cylinder.

Little end The small end of the connecting rod where it joins the piston.

Lobe The projecting part of a cam outside the circular form.

Low-tension magneto An early device before the use of high tension, with points inside the cylinder.

LPA Light pedal assistance, used with early machines to help the engine.

Mag-Dyno A magneto and dynamo combined in one to supply spark and charge.

Magneto In effect a high-tension dynamo producing current for the ignition spark. Now superseded by coil ignition.

Main bearings The bearings in which the crankshaft runs.

Mainshaft Usually the principal shaft in a gearbox.

Manifold   Collection of pipes which supply mixture (induction) or take away fumes (exhaust).

Master cylinder   The cylinder which sends fluid to the wheel cylinders to operate the brakes.

Master rod   Main connecting rod in a V or radial engine which carries the auxilary rods.

MBC   Miniature bayonet cap, a type and size of bulb holder.

MCC   The Motor Cycling Club, formed in 1902, which runs sporting events.

Mechanical efficiency   The relation of the nominal brake horsepower of an engine to its actual output.

Megaphone   An exhaust pipe/silencer shaped like a megaphone, which improves efficiency.

Mesh   Either (1) the fit of teeth together, or (2) a woven grid of material.

Mikuni   A Japanese make of carburetor.

Mixing chamber   That part of a carburetor where the fuel and air are united.

Moped   A light motorcycle of under 50cc with pedals attached.

Near side   The lefthand or curb side looking from the saddle.

Negative earth   Wiring system with the negative side of the circuit earthed to the chassis.

Observed section   A section of a trial where points are lost for touching the ground with a foot.

Octane   Method of measuring the knock-resistance of gasoline on a scale of 1 to 100.

OHC   Overhead camshaft, either single or double.

OHV   Overhead valve engine.

Oil bath   A case covering a chain to keep out dirt and provide lubrication.

Oil pump   A pump which delivers oil to the engine and circulates it.

Oil thrower   A scroll, ring, or plate shaped to throw oil away from a particular area.

Otto cycle   The four-stroke cycle perpetuated by Dr Nicolas Otto in 1876 in his gas engine.

Outside flywheel   The 'bacon slicer' type of flywheel mounted visibly outside the crankcase.

Overhead cam   An engine with an overhead camshaft or camshafts operating its valves.

Overhead valve   A valve mounted in the cylinder head.

Overlap   The period during which both valves in an engine (inlet and exhaust) are open at the same time.

Oversquare   An engine in which the bore is greater than the stroke.

Pawl   A sprag, as in a flywheel, which allows rotation in one direction only, or holds a rack in position as on a car handbrake.

Phased piston   An extra piston in a two-stroke engine used solely for force feeding the engine. It has its own separate bore.

Pilgrim   A type of oil pump with double action, both supply and scavenge.

Pinchbolt   A bolt which squeezes parts together, for example to close a handlebar clip for a control.

Pinion   The small gear in a pair, for example crown wheel and pinion, or any toothed wheel.

Pinking   Distinctive 'pinging' noise from an engine with over-advanced ignition or inferior fuel.

Piston   The component which is driven down the cylinder by expanding gases.

Piston boss   That part of the piston which is built up to carry the gudgeon pin.

Piston slap   Knocking noise caused by wear, or a loose fit for racing, as the piston changes direction.

Pitch   The distance between the rollers of a chain.

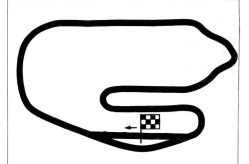

Daytona, United States
Daytona 200
New Speedway built 1959
3.87 miles
First held 1937 on natural circuit

Below: The generally used trochoidal rotor pump.

Bottom: This simple gear-type pump is less efficient and not used often.

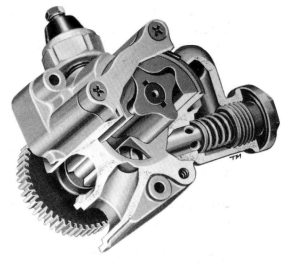

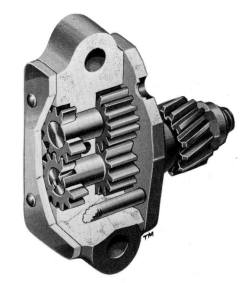

Planetary gear A gearing system in which planet wheels revolve round a central sun wheel. Mostly found in automatic car transmissions.

Plenum chamber An extra reservoir for fuel or gas to help feed an engine.

Plunger A component which moves up and down in a tube like a piston, for example in a tire pump.

Pocketing Condition after valves have been ground in many times so that they sink out of sight.

Poppet valve A tulip-shaped valve on a stem as used in most four-stroke engines.

Port An opening, for example an inlet or exhaust port leads to the valve.

Positive earth System with the positive pole earthed to the frame of the machine.

Post-vintage A motorcycle made after 31 December 1930 and before 1 January 1945.

Pre-ignition Ignition caused not by the spark but by a hot spot. May keep a switched-off engine still running. Otherwise called 'dieselling.'

Pre-load Tension or compression applied to a spring before assembly.

Pressure plate The plate against which the clutch springs react to load the friction plates.

Primary chain The chain from engine to gearbox.

Primary current Another name for the low tension current which induces the high-tension spark.

Primary filter Otherwise a sump filter, which guards the oil pump against picking up debris.

Primary gears Function instead of the primary chain, joining engine to gearbox.

Priming cock An aid to cold-starting on veteran engines, through which fuel could be injected.

Printed circuit A replacement for a wiring harness, embossed into soft insulating material.

Propstand A leg which swings down from one side of a machine to prop it up.

PSI Pounds per square inch, used in measuring tire and other pressures.

Push-rods Operating rods for overhead valves, working from cams below the cylinder.

Quadrant A segment of a circle with teeth, as used in a kickstart mechanism.

Quarter elliptic A spring made up of leaves in a quarter-ellipse, used in early suspensions.

Quill-shaft A hollow shaft often used to carry lubricant.

Radiator Consists of tubes of flowing water to extract waste heat from the engine.

Rake The angle of slope of the steering head or forks.

Ram effect A simple form of 'supercharging' using the wind pressure caused by the machine's progress.

Ratchet A quadrant or bar with angled teeth to take a pawl to limit movement to one direction.

Ratio Relation of one item to another, as in gear ratio, expressed against unity.

Reach Depth of section, as in spark-plug holes, of long, medium, or short reach.

Reed valve A valve like that in musical instruments, opened by pressure or suction, used in two-stroke engines at high speed.

Register Locating dowels or surfaces make one component 'register' with another in assembly.

Relay An electrical switch working on a light current which triggers a heavier switch carrying heavy current, as in a headlight circuit, for horns, or starter motor.

Retard Set the ignition 'back' so that the spark occurs just before TDC. Excessive retard causes overheating. The spark is then said to be 'late,' from the French 'retard.'

Reverse cone A megaphone exhaust with a reverse cone reduces diameter in the final inches.

Revolution counter General misnomer for a tachometer, usually shortened to 'rev counter.'

Rocker A pivoted lever much used in valve-gear operation through rocker arms.

Rocker box The casing holding or covering the rocker arms of the valve gear, on an ohv engine.

Rocker oil feed As its name implies, a supply of oil to the valve gear, at relatively low pressure.

Roller bearing A bearing using rollers instead of balls, confined in cages on prepared tracks.

RON Research octane number, a rating of the knock resistance of a fuel.

Rotary valve A valve driven from the camshaft for inlet or exhaust for either two or four-stroke engines. It is silent in operation and usually a disk or cylinder in shape.

RPM Revolutions per minute, usually marked on a tachometer × 1000.

Running-on Another name for dieselling or pre-ignition, caused by incandescent carbon in the combustion chamber. It means that an engine will continue to run when switched off.

SACU Scottish Auto Cycle Union, which controls motorcycle sport in Scotland.

SAE Society of Automotive Engineers. The initials are used in a system of classifying engine oils as in SAE 30, 10W/50 and so on.

SBC Small bayonet cap, a type of bulb holder for motorcycle light bulbs.

Scavenging Clearing of fumes from the combustion chamber after combustion, which may be assisted, or exhausting oil in a dry-sump system with a scavenge pump.

Scraper ring A piston ring which does not make a seal but collects surplus oil from the cylinder walls.

Sealed beam A light unit made all in one, in which the bulb cannot be changed but the whole unit must be replaced in the event of failure.

Seat angle The valve seat angle in a cylinder head, usually 45 degrees.

Security bolt A bolt to hold a tire firmly onto the rim through an internal pad, mostly used in trials work when tires may be run underinflated and try to revolve on the rim.

Sedan Saloon car.

Seizing When a piston or other component overheats and temporarily fuses to the metal it is rubbing against, in the case of a piston the cylinder wall.

Selector fork A fork to move a dog and hence a pinion to select another ratio in a gearbox.

Separator Plates set between the working plates of a battery to separate them.

Shim Thin piece of metal used to adjust clearances in between two components, for example in an ohc engine.

Shimmy Side-to-side wobble on a motorcycle which may happen at speed.

Shock absorber A device to control up-and-down movement of suspension, or to cushion a drive train. A damper.

Shot blasting A way of cleaning off scale and rust from parts being prepared for re-assembly after stripping, or before painting.

Shuttle valve A valve which slides to and fro like the shuttle of a sewing machine, sometimes used in front fork dampers.

Side-valve An engine with valves at the side rather than in the cylinder head.

Side-wall The part of a tire between the rim and the tread, which carries size markings.

Sight feed Used on veteran machines so that the rider could check through a glass window that the lubrication system was working.

Silencer An expansion chamber to lessen the noise from the exhaust, and may be of several types.

Single A single-cylinder machine.

Single knocker Engine with one overhead camshaft, as opposed to a double knocker which has two.

Skirt The part of a piston below the boss which holds the gudgeon pin and little end.

Slave cylinder Takes its fluid from a master cylinder to operate a clutch or brake under pressure.

Sleeve A cylinder liner, which can be wet (in contact with coolant) or dry.

Slick A wide treadless tire used in drag racing, and also in road racing.

Slickshift Used on Triumph machines, it made the gear lever also operate the clutch.

Slide valve Sometimes called a sleeve valve, it consists of two concentric sliding sleeves between piston and cylinder.

Slipper piston One having the skirt cut away to reduce friction, usually in racing practice.

Slip ring Part of the current-collection devices on a magneto, contacting a brush.

Small end More usually 'little end,' it is the small end of the connecting rod with a bearing of some kind in which the gudgeon pin works.

Snail cam A cam used in chain adjustment which forces the wheel back to taughten the chain.

Sodium-filled valve Valves, usually exhaust, with hollow stems filled with sodium which assists cooling.

Solenoid A remote-control device worked by an electric current to operate a switch.

Solex A British make of carburetor.

Spark plug Sometimes called sparking plug in England, which fires the mixture in the combustion chamber when the induced spark jumps the gap between its electrodes.

Spindle An axle on which a wheel rotates.

Split single Two single cylinders of a two-stroke using a common combustion chamber.

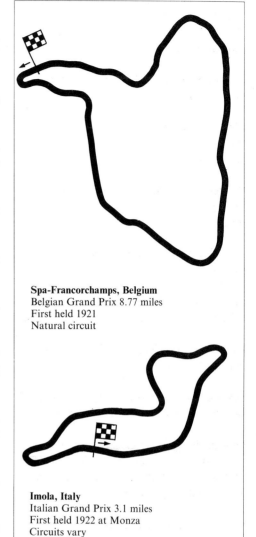

Spa-Francorchamps, Belgium
Belgian Grand Prix 8.77 miles
First held 1921
Natural circuit

Imola, Italy
Italian Grand Prix 3.1 miles
First held 1922 at Monza
Circuits vary

Honda CX500 radiator is typical of water-cooled practice.

Spoke One of the network which links hub to rim, hooked at one end and threaded at the other.

Spray lubrication Or splash lubrication, in which the crank picks up oil as it dips into the sump supply and throws it around the engine. Now long outmoded.

Spring frame Rear suspension, in which the wheel rises and falls vertically.

Sprocket Toothed wheel which carries the chain in chain drives and fixes the ratio.

Squish Achieved by a special type of piston which improves combustion.

Stanchion The rigid member in a telescopic fork, which is attached to the fork crowns. Any similar solid support.

Starter ring The toothed ring attached to the rim of a flywheel with which the starter pinion engages.

Steering head Where the front forks join the frame.

Stirrup brake A brake like those on a bicycle, with a stirrup spanning the tire and working on the wheel rim.

Stove enamel A method of painting frames or other parts where the enamel is baked on to a hard finish.

Strangler A choke for cold starting which cuts down the amount of air mixing with the fuel.

Stroke The travel of the piston in the cylinder; multiplied by the bore gives the capacity.

Stroker Another name for a two-stroke engine.

Stud A screwed rod like that fixed into a cylinder barrel to retain the head.

SU A British make of carburetor with a movable needle rising in the jet.

Subframe Carries the seat and attachments for the rear suspension, or the engine.

Suction stroke Otherwise induction stroke, which sucks fuel/air mixture into the combustion chamber.

Sump A container for oil below the engine. In a dry-sump engine it is scavenged and the oil carried in a separate tank.

Sun wheel Center wheel with planet wheels circling round, most used in automatic car transmissions.

Supercharger A compressor for forcing air into an engine to improve performance.

Suppressor An electrical resistance to prevent interference with TV or radio from car and bike engines.

Surface carburetor A type of carburetor used in very early days, in which air passing over a reservoir was hoped to pick up fuel.

SV Side valve.

Swan neck An S-shaped tube joining a sidecar to its machine from the steering head.

Swash plate A rotating plate at an angle, which can be used as a pump for fuel or oil.

SWG Standard Wire Gauge, a system of measuring wires, spokes and so on, with rising numbers as they get thinner.

Swinging arm Rear suspension by radius arms carrying the wheel, attached to the frame at the other end.

Tachometer A revolution counter which indicates the rate of turning of an engine, in rpm.

Tappet A rod which transmits cam action to the valves, and provides for adjustment.

TDC Top dead center, when the piston is at the top of its stroke.

Template A pattern for making an article, often made in wood to be copied in metal.

Thermal efficiency A measure of an engine's design, showing the work done for the fuel consumed, about 35 percent for a gasoline engine.

Thermo-siphon cooling Relying on the natural action of hot water rising for circulation in a cooling system.

Thermostat A device to control the working temperature of an engine by closing valves in the water system.

Throttle Controlling the amount of mixture of gasoline fed to an engine by a butterfly valve in the throat of the induction tract, or a slide.

Throw The travel of the crankpin.

Thrust face The face of a piston, bearing, or other part which bears the load.

Timing Refers to both valve timing and ignition timing, relative to crankshaft rotation.

Timing chain The chain driving the timing wheels.

Timing chest Where the timing gears or chains and perhaps the cams also are housed in an engine.

Timing gears Used instead of a timing chain to drive the timing wheels.

Timing light A stroboscopic light used to set timing accurately.

Titanium Costly hard light metal with a high melting point.

Toe-in The amount of inward setting when lining up a sidecar on a touring machine.

Torque Twisting rotational force in a shaft, which can be measured to show at what point an engine develops most torque.

Torque converter Used in conjunction with an automatic transmission and in place of a normal clutch to pass on the drive through a fluid coupling.

Torsion bar A rod used as a spring which resists twisting to perform its function.

Track The distance apart of two wheels of a sidecar outfit, the sidecar wheel and bike rear wheel.

Trail The action which keeps a front wheel straight in normal running, and can be set.

Trailing link Front suspension with a pivoted link ahead of the axle.

Transfer port In a two-stroke engine, the port which allows fresh mixture to be transferred from one side of the piston to the other.

Transistorized ignition A method of operation which in some cases eliminates the contact breaker, using transistors.

Transmission shaft Shaft taking drive from gearbox to rear wheel.

Trickle-charger A home-garage device for overnight slow charging of a battery at 1 to 1.5 amps.

Trip speedometer More correctly trip odometer, sometimes trip meter, which records mileage and can be zeroed with a press button or twist knob.

Trunnion A heavy mounting for a spring which permits movement in two planes.

TT The Tourist Trophy races in the Isle of Man, or a car race held at various venues.

Tube ignition More generally called hot-tube ignition, the first form of igniting the spark by a tube projecting inside the cylinder and heated from outside.

Turbulence Swirling movement of the gaseous charge in a combustion chamber which can be artifically induced.

Twist grip Throttle-control device on the right handlebar grip which superseded the throttle lever.

Two-stage blowing Using two superchargers one after the other in the induction line for double compression.

Two-stroke engine A valveless engine firing on every other stroke, unlike the four-stroke Otto cycle type.

Universal joint Joint between two shafts which permits one to move relative to the other but still transmit power.

Unsprung weight Those cycle parts which are not supported by the suspension. It should be kept to a minimum for desirable handling.

Upper cylinder lubricant A once-popular additional light oil added to gasoline to lubricate valve gear and upper cylinder walls.

Valve Device which opens and closes to admit air, fuel, oil, exhaust gases, or whatever.

Valve bounce Induced when an engine is overrevved and the valve springs cease to control the valve. Also called valve float.

Valve cap Small cap which screws onto the barrel of a tire valve to exclude dust and give an additional seal. On veteran machines a removable cap over the engine valve.

Valve core The inner portion of the air-sealing valve in an inner tube.

Valve lifter A once-universal fitting on bigger engines to make it easier to kick start the machine by raising the exhaust valve from its seat with a handlebar lever. Also used to stop an engine before coil ignition.

Valve seat The seating in the cylinder head on which the poppet valve makes its seal when closed.

Vapour lock Blockage in a fuel line caused by overheating of the fuel which induces an air bubble.

V belt Flexible belt used to drive motorcycles before chains, in a vee-section.

V engine An engine with its cylinders in a vee formation.

Venturi Part of a carburetor where depression lifts fuel from the jet.

Veteran Officially a motorcycle made before 1 January 1915.

Vintage A machine made before 1 January 1931.

Vintage MCC The Vintage Motor Cycle Club, a British club catering for riders of old machines.

Viscosity The density of an oil measured on a viscosity index of SAE numbers, the higher the number the denser the oil. Modern oils have a dual rating like 10W/50.

Volumetric efficiency Ratio of the charge which an engine pulls in relation to its theoretical capacity, which is higher in racing engines.

Vulcanizing Method of repairing a puncture in an inner tube with heat.

Wankel engine A valveless and pistonless engine in which all these functions are performed by a rotor revolving in a chamber. Tried by at least three motorcycle makers, and by car makers.

Warranty Another term for guarantee which a maker puts on his products for a limited time.

Water injection Once practiced as an anti-knock device for poor-quality gasoline.

Weber An Italian make of carburetor.

Wheelbase Distance between the front and rear wheels, measured from their spindles.

Wheelie Lifting the front wheel clear of the ground under acceleration.

Whittle belt A transmission belt of the early days, with metal links between the fabric.

Whitworth thread A coarse thread much used before the agreement on international standards.

Wick carburetor An early alternative to the surface carburetor, with air passing over the wicks.

Window Another name for the port in a two-stroke engine through which the gases go.

Woodruff key A slug of metal fitting in slots in two components to key them together.

Worm gear Form of gearing using a gear-wheel and an endless screw on a shaft.

Wrist pin A big-end in a V-twin or some other engines which is mounted on a master connecting rod.

Yard Imperial length unit of three feet or 36 inches, now commonly giving place to the meter.

Y-Drive A link used to drive double overhead camshafts from one shaft.

Yoke A connecting link between components.

Zenith A British brand of carburetor.

PICTURE CREDITS

Richard Adams Front jacket, 36/37, 39, 40/41, 46/47 (*both*), 49 (*top*), 52/53, 55 (*both*), 56, 56/57, 64, 65, 74/75, 82/83, 86 (*both*), 87, 90 (*both*), 94/95 (*both*), 96 (*bottom*), 114/15, 115 (*left*), 118/19, 122/23, 125 (*bottom*), 127, 130 (*top*), 130/31, 134/35, 136/37, 137, 142/43, 143, 145, 147 (*top*), 151 (*top*), 157

AJS 153

Allsport Photographic/Don Morley 44/45, 91, 123

BMW Werkfoto 6/7, 12/13, 14, 60/61 (*all 4*), 79 (*bottom*)

BSA 63 (*top*)

Castrol 15 (*top*), 35, 42/43, 76/77, 77 (*inset*), 89, 111 (*bottom*), 148 (*bottom*)

Champion Photo Service 64/65, 73 (*top*), 82, 104 (*bottom*), 108 (*both*), 115 (*right*), 119, 130 (*middle*), 132, 155 (*inset*), 175

Colin Curwood 4/5, 100/01, 158/59, 161, 168, 169 (*left*), 177

Colorsport 68, 110

Duckhams 38, 50 (*left*), 57

Melvin Eke 170/71 (*both*), 173

Dave Friedman, Photojournalist 147 (*bottom*)

Garelli 88

Goodyear/Marlboro Library 126, 135, 138/39

Honda 97, 142

IPC/*Motor-Cycle* 8/9, 10 (*both*), 11, 15 (*bottom*), 16/17 (*both*), 18, 21 (*top*), 22/23 (*both*), 24/25 (*both*), 26/27 (*both*), 28, 29, 30/31, 32/33, 50/51, 51 (*top*), 54 (*both*), 58, 62, 63 (*bottom*), 66/67 (*both*), 68/69, 69, 71, 74, 76/77 (*top 2*), 77 (*top*), 79 (*top*), 80/81, 84, 85, 92 (*top*), 93 (*both*), 96 (*top*), 98, 99 (*both*), 104 (*top*), 106/07, 109 (*both*), 111 (*top*), 120 (*both*), 121 (*both*), 124 (*both*), 125 (*top*), 128/29 (*all 3*), 132/33, 136, 140/41 (*all 3*), 144, 146, 148 (*top*), 149 (*bottom*), 150, 152, 156 (*both*), 160

Jawa 103 (*top*)

Kawasaki 103 (*bottom*), 165 (*right*), 180

Laverda 105, 165 (*left*)

Lucas-Girling 92 (*bottom*), 112

Tony Matthews 162/63

Minarelli 111 (*middle*)

Bob Norman 169 (*right*)

Norton Triumph 21 (*bottom*), 49 (*bottom*), 70, 78, 154

Olivier Martel/Gamma 166/67 (*all 8*)

Orbis Publishing Ltd 162 (*top*), 183, 184, 187 (*both*), 189

Peter Seddon Back jacket, 2/3, 126/27, 162 (*bottom*), 174

Suzuki 155 (*bottom*)

Trials and Moto Cross News 1, 73 (*bottom*), 116, 117, 149 (*top*), 178

Vauxhall Motors Ltd 20

Vespa 151 (*bottom*)